The  }

News From the Land of the Misfits

Jason Heppenstall

Belenos

For my girls

Cover art by Pernille Christensen

The moral right of the author has been asserted.

Published in association with Belenos Press July 2019

ISBN **978-1-9161828-1-3**

The Olive Press

News From the Land of the Misfits

Jason Heppenstall

Prologue

October 2005, Barcelona. When I moved to Spain I lost my money twice. The first time was quick and painful, while the second time was drawn out and agonising. In the first instance my life did not rush before my eyes as they say it does, but there was a metal bar biting deep into my throat and every blood vessel from the collar up felt as if it would burst under the pressure. I wondered if these were my last moments…

That morning I'd risen at dawn somewhere in northern France. In the cafeteria of the utilitarian road stop I'd placed a plastic cellophane-wrapped croissant, a glass of orange juice and a large black coffee on a tray. Eating in silence I prepared myself for another long day of driving.

By late afternoon I'd passed by the Pyrenees and was making steady progress towards Barcelona. Parking up at a motel near the periphery limits, I'd checked in, dropped some stuff in my room and jumped in a taxi to take me into the city. Barcelona didn't feel like the Spain I thought I knew. This was a growling low-rise city of traffic jams, greasy pavements and hunched figures carrying umbrellas. Bloated clouds moved slowly across the autumnal skies, casting the wide boulevards into patches of shade as we approached the city centre. Having spent the day watching as the green and temperate lands of France slowly transformed into the more brittle and harsh landscape of the Mediterranean, Barcelona seemed like a throwback to some more northerly clime.

I walked along La Rambla beneath the plane trees as people thronged around me. It was a moving river of streetwalkers – of sandaled parents squinting at maps on their phones as their children clutched blooms of pink candyfloss. Gaggles of fresh-faced backpackers milled around, while elaborately done-up girls headed out for the evening and fast-talking men spoke into mobile phones. I slipped down a cobbled side street and found a restaurant. While I was waiting for the food to arrive I sipped a glass of wine and tried to take in the fact that I'd arrived in Spain.

It must have been a couple of hours later when I decided, against all the advice issued in guidebooks, to go for a walk on the beach. Giddy with the idea of the start of a new life, I wanted to dip my toes in the cool blue Mediterranean and give thanks to all the forces in the universe that had somehow aligned to bring me to this point. I'd been living in Denmark for the past four years, struggling to earn a living and getting to grips with being a father to two young girls. Our move to Spain was to be an escape, or so we hoped. On this night the silky water lapped around my ankles and I raised my face to the placid light of the moon, bathing in a feeling of wellbeing.

I didn't hear him coming up behind me.

Actors being choked in films normally get to look imploringly at their killer for a few poignant moments before their tongue lolls out and their eyes close. But my assailant wasn't taking any chances, and was trying to finish me off from behind, assassin style, with a metal bar. The pain was unbearable. My windpipe, which had been cylindrical for its entire existence, was now as constricted as a copper pipe beaten flat by a lump hammer. Nerves, which I had never before noticed, screamed out in protest, sending spasms of pain throughout my body. I didn't even try to breathe – breath stopped in my mouth and it felt like my lungs had turned to hard resin.

The attack was so sudden and unexpected that I'd had no time to react. I clutched at the bar ineffectively, trying to prise it away, but his grip was too strong and apart from flailing around there didn't seem to be much I could do to break loose. How long was I locked in this standoff? Thirty seconds? Unable to breathe, it felt like an eternity.

In this state of panic my oxygen-deprived brain began to hallucinate. I saw my eldest daughter, just two years old at the time, looking at me quizzically, perhaps even with a slight look of annoyance. How had I got myself into this silly situation, she seemed to ask. *Don't you remember our deal about riding horses in the Spanish hills?*

As the water lapped gently around my ankles and fractured sparks of moonlight glinted off the sea, I wondered how many seconds I had left before I blacked out. If I was going to try and save myself I knew intuitively that I had but one chance. I'd never been so aware of the value of oxygen and the dwindling supply I had left. Mess it up and I was done for. My daughter crossed her arms impatiently. *Here goes*, I thought.

I thrust my foot back, finding the gap between my assailant's lower legs, and hooked it there. At the same time I jumped backwards and to the side, hoping for the best. It was a move I'd learned as a kid at Sunday morning judo lessons in a local village hall and I hadn't used it for twenty-five years. He struggled to correct his balance but found his foot locked tightly in position. We fell.

As we went crashing to the sand I drove my right elbow into his stomach as hard as I could. He groaned and shouted something and the grip loosened a little but wasn't released. Feeling his hot breath on my neck I arched my head forwards and brought it crashing back sharply onto where I figured his nose would be. A shriek went up and the hard metal object against my throat went away. It was a merciful release and I gasped for air. But I didn't have much time to appreciate it; I still had work to do if I wanted to get out of this situation. My attacker lay there on the sand. He was yelling about his damaged nose, and he looked angry. Even in the shallow light of the gibbous moon I could see that.

I jumped up and stood over him, still trying to catch my breath. Next to him my bag lay open, its contents scattered on the sand. I realised that in the fray my glasses had fallen off. He was young, just a youth really. As I stood over him he shouted at me and started to get up, anger flaring in his eyes. There didn't seem to be anyone else around and the kid still had some kind of metal bar in his hand, perhaps a tyre iron. He couldn't have been much older than sixteen and I could see now that his lean frame had made it possible for me to topple him. Nevertheless, I wanted this nightmare to be over and I decided there and then to grab my bag and make a run for the safety of the streetlights and the cars cruising along the beachfront. It couldn't have been more than fifty yards away.

"Don't move," said another voice. I was being grabbed again from behind, and I felt another object against my throat. But this was no metal bar, instead I felt a cold and sharp edge. "Sit down and put your hands behind your back." I did as I was told – I was thirty-four years old and I didn't want to die just yet. The first youth came round in front and looked at me in a mocking kind of way. He said something to my captor in a language that sounded like Arabic, and my arm was yanked upwards behind my back painfully. I kneeled down, staring at the beach with the blade against my throat. "We just want some money," said the voice behind me in English. He sounded older than the one I could see. Perhaps he was an elder brother, or a gang leader. His voice was calm, soothing even. "Just relax, and everything will be okay, my friend."

I watched as the first one, still angry about his nose, went through my bag. He found my travellers' cheques, and took out my camera and passport, shoving it all into a bag of his own. Behind me I could feel my watch being removed, then my wedding ring was worked off. Next, my wallet was pulled from my jeans pocket and passed to the younger one, who began to go through it. "Your country?" said the knifeman.

"England," I said. The kid removed a wad of notes and then started to go through my credit cards, examining them one by one before carefully returning them to their allotted leather slits.

"Very nice," said the voice. "Oxford University. Aston Villa."

"Uh-huh," I mumbled.

"Stag?"

"What?" The kid had finished removing the money from my wallet. He waved the notes in the air to his accomplice, happy. He seemed to have forgotten what I did to his nose. I could see my mobile phone poking out of his shirt pocket.

"Please," I said. "Just take the money but give me back my wallet. I need it." The boy looked behind me at his accomplice for approval. He must have nodded as my wallet was returned to my ransacked bag. I was worried about the car keys. Where had I put my car keys?

"What you are doing in Barcelona, my friend? You have lost your friends at a stag do?" I felt the pressure being relieved from my arm a little. They said something

5

to each other in their own language and the youth skirted me, giving me a wide berth. "You should not be on the beach at night, you know. Very dangerous here. You are lucky to have only met us." He was still speaking in his calm, mellifluous way. There was more hushed discussion between the two. I listened to the gentle sound of the waves.

"We leave you now," said the voice. The blade was still pressed against my throat, but not as hard as before. "When we go you stay like you are, okay? Do not try and get up or look at us. After ten minutes you can go to the police, but they will not help you much, I'm afraid." I nodded obediently and the knife was taken away. "Now, my friend, you will count to a hundred. Remember, don't look up."

People walking away on soft sand make no noise. I counted slowly, and by the time I reached fifty I was sure they had gone. I turned around. To my shock, I saw the two figures still there, standing a short distance away and arguing quietly about something. They saw me. "Look away!" the taller one screamed. I started to get to my feet but he sprang towards me. There was nothing for it but to make a run for the lights of the city. That's when he hit me. I didn't feel the blow but the next thing I knew was the gritty crunch of sand in my mouth and a warm feeling in my hair.

"We told you not to look at us." I rolled over and looked up. They were both stood over me again. I saw as the younger one raise the metal bar up, and I tried to shield my head with my hands. There was a sharp feeling as he brought it down on me, and that was the last thing I remembered.

- 1 -

Fools rush in where angels fear to tread – Alexander Pope

The road was dark and the headlights picked out trees and squat crumbling buildings as the car pitched along it. It was too bendy to pick up any speed but, in any case, I wanted to savour my arrival. I pressed a button to open a window, allowing a stream of cool air to rush in. Upon it was the herby scent of a new life. Olive trees crowded in along the verges, their feathery leaves flashing silver as I passed.

I had spent the last two days in the Barcelona motel recovering from my ordeal. When I'd come round my attackers were gone and I had lain injured on the beach until the first rays of the sun had lit the east. I'd needed to find my glasses, without which I felt I couldn't function. A man with a metal detector passed and I asked him to help me. He looked in vain for a few minutes but could not find them. Wearily I set off to find the police station, stumbling through the blurred streets as an agonising headache began to take hold. When I eventually found it I was made to wait in a room with several other victims of the night. The matter of being robbed and beaten seemed routine and not worthy of note to the sergeant who dealt with me. I filled in the police report and left. Luckily, I still had a twenty euro note in my pocket and I was able to get a taxi back to the motel. Luckier still, even though my room key had been taken, the robbers hadn't used it to clear me out, and a shocked looking receptionist issued me with a replacement. If they had been in my room, they might have seen the car keys that I'd tossed on the bed the evening before.

The bathroom mirror revealed a face caked in dried blood. My nose was broken and there was a ring of purple bruising coming up around my throat. My head was swollen and I had a split lip. I looked a mess, but it could have been worse. After a shower, I took some painkillers, and collapsed onto the bed to fall into a deep and dreamless sleep. The next two days were spent in this way, filled with sleep and room service. I called my wife from the hotel phone by the bed and told her what had happened. She was worried, said that it could be a sign we were not supposed to be moving to Spain. She wanted me to come home. I told her not to worry, that I was fine but for a few bruises, and that I'd found my contact lenses and could continue the journey.

Now, two days later, I was almost six hundred miles to the south and nearly at my destination. I could see a town up ahead, clinging to the side of the mountain. Its sprawl was limited by the precipitous geography it sat in, and sodium streetlights cocooned the buildings in a fuzzy glow. Below, in the inky blackness of a ravine stood a fort, in ruins atop a pinnacle and lit up with floodlights. A water truck that had been following me for some time turned off, leaving me alone on the road.

You are Now Passing through the Gateway to La Alpujarra, said the sign at the entrance to Lanjarón. But there were no gatekeepers and this liminal place seemed deserted save for some stray dogs and me. I passed through the town, and re-joined the tarmac ribbon as it wound its way between mountains and valleys. In two thousand miles of motorways I had barely turned the steering wheel, but now I was spinning it as I negotiated a series of switchbacks. A bottle of water rolled to and fro under the passenger seat, clunking against my foot. I passed a ruined building by the roadside on which someone had spray painted the words Alpujarra Libre, adorned with a cartoon cannabis leaf.

The buildings became more numerous as I approached Órgiva, the principal town in the region. Roadside dogs raised their heads out of half-hearted curiosity while, from a rooftop vantage point, a pair of cat eyes hung like green orbs in the darkness. I was almost upon the town and could make out the floodlit twin-towers of the church when I indicated left and swung the car up the minor road that marks the ascent to the high mountain villages. Somewhere up there, at my destination's end, stood an empty house awaiting new occupants.

The road rose sharply and I pressed my foot down on the accelerator, dropping a gear to maintain momentum. The engine's power kicked in, although the weight of the trailer made it feels sluggish and unresponsive. Not for the first time on the journey I had the irrational fear that the load I was pulling would somehow break free, or worse, drag the car down over some precipice. I was tired. I had been driving since before dawn. I told myself to relax, and eased back on the accelerator. This was the final stretch; after five days of service stations, motels and plastic-wrapped sandwiches in five different countries my journey's end was at hand.

My eyes were dry but I resisted the temptation to rub them. I disliked wearing contact lenses, and my eyeballs felt like they were wrapped in cling-film. Just a few more minutes and I would be home. And, yes, this *was* our new home. We were swapping the cold blue of the Baltic for the fierce light of Andalucía. When I arrived I would pour myself a glass of wine and sit on the terrace, breathing in the night air and savouring my lucky escape. This I had promised myself. There would then be a week to get everything in the house ready before the rest of the family came out to join me. But that was something I needn't worry about until tomorrow.

I saw the hitchhiker's thumb sticking out, half angled towards the ground as he trudged uphill with his back to me. As I passed he turned to face me and my foot wavered momentarily on the accelerator. I was so close to my destination yet I felt an irrational urge to announce my arrival to someone – anyone. I found myself pulling over and saw the man sauntering towards me in the rear-view. He had a shaved head with a thick black beard and as he got in I saw he was wearing baggy sequinned trousers that he gathered around him as he climbed into the passenger seat.

"Where to?" I asked, even though I had already guessed the answer.

"Beneficio," he said. I knew the place. It was a place of yurts and tepees, said to have been set up in the 1960s when two American hikers had seen a buffalo in the sky during an LSD trip. They viewed this as a sign telling them to found a commune, and now there were hundreds of people living there, although the place was deemed illegal.

As we eased away the hitcher maintained a silence as if he were a passenger on a bus. Stealing a glance, I noticed a large hole yawning in his earlobe, stretched taught by the circumference of a metal nut.

"Where you driving to?" he asked.

"Pampaneira," I said. "I live up there," I added unnecessarily.

The man carried on looking straight ahead.

"Many British here," he said. I couldn't place his accent.

"You're from Israel?"

"South Africa," he said, shooting me a glance – I'd never been much good at recognising accents. I could sense his gaze lingering on my face, which was still bruised and swollen, with contusions around my neck. There was another long pause as we drove on in the darkness, the illuminated patch of road in front of the vehicle a blaze of bleached tarmac. In the distance, as the road swung to the right, the soft luminescence of some snowy peaks hove into view sitting bright beneath the starry sky. I thought for a moment about turning on the radio. My passenger began to fiddle with something in a floppy fabric bag he had on his lap. I stole another glance. His shambling earthiness seemed so out of place in the anodyne grey interior of the car, and the polished orange sheen of the dashboard reflected the lines in his face.

"Mind if I smoke?" he mumbled, putting one to his lips even as he asked. There was the clink of a Zippo and three or four sharp grinds before his face momentarily lit up and a whiff of lighter fluid crossed the space between us. He flipped the metal cover back and inhaled, bringing the joint to life as he eased back into the passenger seat.

He sat with his elbow out of the open window. "You know you British are everywhere," he said, after his third or fourth toke.

I wasn't expecting this but there was a touch of frank absurdity in his voice and it didn't sound like an accusation.

"You come here and buy all the houses and don't even bother to learn the language. Most of you can just say *por favor.*" He giggled a little and I let his comment hang there in the doped air, knowing we would be at the turn-off for the commune fairly soon. Stealing another glance, I realised he was older than I had at first thought.

"Well, two words is a start," I said. I was thinking I'd picked the wrong person to speak to after my long journey.

"You think you can just buy up these places, these mountains, all this..." he gestured at the world outside the car. I knew what he meant, but I didn't have the inclination to defend myself. He was probably just stoned. In any case I wouldn't bother picking up any more people like him.

"Here," he suddenly said, and I pulled over to the side of the road. He got out, shut the door and then leaned in through the open window. I shook his outstretched hand and he thanked me for the ride. It was a little overly courteous and I wasn't sure if he was ribbing me.

"Remember," he said, his shaved cranium framed by the passenger window "If life screws with you, just come and visit us at Beneficio, everyone is welcome – even you Brits."

"Thanks, I'll remember that," I said. And he bounded off into the dark scrub by the side of the road until just the red wink of his joint was visible, and then he was gone.

- 2 -

After the trauma of my arrival in Spain wore off, things settled down when my family came out to join me. Apart from what I had learned on a couple of prior visits, I didn't know much about the village of Pampaneira where I now found myself living. The German woman we had bought the house from said the villagers were "like the mountain". By that, she explained, they were often as cold as stone to outsiders, but once they liked you they were as amiable as could be.

Following a week spent cleaning out the cobwebs in the old stone house, and with my various bruises and cuts still healing, I drove to Malaga Airport and picked up

12

Michelle, along with our daughters Jasmine (then aged two) and Sofia (three months). Also emigrating was our cat, James, who made it clear how much he disliked being put in a cage and bundled onto a plane.

We soon settled into our little village house, which was part of a crooked row situated on a short alley in the highest part of the village. From the little terrace outside you could see the village church below, and right down the Poqueira Gorge to the distant sea. On a clear day you could just make out the Atlas Mountains in Morocco, although this didn't happen very often. The roof was flat, in the Berber style characteristic of La Alpujarra, although the German lady had put in skylights. The ground floor had only recently been converted from a space where livestock were kept, the idea being that heat from the animals would take the chill off the house in the winter, as well as keep them safe from frosts and snow. In fact, one of our two neighbours had a teenage son who rode a small horse that still lived downstairs in their house. We would sometimes see him leading it in through the front door.

Our neighbour on the other side was a stout man with a leathered complexion and a booming voice. His name was Julio and he usually wore a grey jumper as he chugged around the narrow alleys on a battered orange dumper. Often he would be singing in the clear mountain air as he trundled along with a load of rocks or wood or gas canisters, and he always had a twinkle in his eye. Like some of the other villagers, Julio put his impressive vocal chords to good use by standing atop his house and yelling in the general direction of the rest of the village. This, I was soon to learn, was the standard way of communicating in Pampaneira, for even though this was the start of the twenty first century, it only seemed to be the youths who had phones of any description in those high villages. And so yelling to one another from the rooftops was still the standard form of 'short distance' communication. If one needed to contact people in the other villages in the gorge, Bubión or Capileira, there was a payphone for that purpose.

I soon found out that Julio was Pampaneira's mover and shaker. If you wanted something done, you went to Julio. Not only did he own the house next door to us, but he also had several more that he rented out to visitors from Granada at weekends. Furthermore, he had established a large restaurant – Casa Julio – on the first bend as you arrived at the village, which sold hearty dishes of local fare, including the ubiquitous *papas a lo pobre*, or poor man's potatoes. He had a shy daughter, Julia, who worked in the various family businesses, and his wife was a friendly woman who sang like a songbird in a high, clear voice as she worked.

Approaching me one day soon after I arrived, Julio invited me into his cellar to sample his wine. In the dark, musty interior he handed me a glass of something I would soon learn was called *costa* – a sourish pink-tinted young wine looking not unlike agricultural diesel. *Costa* packed a dangerous punch and would – I discovered – give you an awful hangover. But it was the local lubricant, and given the masses of wild grapes that grew everywhere it cost almost nothing to produce, which is perhaps how it got its name.

To be honest, it was a bit unnerving standing in Julio's cramped and dark cellar drinking from glasses wiped clean with stable straw as he spoke at me with his megaphone voice. I could hardly understand a word he was saying, as Julio had a thick Alpujarran accent and gave no quarter to the fact I was a foreigner. "What's your name?" I figured he was asking me as he filled up another glass with pink *costa*.

"Jason," I said.

"Eh?"

"Jason."

"Eh?" Julio looked at me as if I were speaking Chinese.

"*Me llamo* Jason," I said, dropping the 'j' sound, which is not present in Spanish, and substituting it for an 'h', making it sound like '*Hason*'.

Julio carried on staring at me. He tried to pronounce it but somehow couldn't bring himself to say a foreign-sounding name. After all, most men in the region were called Antonio, so what kind of stupid name was '*Hason*'? I tried to help him out by saying it again. Slowly.

"H-A-S-O-N."

"Eh?"

Suddenly he seemed to have an idea and his eyes lit up with understanding. He started to laugh. "Jesus!"

"Eh?" I said.

"*Si, Jesus!*" He let out a booming laugh as if this were the funniest thing he'd heard in ages, slapping me on the back with a large, heavy hand, and almost causing me to spit my *costa* onto the straw-covered floor. My new neighbour then walked out of the cellar singing some kind of folk song, got onto his mini dumper and, still laughing between verses, drove off down the alley at slightly less than walking speed. I sipped the rest of my *costa* and wondered what was so amusing. Julio seemed like a nice enough bloke, even if I could barely understand him, and he had been very welcoming. It was only then that I noticed a mule peering at me out of the gloom. It was looking at me with an air of expectation, as if I were about to say or do something funny. "What are you looking at?" I slurred.

After our encounter in his cellar, Julio then went and told everyone in the village that the new foreigner living in Calle San Miguel was called Jesus – and so whenever I walked into the village bar or met someone in an alley they would say *hola hay-zeus*!

- 3 -

We settled easily into life in Pampaneira. Our eldest daughter, Jasmine, played in the village with the other children, and there was a small playground beside the church. Often we would sit and watch her, marvelling as she began to pick up Spanish from her new pals. Soon, however, winter loomed, and we found out just how cold it could get in those mountains. I bought a load of firewood from Julio, who delivered to our front door using his dumper. With this I loaded the two fireplaces up and lit roaring fires each day. We draped heavy rugs over the windows for insulation and bought gas powered space heaters. But the stone house always seemed to be cold. We hunkered down, wearing woolly jumpers and gloves and wrapped ourselves in duvets.

Days turned to weeks and weeks into months. After a winter spent shivering in a house that felt like a fridge, spring finally broke and the wildflowers sprouted between the stones in the outer walls. We peeled off the layers of clothing, took down the heavy rugs we had hung on the windows and emerged blinking into the bright sunlight. It was only then that the village baker, Alfonso, told us the trick for keeping the house warm. He pointed out that we should do as he did and instead of short, hot bursts, we should keep the fires burning low throughout the day and the night. After a few days this constant heat would be taken up by the tonnes of stone in the walls and would slowly radiate back out into the house. The process would happen in reverse in the summer, he told us, with the scorching sun never quite managing to penetrate the house's thermal defences. The vernacular buildings in La Alpujarra were, after all, designed with the Sahara in mind.

Pampaneira, the lowest and therefore the first accessible village of the high Alpujarra, did well as a stopping-off point where carsick tourists could get out and stretch their legs after half an hour of bendy roads. Some of the approach roads ran along drop-offs so steep and high that when motorists occasionally plunged over the edge is was debatable whether there was any point calling an ambulance. The village thrived on passing trade, as the number of bars, restaurants and souvenir shops testified. But it could also turn its back on the tourist euro, pulling down the shutters every Wednesday and leaving the visitors to wander around the plaza with their hands behind their backs muttering about the lack of conveniences. Unbeknown to them, behind the locked doors of the village inn El Pilon, the locals could usually be found chowing down on plates of crusty bread and ham beneath the gaze of a large poster of Che Guevara, which was given a prominent place up on a wall above the bar.

Invariably, some of the working men within would be lubricated with sherry and, away from the gaze of the tourists, were free to bang the tables with their fists as they bellowed out tub-thumping songs at the top of their lungs. The residents of the higher-up villages made fun of Pampaneirans for their outwardly liberal outlook. They mocked the progressive mayor, even if she had delivered new affordable housing those village youngsters who were of marriageable age. It wasn't for nothing that they called the village the 'People's Republic of Pampaneira'.

However, by the time we arrived there, Pampaneira was a sanitised version of its former self. Up until the mid-1990s the village had been famed for a yearly event known *as La Gran Matanza* , or 'great slaughter'. From a butchering point of view its sloping aspect and the lack of flies in winter meant it was the ideal venue for slaughtering pigs. The plaza was on a gradient, so any blood that escaped would trickle into the stream that ran down through the village and be washed away into the gorge below. Not much blood escaped. The village women held buckets beneath the open throats of the pigs and would whisk it up with their fingers in order to coagulate it for black puddings. After the slaughter, the villagers would get busy making any number of delicacies from the abundance of pork, and not much went to waste. But at the approach of the twenty first century the EU had shut down *La Gran Matanza* on grounds of hygiene and all that remained of the fiesta were some vintage promotional posters on the walls of bars and restaurants.

Nevertheless, some of the villagers continued the practice behind closed doors and I saw one of my close neighbours and his son silently walk a huge porker into their house one evening. Earlier on I had seen them moving an old enamel bath indoors, although I hadn't given much thought about what they would be using it for. The pig had a scarf tied around its snout and there was something slightly sinister about the arrangement, like a dinner guest being led to his murder. It wasn't long before a series of muffled thumps, human grunts and strangled squealing noises emanated from behind closed doors, followed by silence. After a pause of an hour or so, the odour of charcoal smoke began to drift from open windows, which was soon suffused with the strong smell of roasting flesh. The enamel bath reappeared as twilight fell, half-filled with a thick dark liquid.

Later still there was a knock at my front door and I was greeted by a woman holding what appeared to be some pointed objects wrapped in a tea towel. She smiled and shoved them into my arms before putting a finger to her lips – *shhh!* – before disappearing again. Turning on the light to examine my gift I realised they were a couple of freshly baked baguettes, packed with thick, juicy, smoky, delicious pork. There was a little scrawled note with them and it simply read *bienvenidos* – welcome.

- 4 -

One morning I awoke to find an inquisitive goat looking at me through the skylight in the bedroom. It gazed down with its bulgy eyes, its head slightly tilted to one side as if it were expecting me to do something entertaining, just as Julio's mule had done. Skylights were what set our house apart from many of the others in the village, and from a local point of view this was a curiously northern European thing to do. In Andalucía light was usually considered too fierce to allow into your home and was kept at bay just like the bad spirits they hoped to frighten off with loud fireworks at fiestas. They painted buildings white to reflect the rays back into the sky, and kept the interiors of their homes in near-darkness with shutters and heavy curtains over the tiny windows.

The goat lost interest in me and I followed its movement across the flat roof above by the sound of its footsteps. It wasn't the first time I'd woken up to find an animal looking at me. If anything, it felt like we were in a zoo, with the animals on the outside looking in at us. The nature of living on a slope built into the side of a mountain means your roof is a bit of flat ground for someone higher up. Just above the house was a wooded area of holm oaks and gnarled old chestnut trees and from time to time the local shepherds would pass through with their herds of goats. Even the sheepdogs had started to show an interest in peering through the skylights, perhaps wondering what the goats found so interesting.

I got up and made a cup of tea, taking it outside onto the terrace that overlooked the village. Hanging between two houses below, a string of ragged Tibetan prayer flags fluttered silently in the breeze, diffusing their invocations into the chill early morning air. A black kitten poked its head out from behind a chimney pot to assess the odds of me having some food before scampering away into a half-built structure used to house partridges. I took a sip of tea and listened to the birds' soft cooing sounds.

Down in the village I could see the baker's van parked in the plaza. The baker himself was striding purposefully around shouldering a large plastic crate of loaves, and outside the church a woman was mechanically sweeping the cobbles with a brush. Meanwhile Julio, wearing his trademark grey jumper, was driving the mini dumper loaded with rocks up a narrow alley. If someone chose to make a computer game simulation of a small but industrious Spanish village, this is what it might have looked like.

From this scene of endeavour a thought arose in my mind that I had been trying to suppress: I myself had to find a way to make money. During the first few months after arrival it had felt as if we had landed in a different world. Every day I had to mentally pinch myself to make sure it wasn't some kind of dream. Here, in the clear and pure light of Andalucía it seemed that anything was possible. Was it really that easy to throw off the shackles of a moribund and desk-bound existence? On any typical day I could enter El Pilon and sit drinking coffee amidst the old men of the village and pretend that there was nothing unusual about this arrangement. And if I listened closely to their conversation I could almost convince myself I knew what they were talking about.

But the truth was that until I found a way to make a living here, I was just an unemployed blow-in – a misfit sitting on a barstool drinking coffee with his head in the clouds. Since our arrival we'd been getting our fill of going for walks to collect chestnuts for roasting, drinking *café con leche* in the morning and *vino tinto* in the evenings, and all the other things that you might do if you were on a holiday that you didn't really want to end. But now we were settled, it was time to start branching out and finding a foothold from which to launch our next move.

I wasn't worried. Our house in Copenhagen had sold for a good price, meaning we had plenty of reserves to see us through until we established an income. Most of our ideas involved buying a piece of land and setting up an organic smallholding, while another involved opening up a quirky little café in one of the villages, or perhaps Órgiva. But for now these were just ideas scribbled on napkins, and the task at hand was to make them happen.

We only knew a couple of foreigners in the area. One of them was an estate agent called Emma who had sold us our house. Emma was a vivacious girl who took her young son on viewings for lack of childcare and drove a dangerous-looking jalopy of a car. She had been one of the free spirits who had persuaded us of the sanity of moving to this mountainous village where people seemed to live off ham and wine and nobody had ever heard of an iPod. I literally bumped into her one morning as she was hurrying out of a café. "What are *you* doing here?" she asked. I hadn't seen her for quite a few months, and it seemed she'd forgotten we had planned to move to Spain.

"Well, I live here now, remember – you sold us a house."

She seemed a bit startled for a moment, as if the consequences of her actions had suddenly become clear to her. "That's great!" she enthused. "You'll have to come round and I'll cook dinner. Look, sorry about this but I've really got to dash. Got a client waiting in Bubión and I'm half an hour late already."

Emma's father owned the estate agent in Órgiva through which we had bought the house. On the spur of the moment and before she dashed off, I asked her if her father might have some kind of job that I could do. Perhaps, I figured, it would be a good way to get to know people, and it would be a stepping-stone to something better. "It's worth asking," she said as she climbed into her old Volvo. "Drop in tomorrow morning and have a chat. I'll tell him you're coming."

And so the next morning I drove down to Órgiva, parked the car in the shade of a pepper tree and went to talk about work. The office was on the main street in the town, called Calle Doctor Fleming. In the windows were pictures of houses with enticing descriptions such as: '*Character country house. Lovingly restored in original style with Moorish fixtures and fittings. Situated in the beautiful Alpujarras, where you can go skiing in the morning and sunbathe on the beach in the afternoon.*'

I ascended the three steps outside the office and sucked in my breath; I'd never found it easy trying to sell myself. A young woman with treacle brown hair and a neat fringe was sat behind a desk that acted as a reception: "You must be Jason," she said, speaking with a Yorkshire accent. "I'm Molly. Mel will be with you in a moment if you'd like to take a seat."

I sat on a plastic chair next to a parched yucca plant and wondered whether I'd polished my shoes enough. The door to the street was open, allowing the disorderly Spanish bustle to mingle with the smell of fresh paint and cigarette smoke in the office. Across the road a ragged and emaciated woman, impossible to tell her age, squatted barefoot on the pavement and played a penny whistle tunelessly. Whenever anyone tossed a coin her face would break into a gap-toothed smile and she would put her hands together in thanks before recommencing the erratic melody.

There were two other people in the office besides Molly and myself. In the far corner sat a smartly dressed man with blonde-ginger hair, instantly recognisable as an estate agent. Sitting back in his chair, he was talking into a telephone and gesticulating with his free hand for emphasis. "No it's not often that you get a ruin with such great potential these days. Snapped up ages ago they all were. Aha, yes, like I said the *permisos* come with it. Wait till you see it, the view will blow you away. I was there just yesterday, and I said to Molly 'this'll be gone in an instant.' No, there's no mains water, but frankly, you can get away without it pretty easily – who has it round here anyway? Uh-huh, yes. Like I said our solicitor can arrange all that. Top of his game – and cheap as well. No, the last thing you want to have to worry about is water. No, no you don't need to worry about that either – dead they are. Yes, it's being sold by the children. Madrid. Yes, just want to get it off their hands. Nice people."

A fan whirred slowly above, lazily slicing up a cloud of tobacco smoke that hung up near the ceiling. Beneath it sat a woman, slightly older than the salesman, and with a certain lackadaisical yet proprietorial air. She was at the back of the office typing quickly on a laptop. A cigarette hung loosely between her lips and it jerked up and down like a conductor's baton every time she muttered a curse under her breath, which was often. From her long blonde hair and golden tanned skin I could tell she wasn't Spanish, but when the phone rang she spoke faultlessly into the receiver in the peculiar Alpujarran sub-dialect that I was already becoming accustomed to. She hung up and stared at the receiver for a moment. "Tosser," she said in home counties English before flicking ash into a coffee saucer and resuming her typing. Every so often the deafening din of a passing motorcycle would halt all conversation, although nobody seemed to mind, and they must have been used to it.

"Jason?" I looked up to see Mel standing over me, his hand outstretched. He was a small man in his sixties with swept back white hair and a lazy eye. My first impression of him was that he looked a bit like the comedian Dudley Moore. He led me into his office and asked Molly to go and fetch us coffee from one of the local café bars before closing the door and easing his small frame into a large leather office chair. "Emma said you had a business proposal. Something about starting up a lettings arm of the agency," he said straight off the bat, fixing me with his good eye.

"She did?" I didn't recall saying anything about that when I'd run into her. No, I said, I was just looking for a way to earn some money and, just so he knew, I was no good at sales. I thought it best to be honest to reduce any expectations he might have of me. He paused to consider this and asked if I'd ever been involved with property rentals. No, not really, I replied, although I had *lived* in various rented flats as a student – this was about the top and bottom of my experience. What about website design, he asked. I confessed to once having made a rudimentary blog with a template. It had taken me about half an hour.

"But you *do* want to earn some money don't you?"

"Yes," I replied.

"And you're used to working in an office? Most people who end up here are builders or yoga teachers, and you are neither of those things."

"True," I said, "but I have no experience building websites or working with rentals. I was an English teacher last, and before that I worked in the electricity industry."

Mel listened to my excuses and seemed, if anything, impressed. "None of that matters," he said. "Here, you can be what you want and do what you like. There's nothing stopping you. Just bear with me will you." He began to write down some figures on a desk jotter and a few minutes passed in silence, broken only by Molly opening the door and wordlessly placing the coffees in front of us before backing out again.

I had to concede that he had a point; if I wanted to make a living here I'd have to get outside my comfort zone and do something I wasn't used to. Mel sat back in his chair and pressed the fingertips of both hands together so that they splayed out, giving him the overall impression of a giant tree frog sitting in an office chair. He looked satisfied with his calculations. "Let's say you manage to pull in two hundred properties and we charge two hundred euros apiece as a setup fee. Double that for the exclusive ones – no, triple it. There'll be a small commission on each booking, of course, and I can offer you thirty percent. The new rentals website you create can piggyback off ours, which comes up fourth from the top on Google searches for 'Alpujarra Spanish property'."

I listened to him and tried to work out what exactly he was offering me. It seemed like he wanted me to manage a rentals arm of his business, taking a commission for each property I bagged.

"Just think about the money."

Mel sat there smiling as I did the mental arithmetic. I arrived at a figure in my head, which if true would make our existence in Spain very comfortable indeed. He was looking at me intently, a satisfied smile on his face. "Even lawyers don't earn that kind of money in Spain," he said.

We parted with a handshake. I hadn't promised him much beyond agreeing to start work on the project next week for a probationary period. I'd look into designing a website and we would see if it could work out.

As I stepped out of the office into the bright sunshine and the petrol fumes from the motorbikes I felt a welcome sense of purpose returning to me. Months of idleness over the winter had recharged my batteries after the stress of moving and the aftershock of what had happened in Barcelona, but now I was ready to embark on something new. Passing the ragged flute woman I tossed her a coin and made my way up the main street to the central plaza, pausing to take a drink of water from the small fountain there. It was market day and everywhere was busy with people carrying shopping bags and talking on street corners. One side of the plaza was lined with tattered men drinking *Alhambra* lager from large brown bottles while the town's stray dogs arranged themselves about their booted feet.

I walked up to a large open-fronted café where a group of New Agers were raising a racket banging on drums and dancing while one juggled a set of clubs. It was an almost medieval scene and wanted only for a dancing bear. Inside, men with thick beards were serving halal kebabs and *Mecca Cola* to a line of waiting customers, while an undulating strain of Islamic chanting backed by a slow tempo techno beat infused the place with a feeling of trippy calm.

I ordered an orange juice and sat down on some cushions at a low table. The place was busy with chatter. I could hear Dutch, French, German and English all competing with one another while the staff shouted orders to each other in a mixture of Spanish and Arabic. I looked at the menu on the table in front of me. Along with the couscous and chicken *tajin*, a conversion of faith was also available. The café restaurant was owned and run by an order of Sufis and its name – *Baraka* – the menu explained, could be interpreted as 'spiritual gift'. I'd read about Sufism before, and had a faint awareness that its roots stretched back into the mists of time. It was, in fact, regarded as the mystical arm of Islam, according to the menu. I was sipping my orange juice and flicking through the pamphlets when my phone rang.

It was Mel. I'd only I'd only left him fifteen minutes before. He cut straight to the point: "Can you start tomorrow instead? I've got a job for you."

- 5 -

The next morning I put on an ironed shirt and slipped into my polished shoes for the second day. I left the house soon after breakfast, carrying a leather briefcase containing two pieces of paper and a pen. My task, as dictated by Mel, was simple. I was to drive to a cluster of holiday cottages and convince the owners to part with a sum of money so they could appear on our new rental website. The website in question didn't yet exist but I was to promise them that it would be up and running shortly. I felt nervous, as Mel had described the location of the holiday cottages as 'remote'. How remote? I had asked. "You *have* got a four-wheel-drive, haven't you?"

I drove east for about three-quarters of an hour through the mountainous foothills of La Alpujarra all the way to the whitewashed village of Trevélez, which claims to be the highest settlement in Europe. It's here that thousands of hams slowly cure in the rarefied and dry air, but I had little concern for that or anything else other than the task at hand. As I drove I kept telling myself to relax. But the truth was that I was not confident about my sales pitch, especially as it would have to be done in Spanish and my grasp of the language was basic to say the least. Hadn't I told Mel that I was no good at sales? What's more, given the complicated instructions Mel's younger wife Nikki – she of the blonde hair and cigarettes – had given me on how to get there, I wasn't even sure I'd find the place.

I parked up on a bluff overlooking the deep-sided valley that yawned below the village. Valley? It was more like a giant chasm reaching down into the earth. Deep down at the bottom snaked the Rio de Trevélez and, if the map was to be believed, that's where I was supposed to drive. Descending in to this chasm ran an unsurfaced track, yet from my vantage point it seemed suicidal to drive down it and I looked at the map again incredulously. *Surely* this wasn't the right way, I reasoned. Just then I noticed an old man sitting on a wall and looking at me. I got out of the car and asked him if he'd ever heard of the apartments I was trying to find and he pointed towards the valley. "*Bajo*," he said jabbing his thumb down like a Roman emperor. I thanked him and got back in the car. Well, I said to myself, if other people can drive down that track then why can't I? I shifted the Freelander into four-wheel-drive mode – something I had never needed to do before – and pointed it downhill.

The first section of the track was not as steep as it had first appeared and I trundled along in second gear, feeling the crunch of stones under the wheels and riding the brakes to keep the vehicle in check. Every now and again I passed buildings, mostly hard-up looking farmhouses with the standard barking dog marking the perimeter. The road became steeper in sections and, combined with some torturous bends, it felt as if the tyres had only the slightest purchase on the thin layer of gravelly surface scree. I continued carefully, moving almost at walking speed.

On one particular stretch, as I found myself inching along the edge of a steep-sided and treeless section, the gearbox began to give out alarming noises and a red light – its significance unknown – flashed on the dashboard.

I stopped the car and pulled on the handbrake as far as it would go. Realising that I was certainly lost, I got out and looked around to see where I was. It was a hot day and fine dust had coated the car. I sat on a rock by the side of the track and drank from a bottle of water. Looking up I saw I had descended barely a quarter of the way down into the valley, although it seemed to have taken about half an hour to get here. Was this really the right way? I decided to ring the office for clearer directions but when I got the phone out I saw there was no signal. The engine cooling system whirred noisily. When it stopped the only sound to trouble the mountain air was the trill of birdsong. There was nothing for it but to go further so I got back into the car and continued my descent.

But the further down I went the worse the track became until I found myself driving over ever-larger rocks where small landslips had not been cleared away. The river running below still seemed as far away as when I had started out and I became ever more certain that there was no way the holiday apartments could be down this steep track. I resolved to turn around at the next opportunity but suddenly found myself peering over the steering wheel at the top of a short section of track so vertiginous that I slammed on the brakes and stopped the car for a closer inspection. I got out again and looked at the terrain ahead. Again, it was covered in loose gravel and pebbles and there was no sign that vehicles ever came this far down the track, if you could even call it that. In fact, it was so steep that there was no way, as far as I could see, I'd be able to drive down it without losing control and skidding. It was only about fifty yards before it flattened out again but it would be fifty yards of pure hell. To drive down it would have been like going over the top on a rollercoaster at the funfair, but this time the screams would be for real.

The alternative to driving down seemed even less possible. To get out of my predicament I would have to reverse up a steep bend for about two hundred yards with a drop-off on one side. I cursed myself for getting into this situation and kicked out at a wheel. My shiny shoes were now covered in dust and I was sweating. It was a simple choice: up or down? I walked down the track to confirm my fears that it was undriveable. It was steep, very steep, but there *were* some parallel tyre tracks in the dust so I knew someone must have done it recently. A professional rally driver would no doubt find it a breeze, but I wasn't a professional rally driver, I was just someone who'd bought a four-wheel-drive from a suburban lot and never learned the techniques for driving it off-road.

I trudged back up to the car and sat looking over the steering wheel fearfully. Should I put the seatbelt on or not? Would it be easy to leap out of the door if need be? I checked my phone – there was still no signal – and then looked again at whether I could traverse the steep slope behind me in reverse gear. No chance. I eased the handbrake off and two tonnes of metal began to roll forwards at a sickeningly steep angle. At first I took it so slowly it hardly felt like I was moving. Locked in first gear, the engine kept the car in check as I found myself sloping forwards in my seat at an angle I had never before been at in a vehicle. My hands gripped the steering wheel tightly and my foot hovered above the brake, pumping it every now and again, but not so hard as to cause a skid.

Nevertheless, I was picking up a bit of speed. On the dashboard the red light started to flash again and I saw now that it depicted an out-of-control car leaving two skid marks behind it. The momentum continued to accelerate and I concentrated on keeping to the centre of the track, trying simultaneously to avoid the long ruts that had formed in it and the sharply protruding rocks which could easily rip off the oil filter. There was a slight curve and I turned into it only to be met with a terrible crunching sound coming from deep within the car. It was the sound of metal rods clashing together, and the vibration carried through the pedal and up my leg. The vehicle started to emit a clacking noise like a clockwork toy that had been over-wound. At the same time the brake pedal went floppy and the wheels locked. Brakeless, the forces of gravity took over and I shot forward on a trajectory that pointed directly towards the edge. I scrambled at the gearstick and trod hard on the brake, but nothing happened except the dreadful clacking noise. The handbrake was my last option and I yanked it up as hard as I could. Whatever microprocessor buried deep in the car's anti-skid system was in control seemed to sense my panic and suddenly snapped out of its paralysis. The steering wheel connected with the wheels again, but in those few rudderless seconds I'd picked up too much steam to be able to do much but steer my way out of trouble as the car flew down the sloping track. There wasn't much I could do but cling onto the steering wheel and aim for the bottom.

I hit it with a crunch. The suspension bottomed out and the car came to a standstill in a cloud of dust. For the best part of a minute I just sat there with my heart beating like crazy. As I unlocked my bloodless hands from the steering wheel I decided that no job could be worth taking such risks. Had Mel known I'd have to drive down into this gulley? For a brief moment I wondered if this was some sort of cruel initiation or if, perhaps, he was trying to kill me.

I got out of the car and inspected it for signs of damage. None was apparent, so I got back in and turned it around, the track now being wide enough to do so. It was easy driving uphill compared to down and the engine felt grateful for the torque and the chance to get its teeth into something. I was able to drive closer to the edge that I might have tumbled over a few minutes before. It didn't look quite so bad from this angle. The car would have rolled once, maybe twice, had I gone off it on the descent.

When I reached the top the old man was still sitting on the wall as if nothing had happened. Actually nothing *had* happened. When he saw me he held up a finger, as if he had an afterthought to share. "*Despues Trevelez. Bajo,*" he said, waving in the direction of the other side of the valley. So that was it, a simple misunderstanding. I was supposed to descend the valley *after* going through the village. Instead I'd shot off down what was now quite obviously a mule track. I thanked him and went on my way.

In the village I stopped to freshen up and fill my water bottle from a public spring. My phone had a signal again and I rang the office to say I was on my way. "Good thing," said Nikki, "they called to ask where you were."

I eventually found the place, which was clearly signposted and just off the main road on the other side of the valley. It was run by a couple who'd recently had a baby and moved from Granada to set up their dream venture. The woman proudly showed me the four stone apartments they'd built themselves and had given names such as *Jasmin* and *Buena Vista*. We sat and drank coffee in the refurbished bar while the smiling baby gurgled and bounced in a rocker placed on the table between us. They seemed eager to show off their achievements in realising their dream, saying they wanted to attract foreign visitors and not just locals, but I could sense the woman's apprehensiveness. With my poor Spanish and their valiant English we just about communicated what the deal would be and how much the signup fee was. "*Quatro cientos?*" she gasped, when I told her. She cast a glance at her husband who responded with a wearied look. Perhaps their project had overrun on costs and they were counting every penny. Four hundred euros *did* seem steep, but it was Mel setting the price and not me. This was the bit where I should have told them they'd be fools not to take advantage of the special offer, and that their competitors might get in ahead of them if they dallied.

I got out the printed contract and put it on the table. It was an exclusive agreement, which forbade them from advertising their property with any of the Mel's competition. I pushed it across to them. "Maybe I can take some pictures of the apartments," I said, and went out to fetch my camera from the car. In one of the windows I caught sight of my reflection, noticing the dark sweat stains that had appeared on my blue shirt following my ordeal in the gorge. The arc of the window had the effect of shortening me and, with my sunglasses and scuffed shoes it made me look like a dumpy gangster. Nothing moved in the landscape around me; it was as if the snow-sprinkled mountains, the cerulean blue of the sky and even the silver ribbon of the river below were props in some kind of celestial play in which I played the part of the wicked interloper, or perhaps the fool. I dutifully got out my camera and took some photos of the lovingly created stone apartments.

When I came back the baby was still smiling but her parents weren't. The form had been pushed back in the general direction of my vacated seat and on the table next to it was an envelope that, I guessed, would contain cash. The man gave me a pained look and explained that they could offer me half the money now and the rest when they saw their completed profile with pictures up and running on the website. I looked over the form they had filled out. My hunch was that if I took their money they would probably never see it again. There *was* no website and there probably never would be. Mel had said we'd only bother making a website if we could get enough signups, although he had no idea how long that might take.

I pushed the envelope back across the table towards them. "You pay after your first booking through the website," I said, affecting a lost-in-translation misunderstanding. They looked at me, relieved. The father clapped his hands together. "A brandy to celebrate," he said. The baby gurgled in agreement and waved its feet in the air.

I returned to Órgiva in the heat of the day just before the siesta. I had failed as an estate agent, fallen at the first hurdle, and I wanted to hand in my badge. But when I got to the office everybody was out except Molly. "How did it go?" she asked.

"Awful," I replied. "I just don't think I'm cut out for this kind of thing."

"I know what you mean," she said, casting a glance towards the boss's open office door.

"You live in Pampaneira don't you?" she said. I replied that I did. "Listen, there's no chance of a lift is there? I live in Bubión – we're practically neighbours – and my car's in for repairs."

"No problem," I said. At least I could be of use to someone that day.

On the drive up Molly told me about her life. She'd lived in Spain for several years, teaching English in Madrid and, more recently, Malaga. It was in Madrid that she'd met her husband, another English teacher, who was from Liverpool. He'd ended up teaching the workers in a cement factory while Molly worked at the language school. They'd come over to La Alpujarra for the weekend and fallen in love with the place, abandoning their safe jobs almost immediately. Molly had been lucky to get a new job at the estate agents, she said, what with positions for foreigners being few and far between. Nevertheless, she said, working for Mel was a daily nightmare.

"What about your husband?" I asked. "What is he doing?"

I might have touched a nerve because she became a little evasive. "Marcus? He's, er, well, walking."

"Walking?" I didn't understand. "Walking where?"

"Everywhere," she said. "Every day he's up in the mountains. You know, exploring the *senderos*."

There was an awkward silence as I imagined Molly slaving away answering phones and fetching Mel and Nikki coffee in a hot office while her husband, who looked somewhat like Moses in my mind's eye, led the carefree life of a shepherd, minus the sheep.

"But why not get a job somewhere else if working at the estate agents is so bad?" I asked.

"Are you kidding? There are no jobs round here for *guiris*. Just estate agents and maybe the odd bar," she said.

"For what?" I said. "What's a *guiri* if you don't mind me asking?"

"A *guiri* – you know, someone like me or you. Foreigners. You didn't know they called us that? It's not just the Brits who are xenophobes you know."

"So what are you going to do?" It was none of my business but I asked anyway.

She smiled. "I – we – had the idea of setting up a mobile language school. You know, teaching the people in the high villages how to speak English."

"Sounds interesting."

"Or, failing that, we had another idea. A newspaper. You know, just a local one. A couple in Capileira had one but they just packed it in. Too much work for their liking, they said."

"Do you think it would work?" I asked.

"Oh yeah," she said confidently. "People pay to put adverts in it and you just hand it out for free. Simple really. And Marcus's a journalist. Piece of piss, he reckons. It could really be a success if we worked at it."

"You want to go all the way?" I asked.

"Definitely. We've already thought it through. When it gets successful I'm going to have an interior design section and people will write in to me with their queries. And Marcus's going to write about restaurants and food. He used to work for the *Euro Weekly News*, you know."

"No, I meant, do you want a lift all the way to Bubión. It's no problem."

"Ah, that'd be lovely. Ta."

I drove her back and then returned home. "How did your first day go?" asked Michelle.

"Terrible, I quit," I said. "But don't worry," I added, seeing her eyes widen, "something else might have come up."

- 6 -

Late one evening at our little village house in Pampaneira, just as we were sleepily watching the glow from the dying embers in the fireplace, Michelle stood up abruptly and yelled. It gave me quite a start and I wondered what had happened. She was pointing a wavering hand at the doorway to our bedroom where Jasmine was fast asleep in her cot. "There's an old woman in our bedroom!" she said. A few seconds later, as if by way of confirmation, a shriek went up from within. We rushed in but the room was notably free of old ladies when we got there, although Jasmine was wide-awake and in a flap. When we asked her what was wrong she said 'the granny' had tried to touch her.

It was not an easy sleep that night and I woke up more than once feeling a cold chill in the bedroom and a sense of unease; the last thing I wanted was to live in a haunted house.

But the ghostly visitation proved not to be a one-off. At first it manifested itself in the manner familiar to those who read stories of the supernatural or watch 'ghost hunter' shows on TV. There would be cold blasts in previously warm rooms and sudden bouts of panic in the cat. A standard encounter would see his gaze follow something unseen across the room before high-tailing it out of the house and only creeping back hours later. Michelle said she didn't believe in ghosts, despite having seen one, I was more open to the possibility. It was worrying to think that we might have landed ourselves in a situation straight out of *The Amityville Horror*. I decided to do a bit of research.

The German woman we'd bought the house from had moved to South America, but she hadn't said anything about a ghost at the time. After enquiring with the few people I knew in the village, Antonio, an old man who ran a walkers' hostel told me with gleeful amusement that we did indeed live in a haunted house. "And what's more, Jesus" he said, "everyone in the village knows about it."

I hoped this wasn't true, thinking that perhaps it would die down, but the mysterious visitations continued. Usually, the arrival of the spirit was announced by the scrabble of the cat's claws on the tiled floor as he sought escape. And just like something from stories told around campfires by teenagers, the visitations started to occur at the same time each night, in this case twenty past eleven.

I blurted out our problem to Molly when I bumped into her in town, telling her about the ghostly apparition of an old woman. "Oh, they *love* kids you see," said Molly, referring to elderly Spanish people in general, and not just the living ones. This seemed plausible. Michelle had described what she had seen as an old woman wearing a dark shawl as she drifted across the floor of the bedroom. She had been almost transparent, and was surrounded by a bluish haze. It seemed plausible that an old woman like that might be attracted to a little girl sleeping in a cot for a cheeky look.

"Do you have any images up of the Virgin?" she asked. "Maybe that would help."

We didn't, so I bought a small wooden-framed icon from a souvenir shop and put it on the wall above our daughter's cot. We didn't experience anything unusual for a few days and I thought it might have done the trick until twenty past eleven one evening when a familiar wail went up from the bedroom. Exasperated, I found myself listening to someone recommending the services of an exorcist, which were still considered a public service in parts of Spain. The exorcist, they said, would come round and get rid of any paranormal pests, in much the same way as if the problem were rats or termites.

"You might want to think twice about that," said Maria Jesus, the young woman who ran the souvenir shop where I had bought the image of the Virgin Mary. She pointed out that the ghost, if it existed at all, would no doubt see us as the interlopers in what had probably been her house in the past. Although no official records went that far back, our house had probably stood there since the seventeenth century, and we had only been living in it for the past few months.

Some weeks later, with my ghost story having got around Molly, through her work at the estate agent, found herself in a chance business phone call with the German woman we had bought the house from. She was eager to tell Molly all: "Oh, they saw her then!" she said down the line from Argentina. "I was never lucky enough to catch her, but friends saw her, and of course everyone in the village knows about it. Normally she appears only to women, they say."

I renewed my enquiries with the villagers, who mostly agreed that we had indeed moved into a '*casa de los espíritus*', although it was delivered with a shrug and no one seemed to think it was anything but normal. Julio, our neighbour, had a more pragmatic explanation. "Yes, sorry about that, Jesus," he said. "She used to be mostly in my place but all the building work we've be doing has frightened her through the walls into yours." That figured

– Julio was busy demolishing his own house with a pneumatic drill, and was planning to rebuild it as a modern guesthouse. The racket he made on a daily basis was enough to not only wake up the dead but also cause them to move somewhere more peaceful.

We decided to move Jasmine into another room. I'd noticed that the ghost only ever seemed to frequent the two main bedrooms, and the cat had also learned to avoid these rooms, instead preferring to curl up in the lounge.

I did some research into what ghosts might be. Nobody seemed to know for sure, but the theory that made the most sense was that they were some kind of projection or recording. For the most part they tended not to interact with the people who saw them, and it appeared they somehow drew their energy from their surroundings, which would explain the cold spots in rooms. Most occult researchers agreed that they were a kind of low-level paranormal occurrence and probably nothing to do with departed souls or anything like that, and were likely some kind of memory stored in quartz stones. Despite this, there were some signs that they could be interactive, and some displayed traits of intelligence.

Over the next few months our own ghostly presence – whatever it was – seemed to dwindle and then disappear as if her batteries had slowly run down. Perhaps she had become bored with checking us out. I was becoming bored with the matter too. Ghosts, it turned out, were as common as wild boars around La Alpujarra, especially in the higher villages where it was a lot damper than other places; something that apparently encouraged them. A man who owned a restaurant in a nearby village told me matter-of-factly that he often saw his dead father walking in the hills. "It is normal in these parts," he said "my father used to walk with the spirits too when he was alive. If you are to live around here you must get used to it. Here, in La Alpujarra, the spirits walk amongst us."

Local legend had it that there was the ghost of a girl who enchanted shepherds and lured them into a deep lagoon where they drowned. This didn't seem like the kind of ghost I was keen to encourage in my house. Others claimed that the spirit of the poet Lorca roamed the *senderos* and lived on in the sparkling streams that added music to the soundtrack of the hills.

And so gradually we learned to accommodate our apparition, although we never mentioned it to guests when they came to stay.

- 7 -

The high villages of La Alpujarra had been home to disaffected Englishmen for nearly a century. Suffering from shell shock after the First World War, the writer Gerald Brenan had sought peace and solitude in the Spanish mountains, moving himself and thousands of books to the remote village of Yegen. Taking up residence in a house not dissimilar from the one I now found myself living in he would look out south over the hills and mountains, describing the unusual moonlike terrain as possessing a billowing quality like the convulsions in a thin sheet as it is shaken and aired.

Those kinds of hills are not visible from Pampaneira, which is too far towards the western end of La Alpujarra. Instead, on a clear day with no cloud, one can see the summits of the first and third highest mountains in Iberia. Mulhacén is the highest, at almost three and a half thousand metres, but its rounded dome looks less striking than its sister, Veleta, which is truly Himalayan on account of its craggy peak. Perhaps it was this visual similarity that had also attracted fragments of displaced Tibetan Buddhists to the region and why there were so many prayer flags tied to the whitewashed houses.

We had been living in the village for a while and assumed we were the only foreigners, so it was a surprise to hear some English voices coming from an open window one day. A middle-aged man appeared at a balcony holding a gas bottle and I called up to him to say hello. He invited me in and introduced me to his wife, Maureen. Tony and Maureen were only in the village for a few months each year, they said, which would explain why I hadn't seen them before. They chose to spend time in Pampaneira to be close to their son who was 'up there' as Maureen put it, pointing skywards and making a strange face. Puzzled as to her meaning, and perhaps assuming that their son had passed beyond the veil, I asked when was the last time they had spoken to him. They replied that only two evenings before he had 'come down' to help sand down some of the ceiling rafters in preparation for chemical treatment. Maureen got out a picture of him. It showed a shaven-headed young man wearing a monk's cowl and holding a dog on a leash. Now it all made sense; their son was clearly a monk living up at the Buddhist place on the other side of the Poqueira Gorge. I had heard about the retreat but had never been up to visit. It was perched high up on a ridge opposite Pampaneira and blended in so well with the surroundings that it was practically invisible without decent binoculars

Intrigued by the idea of a Tibetan Buddhist sanctuary in such an overtly traditional Spanish region, I went away to find out some more. The retreat on the mountain was called O Sel Ling, meaning 'place of clear light' and it had been set up in the 1970s by a couple from Bubión. Maria Torres and Paco Hita had received instruction by a Tibetan Lama called Thubten Yeshe who founded a centre in Nepal where western seekers could study ways to achieve enlightenment. Yeshe's teaching methods were described as unconventional and the man considered himself somewhat offbeat, joking that he was a 'Tibetan hippie'. But his teachings made an impression on Maria and Paco, and so they set up their own centre on the slopes opposite their village. Yeshe then died in 1984, and the hunt was on for his reincarnation.

A year later Maria and Paco had their fifth child, whom they named Ösel, and as soon as he was born they began to harbour suspicions that he was the reincarnation of Yeshe. The boy never cried and there had been little pain during the birth, and formal tests to validate their theory ensued. A little over a year later the baby was indeed proclaimed by the Dalai Lama to be the reincarnation of Yeshe. The story caught the attention of the world's media and little Ösel Hita Torres was renamed Tenzin Ösel Rinpoche. He was immediately whisked off to India, where he would spend most of his childhood and adolescence ... and then the unthinkable happened.

Aged twenty-four, Ösel had had enough of being a famous reincarnated guru and went AWOL. When he resurfaced he had long hair and a goatee beard and was said to be living a free and easy life in Madrid, 'catching up' on what monastery life had denied him. In a magazine interview Oz, as he now called himself, had rejected Buddhism and said that he had run away from the strictures imposed on him against his will and that his youth had been 'stolen'.

The media had its field day. But perhaps the ultimate irony was overlooked: the boy who was said to have been the reincarnation of an individualistic dropout had ended up rejecting the whole idea, thus actually becoming just such an individualistic dropout. Perhaps he was the reincarnation of Thubten Yeshe after all.

- 8 -

Thinking about Bubión and hermits gone AWOL got me wondering again about Molly and her wayward husband, Marcus. It had been a couple of weeks since I had spoken with her and I wondered if she had yet managed to talk him down from his mountain peregrinations. I had been thinking a lot about the idea of setting up a local newspaper and was eager to talk to her about it. Truth be told, I'd been madly scribbling down ideas in a notebook, yet because I had no knowledge of journalism beyond taking a minor correspondence course once, I liked the idea of enlisting the mysterious Marcuswith his experience and journalistic knowhow. I called up Molly and asked whether she'd be able to catch hold of him and bring him down to Pampaneira the following Sunday. I said I might have a proposal for them.

Sunday dawned crisp and cold. There was ice on the windows but the sun shone bright as the village cats huddled against warm chimneys and the pure air was suffused by the delicious smell of olive wood smoke. By late morning Pampaneira was pulsating with life, as it did every weekend. We walked down, *en famille*, to El Pilon and found a table at the back beside a roaring log fire next to which slept a large black dog. I ordered coffee and sherry, as well as a *rosca* – which was a large ring of crusty warm bread stuffed with dried ham and goat's cheese, cut into biteable sections, and served up dripping in olive oil.

Molly appeared with Marcus walking behind her. She introduced him and they pulled up chairs to sit with us. Marcus bore no resemblance to the image I'd had of him in my mind's eye. Instead of being a rugged and bearded mountain man, he was smooth skinned and angular, wearing brown corduroy trousers and polished shoes. His face was rendered small by the large glasses he wore and his curly brown hair had been neatly trimmed. He looked more like a librarian than a survivalist. 'Pleased to meet yous,' he said revealing a Merseyside accent as we shook hands. We sat and exchanged small talk about life in our respective villages and ordered some sherry and *tapas*. Small bowls of green olives were placed in front of us, along with little plates of cheese and ham. "Granada's the best place for *tapas* in Spain," said Marcus, poking at the olives with a toothpick. "Everywhere else you have to pay for it, but not here."

We chatted, filling in our back-stories and getting a feel for one another. Although they had lived in Spain for a few years, like us they had only recently moved to La Alpujarra, mainly for the fresh air, the food and the mountain life. We all agreed that the idea of living anywhere else was now unimaginable.

When it seemed like enough time had elapsed, and the effect of the warming sherry had begun to course through us, I floated the newspaper idea to the two of them. Molly looked excited "I *knew* that was why you wanted to meet up. We've been talking about it too." She was full of ideas, and talked excitedly of the different sections we could produce and all the articles we could write. I pulled out my notebook full of scribbles and read out some of the ideas I'd come up with. The thing that we all felt, right there at the beginning, was that there was a niche for a newspaper that delved into Alpujarran life and culture. It would be a community newspaper that reported real local news, and it wouldn't just deal with the fluffy stuff. As far as any of us knew, nobody had ever done that before, so it would be something of an experiment.

When we'd been gabbing on about it for an hour or so I said, "So, we're going to do this, are we?"

"Of course we are!" squealed Molly.

"Sounds like a plan – gotta do something to earn a crust," said Marcus, poking olives around on his plate.

We ordered glasses of *Rioja* and toasted the venture. The rough plan, we decided, would be that myself and Molly would be the ones to become business partners, while Marcus with his journalistic know-how would head up the news production side of things and I would manage the newspaper's creation and write some feature articles. Molly would keep her steady job with the estate agent until such a time as Marcus and I had made a success of the newspaper, when she would join us. Michelle, not having any interest in newspapers or writing, said she would be in a 'support role'. Before we parted company that day we agreed that Marcus and I should meet every Wednesday to put some plans down on paper and discuss ways to get the ball rolling. On that cold day in early February we gave ourselves a target for getting the newspaper in the hands of readers before the end of spring. I went away buzzing with excitement and filled with ideas.

- 9 -

When Wednesday came around Marcus seemed like a different person to the one I had met in Pampaneira. I had arranged to meet him in Baraca, the Sufi café in Órgiva, and we were going to hash out some concepts and ideas. We had already figured that if it was to be taken seriously, the newspaper should be run from Órgiva, the main regional town, rather than some tiny village up a mountain. Marcus seemed diminished and fidgety when he turned up, casting uneasy glances around him and muttering about the 'weird looking' clientele. The previous weekend in El Pilon he had seemed almost overly polite and accommodating but today he cast sideways glances and wouldn't make eye contact. I wondered what was putting him on edge.

I asked him about his experience and he told me he had studied journalism at college and then gone on to be a cub reporter at various local papers in Liverpool before moving to Spain and writing for a newspaper on the Costa del Sol. As we were speaking he had the habit of abruptly standing bolt upright and digging his fists into his pockets as if he was about to suddenly walk away, before sitting down again and fiddling with whatever he could find on the table in front of him. He seemed inordinately nervous and steered talk towards restaurants and *tapas*, which seemed to animate him. When I tried to move conversation onto the topics I thought we should be discussing, such as how we'd get advertising revenue and where we'd find writers, Marcus didn't seem to want to talk. He'd more often than not respond with evasive rejoinders: "You've got to be in it to win it" or "It'll be alright on the night."

By the time I left I felt the way ahead was no clearer. I went home feeling a bit dejected about our meeting, hoping perhaps that it was just a case of nerves and that Marcus would become more relaxed around me in future. In hindsight, this was perhaps the point where I should have followed my gut instinct and walked away. Whatever was bugging Marcus was his business, and maybe I should have left him to get on with his life and focus my energies on something else instead.

My worries increased the next week when Marcus failed to show up at all. I called Molly to ask where he'd got to and she apologised and explained that he'd probably run into some problems walking down the mountain. I asked her why exactly he would be *walking* all the way from Bubión to Órgiva – a hike that would have taken hours – when he could have driven or simply asked me for a lift. Molly explained patiently that he had never learned to drive a car, wasn't keen on taking lifts off others, and that there was no way to contact him as he didn't possess a mobile phone. "In fact," she added, "he doesn't even own a wallet."

A week later and he *did* show up this time, albeit looking a bit sheepish. I was glad he'd decided to appear but my relief soon turned to frustration when I tried to go over all the issues I thought we needed to straighten out. Who would write articles for us? How much should we charge advertisers? What geographical area would we cover? Who would be our target readers?

All these questions seemed important to me, but Marcus, slouching into his denim jacket with his hands in his pockets, could barely make eye contact. To each of my questions he would respond with some flippant remark that seemed to bear no relation to the matter at hand. "Chill out chuck," he said.

I was growing frustrated with his unwillingness to discuss the newspaper idea. Perhaps the whole thing was a mistake and I should abandon it and set up my café, or else ditch Marcus and try to do it alone. But without Marcus I wouldn't have the first clue about how to proceed, so the latter option was no good. My frustration must have been visible because just as I was about to call off the rest of the meeting and go home he reached into the leather satchel he carried with him everywhere and pulled out a sheaf of papers, slapping them down on the table. "You see," he said "I might not be much good at business planning and all that shite, but while you've been doing nothing I've actually gone and done some work."

I looked through the papers. Page after page of lined A4 was covered with a thin spidery handwriting, much blighted by crossings out and straggled arrows leading from footnotes and sideways-written comments. Some pages were stained red in parts by the base of a wine glass and the whole lot was dog-eared. It seemed to be about some gangster or other from Marbella, and there were lots of references to drugs, ostentatious villas and incidents of violence. "Voila," said Marcus as he picked up his coffee cup "our first crime feature."

- 10 -

When the door swung open into what would be our new office it revealed a scene that suggested the previous occupant had left in a hurry. The brass plaque with the lawyer's name was still attached outside the entrance and the picture from his law school graduation remained on the wall above the desk, but of the man himself there was no sign. Next to the picture stood a bookshelf packed with leather-bound tomes of the type lawyers like to be pictured sitting in front of. It was difficult to overlook the fact that the splintered wooden door had a boot-print on it, and an upturned chair lay on the floor surrounded by scattered legal papers.

The elderly landlady was showing us around. Mercedes was a sturdy-footed senior with a booming voice and a cast iron hairstyle. She was speaking so fast that Marcus had to translate for me as we inspected what was clearly a residential apartment rather than an office, complete with floral curtains and a kitchen sink full of washing up. "These books," she shouted as if we were deaf, "are included in the rental agreement." She waited for our reaction, and failing to detect one, started again, a little louder this time. "These books are included in the price of the rent."

"We're not lawyers," I pointed out "but thanks for the offer." The landlady didn't seem to understand my Spanish but repeated the offer again very slowly as if we were both deaf *and* dumb "THESE BOOKS ARE INCLUDED IN THE PRICE OF THE RENT. They are very valuable. Maybe you will need them here in my country so you can understand the law."

"Fuck sake," grumbled Marcus, "why do these old Spanish people have to say everything three bloody times?"

We had been searching in vain for an office. After writing his first article, Marcus had got on board with the newspaper project and, perhaps deciding to trust me, buckled down to the nitty-gritty of helping set up a business. Having considered cutting costs and working from home, the prospect of possessing an office in Órgiva would lend us at least some credibility we figured. After all, a physical address would be an indicator of stability in the eyes of advertisers. But office space was in short supply in Órgiva, a town unaccustomed to white-collar employment, and we had almost given up the search when Molly had put us onto Mercedes. The space we were being shown was a couple of floors above Mel and Nikki's estate agency where I had briefly worked, and Molly still did. Surveying the wreckage in the office before us the question had to be asked, and Marcus duly obliged: "What happened to the lawyer who was here before?"

She eyed him suspiciously. "Gone. He is gone away," she said with a dismissive flick of the wrist. "To Madrid." I got the impression that 'Madrid' was a euphemism for 'away: destination unknown'.

"So he's not going to come back and find us in his office?" I asked, a little hesitantly. In truth I was more worried about people coming in looking for the man than I was of the lawyer himself who, from his picture on the wall, looked a bit wet behind the ears. Whoever had kicked in the door and smashed the place up probably didn't look wet behind the ears.

"He will not be coming back," Mercedes replied with a wry chuckle that sounded a little sinister. "If you want his books I will also throw in the desk blotter as well."

"As if we'd fucking want that…" muttered Marcus.

"What are you doing here in my country?" she suddenly demanded, her penetrating stare putting us both on trial.

"We making a newspaper," said Marcus.

"An estate agent?" she replied, as though that was the only reasonable answer.

"No a newspap…"

"Yes," she interrupted. "You estate agents come here to sell the land from under our feet. Just as I thought. Well, you may rent my office while you go about your unsavoury business, but on my word, I trust you only because of your German heritage."

"We're English," I interjected, feeling that perhaps I'd missed some part of the conversation.

The old woman's eyes narrowed as she scrutinised my face for signs of dishonesty. "*Ingles?*" she said, her voice softening. "If you were English, as you say you are, you'd be *pirates*. And I do not let my office out to *pirates*!" She spat the word *piratos*, disgust flashing in her eyes.

She continued, almost at a whisper. "No, you are nothing more than babies. But at least you are not English and, I must admit, I respect what you Germans have done in the past."

"We're not fucking Germans," said Marcus, in English.

She reached out and squeezed his cheek, causing him to blush, continuing almost in a whisper. "You may rent my office but, by the Lord, the rent I am charging you is so low it pains me. You hear me, it pains me! And me, a pensioner being held hostage in my own country by foreigners!"

We both looked at her. She seemed to be completely mad, but an office was an office, even if it wasn't really an office and was a bit on the pricey side.

"You may pay me a deposit of three months' rent and the first month's rental in cash, plus a breakages deposit. But do not push my generosity, if I do not hear from you by tomorrow I will give it to someone else." And with that the old lady turned and left us on our own. We looked around the apartment unimpeded. It was large, consisting of a spacious reception room and two smaller ones, including the hapless disappeared lawyer's space. There was a small kitchen that was stacked to the ceiling with cardboard boxes, and an avocado-coloured bathroom with a leaking tap, no light and an unflushable toilet. The one large window looked down from the second floor onto an abandoned litter-strewn courtyard in which a lone fig tree had sprouted from a gutter. Stray cats sunned themselves atop a graffiti covered wall beside the church.

"Órgiva really is a shithole isn't it?" said Marcus.

Naturally, we took the office.

Acquiring an office in which to do business was the easy part compared to the complications of setting up a company. Without a company number we would not be able to conduct even the smallest business transaction so it was essential that we submitted a name with the mercantile register in Granada. To help us we employed the services of a solicitor, Pablo, an Órgiva native who could be found in a large office overlooking the town's plaza. Far from being the kind of fast-witted legal knife one might imagine, Pablo liked to take things at a more sedate pace. With his polished, clean-shaven face, he was more Volvo than Ferrari, but he knew inside out the procedure for setting up a business. Thanks to his efforts the slow wheels of the Spanish legal system began to turn and the minting of our small media startup began.

We needed a name for the newspaper, and racked our brains to come up with one. As it was originally conceived we wanted to cover no more than the news and happenings in Órgiva and the surrounding villages, so I thought the *Órgiva Post* seemed an obvious moniker. This, however, was swiftly rejected by Marcus and Molly who disliked the association with Órgiva, which they regarded as a Spanish version of Mos Eisley spaceport from *Star Wars* ("*You will never find a more wretched hive of scum and villainy…*").

The next proposal was the vaguely communist-sounding *Voice of the Alpujarras*, which had a pleasing resonance and seemed to fit in with the area's self-regard as an enclave of radicalism. Michelle pointed out, however, that the name was likely to put off people who lived further afield, such as those living on the coast. And although the newspaper wasn't aimed at them, we felt that we shouldn't exclude potential readers right from the outset, so we tried to think of something more generic. I looked around at the landscape with my foreign eyes for inspiration and came up with *The Lemon Tree*. Nobody could find a good reason *not* to dislike this title and so it remained *The Lemon Tree* for quite some time prior to the first issue. But then, one day, standing in the kitchen of one of my neighbours and listening as he lamented the amount of work he had put into harvesting his olives compared to the puny amount of oil he had received as payment from the olive press, a new name struck me.

I texted Molly: "The Olive Press?" She texted back immediately: "We have a winner!" And so from then on it was *The Olive Press*.

Aside from getting a name, an office and a solicitor, we also needed to find a few other things that would be necessary for running a newspaper. I wrote a list of what I thought was essential:

Accountant
Computers (4 – cheap as possible)
Inkjet printer
Desks and chairs (4)
Desk Top Publishing software
Paint and brushes (white, to cover nicotine-stained beige walls)
Sofa
Rug
Wall map of Andalucía

The accountant was easy enough to find; Órgiva had three of them so it was just a case of picking one that nobody could say anything bad about. The furniture came from Ikea in Seville, shuttled over to us by some friends in a large van. The computers were discounted display models from the supermarket on the coast and the software we needed to make the newspaper – *QuarkXpress* –was bought on Amazon. I also bought a copy of the book *QuarkXpress for Dummies*, and attempted to get to grips with it over coffee each morning.

One thing that wasn't on our shopping list was a dog, but when I drove down to the coast with Jasmine to pick up the computers, we noticed something very odd in the supermarket: a husky puppy was cramped inside a small cage in the pet section amongst the budgerigars and gerbils. It just didn't seem right that an animal bred for the cold northern latitudes should be confined in such a way and so, predictably enough, I found myself using my credit card to pay for four desktop computers, a week's shopping and a husky. My daughter immediately fell in love with this blue-eyed bundle of fur and soon we were driving back to the mountains with our baby wolf, which we named Zac. Quite what a husky was doing on a supermarket shelf in Spain is anyone's guess, but we figured it would be better off living in the cooler mountains. What's more, we figured, Zac could be the office dog, and when he got bigger he might even protect us against anyone who came looking for the lawyer.

The office was almost ready for us to start work in, although there still seemed a hundred things that needed to be resolved before we could actually print a newspaper. The questions turned around in my mind at night and, the further along the line we went, the more worrisome they seemed. Where would it be printed? Who would write stuff for us? How many copies should there be? How do we get sales? As the questions and uncertainties jostled in my mind it occurred to me with each passing day that, quite frankly, we had almost no idea what we were doing. Marcus was already scribbling away amassing a bunch of stories, mostly about crime and corruption, so at least we had some content lined up, but it was Molly who was the more useful from a practical point of view. Even though she was still working for Mel and Nikki, she would surreptitiously be drumming up potential business and putting the word out about us through her contacts.

I printed off some some fliers announcing our forthcoming arrival in the hope that local writers would step forward. Making sure the launch date was as vague as possible – 'Coming in late Spring' – I spent a long day driving around the whole region, sticking the fliers up in cafés and bookshops or wherever I thought any English speakers might congregate. In so doing I was asked more than once whether *The Olive Press* would be a bi-lingual publication, with articles translated side-by-side on the page. When I got back I mentioned this to Marcus, thinking it might be a good way to draw in extra business.

"That's a fooking stupid idea," said Marcus, with what I was beginning to realise was his characteristic acerbic manner. "The Spanish already have dozens of newspapers to read – why would they bother to read one made by a bunch of *guiris*?"

"Okay," I said "but what about writers? We don't have any and we're going to have to actually publish our first issue sooner or later before we run out of money."

"It's alright, we don't need writers," he replied. "We'll just buy ready-made articles from the Associated Press to begin with. After that we'll be inundated with the bastards. Every Tom, Dick or Harry thinks they're a writer, you wait and see."

But printing pre-fab articles seemed too easy to me, and it hardly fitted with the plan of making it a community newspaper covering local issues. A quick look at the kind of articles Marcus was talking about showed them mostly to be generic and insipid ('Eat Healthy to Avoid Allergies' or 'Five Steps to a Better

Love Life' etc.) – there would be nothing to distinguish *The Olive Press* from the numerous other advertising vehicles out there. No, I figured, here was a chance to be bold and take a gamble. In any case, the likely readership would be an independent-minded bunch who would probably not settle for spring cleaning tips, listicles and celebrity sightings on the *costas*. Furthermore, it appeared pointless to focus on news from 'back home', like all the Brit-centric newspapers up and down the coasts did.

"Don't worry," said Marcus, sensing my unease. "There will be people queuing up round the block wanting to write for us soon – we'll have to set that dog of yours on them."

And he was right. Writers began to appear out of the woodwork. The first one to turn up was John. John was a somewhat avuncular-looking Australian who turned out to have a deadpan sense of humour. He said he freelanced for a magazine in Nerja, meaning he was already well known in the area and would have to write for us under a pseudonym so as not to annoy his other employer. Newspapers, I was later to learn, avoided stepping on one another's toes. John said he had lived in Spain for decades and claimed to have a 'pretty good idea' about the country. I read some of his articles and insights into the local ways, which were laid out with an Antipodean wit not unlike that of Clive James.

I figured John would make an ideal contrarian, with a license for barbed repartee. We'd put him on the back page and his job would be to be controversial yet funny. So, inventing a *nom de plume* for him became the challenge, and it came to me when sitting in a bar pondering the multitude of drying legs of *serrano* ham that hung from the ceiling. Still being new enough to the region to remark upon the macabre spectacle of so many severed limbs, each with a small inverted plastic umbrella to catch any putrefying dribbles, I found these dripping meat ceilings worthy of comment. With so many legs dangling there it seemed only reasonable to wonder where the rest of the animal was – so far I'd only seen a single live pig in the region, and even that hadn't been alive for very long. I imagined somewhere out there beyond the horizon there must be a landscape swarming with three-legged pigs hobbling around on crutches. Thus *The Amputee* came into being; an irascible cartoon pig on crutches whose wisecracking sarcasm went – like the legs hanging up on the ceiling – over most people's heads.

Marcus said he knew another likely writer, an American 'Flower Power' survivor and Vietnam vet living in Bubión who spoke barely a word of Spanish and lived like some latter-day Ernest Hemingway. He'd written a book about his time in the 1960s, and he was apparently keen to do some more writing. When I met him, Paul McGwin, a man with a crushing handshake, said he was a poet and couldn't write without a bottle of bourbon in front of him. He had that gruff American directness about him, and he wasn't short of opinions and anecdotes. But he was passionate about Spain and its history and seemed glad, when asked, to have the responsibility of writing about local history and culture. He immediately got down to writing an article about the time when the poet Lorca lived in Bubión.

Another writer came in the form of Gill, a vegan who was living the good life on a smallholding out in the eastern Alpujarra. This was an area that was remote even by Alpujarran standards, and she lived there with her photographer boyfriend, Steve, who wore a bandana and, for reasons unknown, insisted we address him by the name Zenon Zappa. Gill, who just like us was a recent arrival, would write a column about growing food and living sustainably in what was for her a completely new setting. She said that locals had started to call her 'Goat Girl' for her habit of following the animals around with a pair of tights in which she collected their dung to use as fertilizer on her vegetable patch.

We needed someone to write about ornamental gardening, and for a while it seemed like we wouldn't find anyone qualified to do it. But then Richard, a genteel man from Dorset who ran a cleaning firm with his partner Tim, mentioned that he had plenty of experience gardening, if not writing. Tickled at the prospect of writing a column, his only request was that we substitute his surname for the pseudonym 'Duende' – a *duende* being a kind of magical Spanish pixie invoked during Flamenco performances. To that end I used Photoshop to give Richard a set of pointed ears for the profile picture that would accompany his gardening column.

Kim was another local writer. She came into the office saying she wanted to write about spirituality and ecology. In particular she wanted to write about the local alternative school, which had been set up on the banks of the river. The school took the form of a series of yurts in which the children were taught to think along the lines of the Austrian mystic Rudolf Steiner. Marcus reacted with suspicion to her proposal, pointing out after she'd left the office that she hadn't shaved her legs or armpits. "We're not going to be some bloody environmental rag for hippies," he said disdainfully. But, then again, Kim was certainly qualified to write about such things, as she was already a regular contributor to the Andalucía based spirituality magazine *La Chispa*. What's more, she was the daughter of Wendy Henry, the erstwhile *News of the World* editor, known in some quarters as 'Fleet Street's killer bimbo', so she must have known a thing or two about journalism.

"She can write for us on a trial basis," grumbled Marcus. "But too much hippie shite and she's out the door, hairy armpits and all."

Another female writer came in the form of Lisa, who lived over the other side of the Lecrin Valley in Alhama de Granada. Lisa wanted to write about social issues. She was a good writer and had written for a number of other publications so she was a shoe-in.

We also hired a cartoonist by the name of Dave. He was already known as something of a satirist and did a series of cartoons for us based on the famous silhouette of the Osborne sherry bulls that you see scattered around the hillsides of Spain. Dave was a retired union representative and, for reasons best known to him, would take any opportunity to dress up in a realistic-looking gorilla suit. He could sometimes be found wandering around the streets of Tíjola thus attired like a rural Spanish Yeti. The locals were puzzled by this behaviour, but they tolerated it as long as it didn't get any weirder.

Finally, a section on learning Spanish was to be headed up by Joachim, a flamboyant young Mexican with a ponytail reaching most of the way down his back. Mel the estate agent at that point employed Joachim as a property scout, and his job was to walk around the hills seeking out picturesque properties and attempt to convince the usually elderly residents to part with them for a fistful of euros. As a card-carrying left-wing radical with a wardrobe full of Che Guevara t-shirts, his job at the cutting edge of capitalism had been playing on his conscience for a while. And so a new role as a Spanish teacher suited Joachim fine.

After all the palaver of finding writers and figuring out what they should write about it seemed logical at that point to decide what our respective roles should be.

Marcus said he didn't care about titles, but I wanted us to look professional and thought there should be a list on the inside front page with our job titles. "Fine," said Marcus, "I'll be the News Editor." It made sense, because his focus was on the news and *The Olive Press* was, after all, a *news*paper, as opposed to a magazine. I settled on the title of Features Editor, being more interested in the feature article aspect of things and having found most of the columnists.

We needed someone to fulfil the role of office administrator, receptionist and salesperson. And so Vicki, whom I'd met at a local group for parents with toddlers, was employed on account of her language skills and organisational nous. Molly was supposed to have filled this role but she was still working downstairs and didn't want to commit to our venture until after we'd launched. I'd offered Vicki the job and she had accepted immediately, after all it was extremely hard to get a paid job as a foreigner, but Marcus was lukewarm about her appointment. Vicki was over six feet tall and blonde, and he just didn't click with her. But the important thing, as far I was concerned, was that she could do the job, and do it well.

The weeks that followed were filled with activity. Furniture arrived and was set up, the walls were painted with a fresh coat of white paint and the brass plaque bearing the name of the previous occupant was unscrewed from the door. Someone came and repaired the bathroom fittings and our landlady carted away the lawyer's books two at a time, muttering about how ungrateful we were. With word spreading about the impending first edition, people began to contact us hoping to be involved in some way, invariably for money.

On the wall above my newly installed desk I had Sellotaped thirty-two blank pages which were now covered with scrawls and pictures, giving a rough outline of how the first edition would look. There was still a worryingly large number of holes that needed filling, but Marcus didn't seem concerned and said we'd fill them somehow, even if it was with cute pictures of Zac the husky. Vicki turned up for work every day, dressed smartly and with a long list of potential advertisers to contact. Soon enough the phone line was connected and she started to work her way down the list, bringing in a few promises.

It was by now May, and things were finally starting to happen.

- 12 -

We fixed a date for the first issue as a Thursday in late May and began to work towards it. Thursday, we figured, would be the best day to reveal ourselves to the world, as this was when everyone came into town for the market. Aside from trying to learn how to use the desktop publishing software, I also had to learn how to tally accounts and deal with the other responsibilities of running a small business. The task fell on Vicki to find us a printing firm, and so she rang around and asked for quotes. Soon, it became clear that there was only one real option available to us, and that was to use the services of the main regional newspaper, *Ideal*, based in Granada.

When the day came for us to go and meet the production manager and discuss our requirements, we drove the hour or so from Órgiva to an industrial estate in the northern reaches of the city where the newspaper was based. Carlos, the production manager, showed us around the printworks before leading us into the offices where the editorial department was based. It was the first newsroom I had ever been in. There were desks for up to a hundred journalists, but at ten in the morning the place was almost deserted. "In Spain, journalists work late into the night," explained Carlos. "Translation – lazy bastards," muttered Marcus into my ear.

After the tour, which included seeing the huge mechanical printing press in action, we repaired to Carlos's office to talk business. The important things for us to consider were the paper quality, the page size and how many sheets it would be comprised of. Vicki did most of the talking, as my Spanish was certainly not up to the level of negotiating a printing contract, while Marcus said he was a writer rather than a businessman. We left with a deal to print five thousand copies of *The Olive Press* on a fortnightly basis, with an initial print run of ten thousand so we could saturate the region and get the message out that we existed. The size of the paper was to be slightly less than a tabloid, and was based on a brochure for a computer retailer that I had seen lying on Carlos's desk. I had held up the brochure for inkjet printers and desktop workstations and said, "We want something this size, and on the same type of paper."

On the way back I felt excited about what lay ahead. It was late spring and the snow had melted on the mountains, while the countryside was refreshed and seemed full of pent-up energy. A profusion of wildflowers turned every verge, ditch and hillside into a scramble of colour, and clear streams rushed through ancient channels, flooding into fields and staining the earth a dark shade of ochre. With the burst of spring and the clear, open landscape around us, it seemed like anything was possible. New horizons stretched out before us like the long lines of orange groves we were driving through, the trees frothy with blossom, and their perfumed scent carrying in through the car windows.

We passed an old working olive press and I made a note of the deep green colour of its painted metal doors. It seemed to be the standard colour across the region to advertise your olive press to passing traffic, and so we agreed this would make the perfect colour for our masthead. When we got back to Órgiva, Vicki went back to work while Marcus and I met up with Molly in a café. It was here that she and Marcus dropped some unwelcome news on me. They had decided, she said, that it would be better if Marcus was on the deeds as a co-owner of the business rather than her, given that she was still working for the estate agent. Marcus was more involved in *The Olive Press* than was she, so it would make more sense.

This adjustment to the deal came as something of a blow to me: I had justified sinking a sizeable sum of money into our project on the basis that I would be dealing with Molly as a business partner, rather than her husband. Now, at the last minute and just as we were about to go into print, it seemed they wanted to switch the deal around.

I went back home and discussed the matter long into the night with Michelle. Neither of us felt happy about the sudden change, but it was clear that the newspaper wouldn't be going anywhere without Marcus's experience. What's more, Marcus was never willing to discuss the ugly topic of money, and it had been Molly I'd been dealing with up until then on all matters to do with financing our venture. Perhaps Molly would still be the significant partner, even if her name were not on the deed. That's what we hoped.

And so, despite misgivings, I found myself a few days later sitting in the local notary office next to Marcus and signing the company deeds. The *notaria*, a busy woman from Granada, was polite enough to complement us on our decision to dispense with an interpreter. Clearly, she said, we were not like the other *ingleses*. She turned the pages of the deeds over in her hands, reading out the Spanish legalese at high speed and making little sounds every now and then to indicate that she was impressed with some detail or other. I hadn't got a clue what she was saying. Pablo, our fresh-faced solicitor, sat in the corner looking in on the proceedings with a fixed smile. I glanced at him every now and again, perhaps for reassurance.

"So," said the notary, reverting back to speaking at a normal speed as she handed a couple of pens to Marcus and myself, "I wish you luck with your venture. Times are good for the real estate sector." I looked at Pablo, nonplussed: had I misunderstood something? I had been under the impression we were setting up a newspaper, not a property business. Pablo coughed politely and indicated that I should just sign the title deeds, which, I now noticed, described our business purpose as 'media estate agent' whatever that meant. Marcus looked equally alarmed.

"This way," Pablo explained, "if your newspaper goes bust, as is likely, you can still buy and sell houses to pay off the debts."

"Fucking great," said Marcus sarcastically. "That's very clever of you."

"In any case," continued the solicitor, "the authorities in Spain are not keen on foreigners owning newspapers, so this is for the best. Most of your money will come from estate agents placing adverts, so it is not entirely untrue that you are an *estate agent media company*."

There was a moment of silence in the office as Marcus and I stared at our solicitor while the *notaria* held out the two pens to us. Shouldering a mountain of misgivings, I took the pen and signed my name. Marcus did the same.

"*Que bien*," she mewed, "congratulations on your new status as business owners in Spain."

After our appointment at the notary office I left Marcus and found a small bar down a side street. I went in and ordered a large whisky, and then another one. There, I sat on a barstool and wondered what the hell I'd just done. I had a terrible feeling that we'd just set something clockwork in motion, and I wasn't entirely sure where it would lead or how it could be stopped, but I knew I'd probably regret it.

- 13 -

Like us, there were plenty of other people who had just arrived in the region and were setting up small businesses that needed publicity. Some of them were estate agents but others were dog groomers, life coaches and restaurateurs. However, the hills were alive, we soon found out, with healers and yoga teachers of one sort or another. Judging by the noticeboards around town, which bristled with torn bits of paper advertising everything from quantum hypnosis and reiki, to aura massage and sacred drum birthing, every kind of alternative therapy was on offer by an army of practitioners. "There's so many fucking yoga teachers here," observed Marcus "they must be teaching one another."

And although a lot of these practitioners wanted to place adverts with us very few of them seemed to be able to pay with actual cash. But cash was what we needed, and so we had to politely turn them down. One man, who claimed to be able to see people's auras, came in and offered an analysis in return for a free ad. As he was speaking to me his gaze was, somewhat unnervingly, fixed about six inches above my head.

There were builders, gardeners and handymen too – and at least these practical people offered us money and didn't attempt to get six months of free ads for cleaning our chakras and giving us Tarot readings. But they too proved to be a dead end as far as advertising went. For the most part they preferred to take on jobs by word of mouth and were averse to having any mention of them put down in ink in case the tax authorities saw it. And those who trusted us enough to place an advert invariably said they'd pay for it if and when they had seen 'results'. Invariably we had to say 'no' to them too.

Both Marcus and I were coming into the office on a daily basis by now. I sat in the smaller office on my own, while Marcus positioned himself at a desk as far away from the main door as possible and sat facing a wall while tapping away at the keys of his computer, a spread of the day's papers arranged around him. He didn't like to speak when he was working, although he said he couldn't concentrate without some type of music playing. Marcus's idea of 'some kind of music' was usually *The Fall*. When it wasn't *The Fall* it was usually Nick Cave or else some sort of avant-garde audio production, which could take the form of anything from bursts of static feedback to strange wailing noises interspersed with random sounds. But the peculiar music must have helped him concentrate, as the pile of finished stories grew daily. Most of them involved local crime and corruption, and Marcus seemed to have a thing for long, complex sagas involving the downfall of crime bosses who lived in lavish mansions with gold taps and racehorses. When I commented that maybe we should try and strike a balance, perhaps with something more light-hearted for our first issue, he was aghast.

"Light hearted?" he said, incredulous. "There isn't any light hearted news, this is Spain, you know!" I decided not to raise the issue again for the time being. After all, he was the one with experience of writing news stories. At least, I considered, a mix of interesting feature articles might balance out the gloom and doom, which judging by the stories he had ringed in the local papers were going to be filled with pictures of starved horses, hunting dogs hung from trees and the corpses of poisoned birds. "I'm only reporting the news," said Marcus, defensively. "It's not my fault that it's nearly all bad."

But there was one local news story in particular that caught my attention. We pieced together what had happened from a media report, as well as from local gossip in town. It concerned Beneficio – the commune up the mountain near Cáñar – and a South African man. The man had turned up there some months before, and had quickly muscled his way onto the community council and seized the talking stick, meaning nobody else was allowed to speak from then on. In this way he had established himself as a kind of mini tyrant and nobody had dared to challenge him.

At some point it all come to a head when he accused a British hippie of sleeping with another man's wife. The South African exacted punishment on the man by tying him to a crucifix and keeping him there for several days inside a 'prison tepee'. Eventually the man was released but the South African decided to run him out of town, chasing the poor man stark naked down the mountain with a bull whip in the middle of the night. This was enough for the local police to go up to Beneficio and arrest the man, who was taken in and thrown into the cells, much to the relief of the other residents of the commune. Further investigation revealed he was a fugitive wanted in connection with a serious crime and he was later jailed in Granada. Whether or not he was the hitchhiker I had picked up I'll probably never know as

Spanish media only revealed the initials and nationalities of people involved in criminal proceedings and I couldn't find any pictures of him. In time, we learned, there were a lot of things going on like this, but more often than not they were never reported upon.

As the date grew closer of our first edition I asked Marcus what he thought the main story should be on our front page. He said he had a crime story about the police station being closed in Bubión, meaning there would be no officers to handle any outbreaks of criminal behaviour.

"But there *is* no crime in Bubión," I said. "It's a sleepy little mountain village where nothing happens."

"That's immaterial," he replied. "You never know when something *might* happen. Besides Molly took a picture of the police station, so we can use that for the main article."

I began to protest that this was possibly the most boring story I'd ever heard and that our first story should be something of a splash but he cut me short. "Look, I'm the News Editor, remember? I get to decide what news goes in."

With some misgivings, I decided to keep my focus on the feature articles and let Marcus get on with the news aspect. Perhaps we'd get feedback from readers and after a few issues he'd publish something a bit more interesting. That's what I hoped, at least.

We thought it would be a good idea to have a small headshot of each of us to go on the inside cover. We all posed, and when I'd got one I was happy with it was Vicki's turn, and then Molly's. When it came to Marcus's turn I held the camera up and said 'smile'. But instead of smiling, Marcus put on his most serious face, pursed his lips together and glared at the lens in an expression that seemed to ask 'Did you spill my pint?' The resulting picture made him look like a football hooligan, or maybe a violent offender, and it seemed like he might leap out of the page and head-butt the reader. "Perfect," he said, examining the digital image. "The last thing we want is anyone thinking we're a soft touch."

- 14 -

The build-up to our first issue was quite stressful, beset by many niggling technical and administrative problems. There were salespeople haggling over commissions, writers forgetting to hand in their copy and issues with the publishing software.

I felt I needed to get out of the office and clear my head, and so I decided one day to go for a strenuous walk. It was mid-May, only ten days or so before our first issue, and most of the snow and ice had melted from the summits of the mountains. Michelle had gone off to Denmark for a few days in order to attend a wedding and she had taken the children with her. So, with no domestic commitments and only a cat, a husky and a ghost for company, I was free to do as I chose. I thought: why not walk up to the top of Mulhacén?

Following a light breakfast at the village *hostal*, served up by the po-faced waiter Paco, I put Zac the husky in the car and drove up to the pine forests on the high slopes above Capileira. Up there the light was so luminous and the air so fresh and clear that it seemed like I had driven up into some higher plane of existence. I parked the car and opened the boot, letting Zac fly out like a coiled spring. I was in a silent landscape of lichen-covered boulders on the edge of a dark forest of trees that dripped with strands of hanging moss. Despite it being a fine sunny day, the air still held a cold chill, as though the last remnants of winter lingered on. It felt as if I had the whole mountain to myself and I stood on a rocky ledge looking out at the valleys below me, which were blanketed with layers of swirling cloud that swaddled the lower slopes. Turning around and looking towards the summit I knew that I would be walking for several hours to reach it and so I set off with Zac running ahead to make sure the way was safe.

For the first part of the journey we walked through an eerie and silent pine plantation. In the winter this place had felt magical, but without the softening effect of the snow, winter's spell had dispersed leaving only the darkness and damp of the pines. It took an hour or so to pass through them, when we emerged onto the upper reaches of the mountain. At 2,600m the air was noticeably thinner and I felt a little giddy as I walked. Lower down I could make out the large stone building that served as a refuge for walkers, and I remembered that there had been three British climbers who had died up here only a couple of months before. The men had been unlucky to be caught out by a sudden blizzard which had made it impossible to know which way they needed to go to find the safety of the refuge. After wandering around in circles they had eventually given up and tried to shelter in place. However, the son of one of the men realised that certain death lay in store unless they got down from the mountain and so he waded alone through the snow to seek help. Eventually, half-crazed with frostbite, he stumbled into Capileira late that night, raising the alarm about his father and friends. The authorities quickly mounted a search for the three older men but the weather was severe and the seasoned rescuers knew there was no chance of finding the men while such conditions persisted. I had experienced that same blizzard way down in Pampaneira and it had been pretty bad even there, so it must have been terrible for the men trapped on the upper slopes that night.

Following the abandoned search of the night before, the skies had cleared enough the next day to allow the hunt to continue. Alas, they were too late, and the dead men were found where they had tried to make camp. Their frozen bodies were taken by helicopter down to a mortuary on the coast. I recalled seeing the helicopter pass over Pampaneira with its grim bundle of cargo hanging below it from a rope. The men had died from hypothermia, what the Spanish term the 'sweet death' – so-called because of the feeling of peace and bliss that is said to envelop you as you approach death by freezing, which causes you to discard items of clothing in the belief that you are too warm. The men's death had been a warning to others that walking in these mountains was not to be undertaken lightly.

Now, however, the snows had gone, except for the odd frosty patch wherever a boulder had prevented the sun from reaching. Walking was easy as there was a track that seemed to go right to the top of the mountain and, although at one point I had convinced myself I must have been the only person up there, I was surprised when a small off-road jeep drove past me with four passengers in it. But these were the only other people I saw on my ascent, and by the time I neared the summit it was just Zac, the occasional mountain ibex and myself in this spectral landscape of boulders, lichen and silence.

When I heaved myself up onto the summit, which was a tor-like slab of rock with a concrete pillar set into it, I lay flat on my back to catch my breath. Although it had been no means a difficult walk, the air was thin and cold and there had been a blind summit near the end that had fooled me into thinking I had been a lot closer than I really was. When I had regained my breath I sat up and looked around. The view was incredible, and the dusty yellowish expanse of Spain stretched away in ever direction. To the north, the city of Granada was little more than a greyish smudge in the vast landscape, and when I looked to the west I could see a chain of volcano-like mountain stretching away from me into the far distance of Malaga. At the foot of these mountains the shining sea was laid out like a huge silver lake, with distant Morocco fringing its far shore. The sides of the nearest mountains were riven by gashes of green, and even the largest villages were barely visible as small white splashes on a vast green canvas. The silence was no less immense, and all of a sudden I felt incredibly small in this grand landscape, my presence in it about as significant as a microbe. For a moment it seemed as if this bird's eye view of my surroundings had given me a glimpse of something beyond the physical world, as if I was a lonely soul that had somehow drifted up above the earthly plane.

But it was when I turned my gaze to the east that I was brought back down to earth again. At first, my conscious brain couldn't compute what I was looking at, for it seemed I was gazing down upon a vast snowy plain that stretched off into the hazy distance. But there was no way it could be snow; this was the middle of May and, in any case, it never snowed in Almería, as far as I knew. And then it struck me what I was looking at: it wasn't snow, it was plastic.

I had heard about the plastic greenhouses of Almería, knew that much of the salad we were used to buying in the supermarket was grown in that region, but nothing had prepared me for the immense scale of it all. It was as if the entire landscape had been put under plastic, shrink wrapped and packaged up. And the more I looked at it, the more abnormal it seemed. It looked like a big 'screw you' to nature, and the alarming thing was that it seemed to be spreading towards La Alpujarra. Even at this distance I could see the plastic creeping out from Almería, its tendrils feeling their way down valleys and across mountaintops. From the top of Mulhacen, it looked like it wouldn't be long before it began to creep into La Alpujarra, sucking it dry of water and displacing every living thing in its ongoing thirst to consume the earth.

I descended from the summit on shaky legs. It was as clear as day – the salad business was going to eat up La Alpujarra. Yet nobody seemed to be bothered by it, and I'd heard few people talk about it. And if nobody was bothered by it then who would stand up for the area as the plastic tide flooded over the hills and down into the valleys? The traditional small-scale farmers, it was said, were all growing old, while the young were heading off to the cities. Sure, lots of foreigners had moved in to the region, attracted by the peace and quiet and the natural beauty, but they were hardly a political force to be reckoned with.

By the time I reached home again that evening my legs ached from the exertion and Zac was exhausted and quickly fell asleep on my bed. I went down to the *hostal* in the village and ordered a plate of poor man's potatoes from miserable-looking Paco, who was still working his shift and was uninterested in the fact that I'd just scaled Iberia's highest mountain. He brought over my dinner and a glass of red wine, and as he turned away I called out to him.

"Paco," I said. "Have you ever climbed up Mulhacén?"

The glum waiter looked at me. "No, why would I?"

"So you have never seen the greenhouses in Almería?" I asked.

"*Los invernaderos?* Yeah."

"Do you think they'll come here? I mean, will they be everywhere, like they are further east?"

"Probably," he said, with a shrug. "Who cares? It'll bring more jobs." He turned away and went back behind the bar to watch the football on TV.

Who cares? I thought. Well, I cared. And I was pretty sure many people who had moved here cared. If most of the local people displayed the same attitude as Paco the whole region would be bulldozed into oblivion in no time.

The thought of the region being despoiled by those plastic pirates rolled around in my head all evening. That night, I found I was unable to get to sleep from thinking about it. I got up, made myself a cup of tea and opened up my laptop. For the next couple of hours I did some research into the plastic greenhouse industry that had eaten up much of Almería and was threatening to eat La Alpujarra. What I discovered was concerning. Not only was the industry spreading rapidly in each direction, but wherever it went it left behind a toxic mess of discarded plastic, poisonous chemicals and depleted aquifers. The controversial American biotech company Monsanto had a research station there, and who knows what they were experimenting with inside those plastic tunnels. Worse still, there were actual slaves working in many of the greenhouses in Almería. Invariably Africans, these modern day slaves might not be wearing a ball and chain, but they were nevertheless not free to leave and were being forced to work long hours in dangerous conditions for little or no pay.

Of course, I read on, the authorities turned a blind eye to all this abuse of humans and the environment. The industry produced a valuable export commodity in the form of tomatoes, cucumbers and salad leaves, and was the main reason you could buy fresh tomatoes in Yorkshire in January. Or, at least something that looked like a tomato, even if it didn't taste like it.

I shut my laptop and went back to bed. In the strange quasi-mystical state between waking and sleeping, I half dreamed of a loud and clear voice that spoke out against these abuses; a voice advocating on behalf of the animals, the flowers and the very rocks and soil of the land. It took the bizarre form of a computer catalogue – many of them in fact, strung together and fluttering like prayer flags on the breeze in the cold, clear air of the high mountains. It gave voice to the people who saw value in protecting and restoring nature, and in nurturing the land that sustains all of life.

I snapped out of my weird reverie just before sleep overtook me. Sure, it sounded like a potty idea, but after what I had seen from the summit that day I couldn't just sit idly by and say nothing.

- 15 -

"This is not going to be some fucking hippie rag for do-gooding nimby fuckwits," said Marcus. He wasn't angry, that's just the way he spoke. I had been telling him about what I had seen on top of Mulhacén and how I thought we should focus on protecting the region from rapacious developers.

"But saying that," he said, "the last thing we want is for this area to turn into a shithole like Almería, so perhaps you've got a point."

I had suspected Marcus wouldn't be overly keen on the idea, but this was at least a start and he hadn't rejected it out of hand. Maybe if our newspaper got kudos for being a defender of the environment then it would reap benefits in other ways. The proof would be in the pudding, I hoped.

But, for now, we didn't have much time to wrangle over the ideological direction of *The Olive Press* as the time to print our first issue was upon us. The day duly came and myself, Marcus and Vicki set off to the print works to watch it come off the press. The night before had been a late one, with many last-minute changes and technical gremlins to sort out. The newspaper was finally 'put to bed' when the graphics files had been processed and sent over to *Ideal's* servers at around one in the morning.

I was nervous not only about how the print process would go, but also about how people would react to the first issue. The date was May 26th 2006, and a launch picnic was planned for later that day next to some natural pools in the gorge just below Pampaneira. But first we had to get the newspaper printed and distributed.

The appointment with Carlos was set for eight o'clock at the busy industrial estate where the *Ideal* headquarters was located. Marcus, Vicki and myself arrived early, having time to nervously drink down a coffee in a nearby café amongst local factory workers coming off their night shifts. The printworks was next to the Jaén motorway on the northern outskirts of Granada, and as we arrived trucks and vans burdened with freshly printed newspapers were easing out through the factory gates. Standing outside the building was an old metal printing press, reminding visitors and staff alike how the first edition of the left-leaning *Ideal* had been produced in 1932, a year before Franco began his inexorable rise to power.

Carlos greeted us and led our party inside the facility. Here, a handful of tired-looking print workers wearing blue boiler suits were leaning against different parts of the mechanical contraptions that filled the cavernous space. He led us around, pointing out the functions of the machinery that would print *The Olive Press*, explaining where the vats of ink went and inviting us to examine the large metal plates that a different machine had fabricated. Each metal sheet was a negative of a double page of our first edition. A worker yawned loudly, and Carlos apologised, telling us that they had just spent the night printing two hundred thousand copies of *Ideal*, as well as various magazines and books, and all that stood between them and their beds were ten thousand copies of *The Olive Press*. The man said something to his mates and they all burst out laughing. Carlos looked embarrassed. "What did he say?" I asked, and Marcus explained that he'd said printing our newspaper would be "like a little fart at the end of a long shit."

And thus, with that thought in mind, and without any fanfare whatsoever I was invited to press a large button, setting in motion the entire printing press. The cacophony was enormous, like being inside an immense metal tank while men with jackhammers tried to smash their way out. A huge roll of paper, like a giant toilet roll, span around and a single continuous sheet of printed paper flew above us at speed as it was fed into a box. It appeared from this box just a fraction of a second later chopped neatly into small piles and recognisable as a newspaper. These newspapers flew onto a high speed conveyor belt, which took them around the warehouse at a dizzying speed before they emerged on another belt at table height where a man with a magnifying glass picked copies off at random, inspecting the colour balance with one bloodshot eye.

Carlos walked over and grabbed three copies, handing one to each of us. It was an incredible thing to see months of work realised in vivid colour among the cacophonous din of the printing machinery. Feeling it, one could certainly appreciate the term 'hot off the press', and the newspaper smelled of hot ink and paper. "Hold on," said Vicki, a frown on her face, "where's the '*The*'?" I looked at the front page again. Instead of *The Olive Press* it simply said, *Olive Press*. The '*The*' was supposed to be a light shade of green set on the deeper green of the banner, but due to some miscalculation with ink shades it had simply disappeared altogether. Carlos had previously explained to us that greens were often a problem with printers, where every shade is made from a palette of blue, red, yellow and black; it had been one of the main technical gremlins we'd had to sort out the night before. Before I could point out the problem however a loud bell rang and the printing press ground to a halt.

"What's happening?" I asked. "Finished," said Carlos triumphantly. The whole process had only taken a few minutes. Behind him was a stack of papers the size of a small car, and the newspapers were already trussed up into bales with plastic binders. Feeling somewhat pedantic I pointed out the ink error to him. Carlos looked at the front page with the air of utmost seriousness for a few seconds before berating the colour technician with the bloodshot eye, waving a copy under his nose.

"How am I supposed to spot something that isn't there?" the technician protested, reasonably. We quickly debated what to do. Marcus and I were of the opinion that the error was no big deal and could be corrected in the next issue, but Vicki, whose standards were higher than ours, thought we should insist on it being fixed here and now. I felt the impatient eyes of the workers on us as we debated what to do. Carlos began shouting orders at them while we stood around nervously. Suddenly the clanging started up again and the massive machine came back to life.

"What's happening?" I asked Carlos.

"I have adjusted the colour settings and we will reprint," he explained. "It's no bother." A moment later a man in a fork lift truck picked up the ten thousand defective newspapers and drove them over to a far corner, where they were dumped in a huge skip labelled '*Basura*' (garbage).

"There go your green credentials," said Marcus.

Afterwards, when the second print run had passed muster and the night shift workers had been dismissed, we loaded the papers into my car. The suspension groaned under the weight of three hundred and twenty thousand pages. Marcus hitched a ride with Vicki, given that the passenger seat in my car was stacked to the ceiling with newspapers, and I had to take the road back to Órgiva slowly to avoid tipping the top-heavy car over on tight bends. When I arrived, we unloaded and lugged the bundles up the stairs to the office, finding that when they were all stacked up they covered a significant area of the office floor space. An uneasy question arose: just what the hell were we going to do with all these newspapers? I'm not sure what we had expected when we ordered ten thousand copies, but it seemed like rather a lot now they were stacked up in front of us.

"Better get to it," said Marcus.

He went out first, carrying as many as he could and going into all the cafés and bars in Órgiva, of which there were around forty, placing a stack in each. As the newspaper was free, none of the owners seemed to mind having copies of it lying about. When Marcus got back I went out next, handing copies out to people walking past, and delivering a load to the Sufi café Baraka, where we had first discussed the idea of starting a newspaper.

Other distributors arrived at the office and began loading bundles into their cars to be spirited off far and wide to the villages and towns of the region. One distributor, Jerry, turned up to take a carload out to the eastern reaches of La Alpujarra, while Patrick, Vicki's husband, arrived in a shiny new Land Rover to take several thousand down to the coast, and yet others took bundles away to Granada, the Lecrin Valley and beyond.

Órgiva was thronged with people coming into town for the market and by lunch time, after we had handed out over a thousand copies, we were rewarded with the sight of people walking around with a copy tucked under their arm, while some sat outside cafés reading it. After all the effort we'd put in, it was a marvellous sight to see so many people reading it.

When we felt we had saturated the area with as many copies as possible we decided to call it a day. We retreated outside and sat in the sun, drinking a celebratory glass of sherry or two and nibbling on the dishes of *tapas* the waiter brought out. Molly joined us and together we toasted the birth of our newspaper.

"Here's to *The Olive Press*," said Molly, raising her glass. "Long may it last!"

- 16 -

I found it was easy to be fooled by Spain. The Spain of popular imagination was a place of clear bright light and refulgent colours where matadors pierced the hearts of raging bulls and the gypsy *cante jondo* suffused the red earth with its melancholic tones. This, I discovered, was the romantic version. The more prosaic modern day one might involve concrete, cars and *Nescafe*.

While living inland and away from the coast, I never saw a bullfight or heard traditional gypsy flamenco, never ate paella and didn't once attend a raucous fiesta into the early hours. Although Spain is cited for its high drama, the truth of where we lived in La Alpujarra was that people there didn't have much time for shenanigans. Although most of the inhabitants were aware of the cultural drama taking place somewhere over the *sierras*, they seemed to be quite happy to let it stay that way, making do with the various *ferias* and firework displays that periodically set the villages ablaze, sometimes literally.

The good thing about living in a quiet backwater was that you could more or less do what you wanted. Those who valued liberty and freedom were attracted to the idea that you could move to Spain and become who you really felt you ought to be, free of many of the strictures and regulations elsewhere. Sure, the bureaucracy could be a drag, but even then most of it was so inefficiently organised that you could probably get away with more than you dared to admit in public. Better still, there was plenty of space to be yourself, and in Andalucía nobody would question your motives. If your wish was to found a tepee village and bring up your home-schooled children venerating Hindu gods, that was fine as long as you kept your head down and didn't get involved in a water disputes with the citrus farmer slightly further up the hill. Not for nothing had Andalucía earned the reputation of being Europe's California – a Shangri La for misfits, visionaries and the just plain odd.

For many, it was simply the peace and quiet of the countryside and the satisfyingly achievable challenge of rearranging whatever neglected jumble of stones they had acquired into a house that would be unaffordable at a more northerly latitude. People in La Alpujarra, on the whole, seemed to be puzzled by this urge, although usually they were too polite to say so to your face. Since the great wave of modernisation that had swept over the country, the movement of Spanish people has been mostly one-way: from the countryside to the cities. Not only were there more jobs and conveniences in the urban areas, but most Spaniards seemed to find the traffic fumes of the *pueblo* far preferable to the incessant ennui of the *campo*.

But it was definitely peace a quiet that we sought, along with a bit of land to grow our own food and perhaps raise a few chickens, and so I set out looking for a ruin to do up. Estate agents said we were too late and all the ruins had been snatched up, but all it took was a few minutes surveying hillsides with a set of binoculars to see that this was plainly not true. In fact, the countryside was full of buildings in stages of disrepair, from the merely abandoned to those that had already fallen to pieces and were lying in fragments. It was often very hard to find out who owned these abandoned buildings, although sometimes a phone number and '*Se Vende*' would be spray painted onto a crumbling wall on the off chance someone mad enough would one day pass by and want to purchase it.

The ruins fascinated me. I spent hours wandering along little-used tracks, poking around to take a closer looks at some of the crumbling and silently decaying buildings. What was clear was that – given enough time – when a traditionally built Alpujarran house loses its corporeal form it leaves very little evidence of its existence behind. Some were mere patches of brambles beneath which the lumpen shape of fallen rocks denoted a building on its journey back to the earth. The landscape surrounding us was scattered with such derelictions, and buildings abandoned for reasons of hardship, war or simple exhaustion could be found on the sides of *barrancos* or hidden at the end of overgrown tracks.

Around them stood the aloof *sierras*, which over the ages had observed human habitations come and go with implacable cool. But there they were regardless, the humble remains of human habitation, huddled on the slopes of misty valleys, surrounded by dusty trees and rusting vehicles, or sometimes embedded, invisibly, in the midst of the busiest towns.

I looked at lots of these falling-down buildings and I could see the process by which they would dissipate and dissolve if nobody stepped in to rescue them. As soon as the humans had left, the buildings would soon revert to habitat for the wildlife that up until then had been kept at bay. With no one around to make repairs, it would only take a year or so before a heavy storm washed away enough roofing *launa* to make an entrance hole. It wouldn't be long before *Hylotrupes Bajulus* – a type of long-horned beetle that the Spanish call a *carcoma* – moves in and begins laying eggs in the chestnut beams that support the ceiling. Over the next two or three years a highly-audible munching noise would be heard night and day as the white grubs bore out tunnels through the woody cambium and deep into the heartwood of the dead tree, causing slow motion puffs of sawdust to sprinkle the floors, catching in the sunlight as they trickle.

In an abandoned house there is no one around to take such radical measures against the grubs and the *carcomas* sooner or later bring down the roof, throwing the newly-exposed house open to all manner of other interesting species. Once the roof has collapsed rainwater gets into the walls and they erode from the top down, shedding the mud and *launa* that binds them together. Birds excrete fig seeds onto wall tops and when the trees grow, their roots prise the walls apart. Snuffling animals, snakes and colonies of ants also play their part in undermining the mud between the rocks that bind the walls together.

The one I was led to and ended up buying wasn't exactly a ruin. Instead it was a collection of buildings, some fairly modern, comprising of a couple of serviceable stone buildings and a sizeable concrete house with a single ancient solar panel that was powerful enough to illuminate the property's lone light bulb. A small twelve-foot by nine building just below the main house was teetering on the edge of ruination, its form as a human habitation still clearly visible but its future as a pile of rocks for lizards to set up home in not long off. The roof had gone, leaving the four walls standing although one of them was leaning at an alarming angle above an unruly patch of *chumba* cactus. There was a rusting tin door that creaked when opened, and the gloomy interior was populated with numerous geckos, like some sort of reptile zoo.

I didn't want this house to disintegrate and fall back into the earth – it was too good for that. A human was needed to stop it slipping any further, and I fancied myself as just the one for the job. Miguel, an estate agent from Barcelona, showed us around, and when we went to view it we discovered there was an old man living in it. As we were shown around the different buildings and rooms this old man joined us, pointing out features and warning us about where was unsafe to walk. It seemed like he was from a different world. Later, we found out he had been there most of his life but, with his trembling hands and his lack of balance, he clearly could not go on living there much longer. He slept on a hard, urine-stained mattress in a small room with just a bedpan and a picture of the Virgin Mary – a room that would be our future pantry. His eyesight was going, which I suspected might account for all the geckos in the house, and he was bow-legged. Apart from a few cooking utensils and a room filled to the ceiling with almonds there was nothing else in the house, except for some chunks of putrefying animal flesh hanging from hooks in the ceiling. If we wanted, he indicated, the meat could be included in the deal, but he regretted he couldn't offer us the store of almonds, which represented a season's work. The old man's name was Augustin, and this was but one of his family's ancestral farmhouses.

The main building was made up of three houses that had been cobbled together during different eras. Along with various sons, brothers and nephews, Augustin had constructed a crude bathroom designed to heighten the appeal and sales potential for *modernistas* like us. In truth, it wasn't much more than a breezeblock privy with a corrugated tin roof and a hole for the sewage to soak away into one of the terraces.

But whatever the house lacked in finesse it made up for in its potential and the state of the land it sat in. The old farmhouse was embedded into the side of a hill and was half obscured by mature olive and almond trees, of which there were about twenty of each. A number of terraces had been cut away and on these grew handsome, well-spaced citrus trees. Mostly they were oranges, but there were also several lemon and grapefruit trees that had enormous fruits hanging from them. The hill was called *Cerro Negro* – meaning 'Black Hill' – although nobody could explain why it was called this as it was mostly yellow and ribbed with green trees and not black at all. A single dusty track, said to be the roughest in the whole area, wound its way up the hill from the paved Tíjola road that ran parallel with the river along the bottom of the valley. It went up through expanses of olive groves and eventually arrived at the rosemary-covered brow of the hill from where an astonishing view of the white villages in the Poqueira Gorge could be seen, as could the snowy summits of Mulhacén and Veleta.

It was scarcely three miles from the bottom to the top of Cerro Negro along the bumpy track, but its parlous state meant that the journey could take half an hour, and that's assuming you were in a four-wheel drive. At some point in the not-too-distant past the houses on the hillside had constituted a kind of spread-out village, and the remaining residents, when we got to know them, spoke fondly of times as late as the 1980s when nightly socials would be held in a building that was now an imploded relic with a palm tree growing out of it.

But the house was everything we had been looking for, and when I went into town the next day I called in to see Miguel the estate agent and put in an offer. It was accepted almost immediately. That's how we ended up owning a farmhouse called Los Pechos.

- 17 -

There had been a great flurry of excitement in the first couple of weeks after our newspaper launch. Everyone I bumped into wanted to talk about it and I found myself more often than not shaking hands with strangers wishing us luck. There seemed to be a great amount of pride that something new should come out of Órgiva, which had been down on its luck for so long, and I was happy to be a part of it.

Marcus got straight down to writing new articles for the second issue, while I focused on the tricky job of filling boxes on a screen using the DTP software. The occasional person would find their way up to our second-floor office to place a classified advert, while others came in to talk about whatever venture they were starting out on in the hope that we might do a write-up on them. One such person who popped in was a placid-sounding man called Patrick who lived just outside of town, and he said he knew something about growing food and looking after the environment. Like many, he seemed intrigued that *The Olive Press* was rumoured to be a 'green' newspaper, and wondered if he could help in some way. I was happy that people such as Patrick had got the right idea about *The Olive Press*, because I figured that if we were going to make a newspaper that focused on protecting the local environment then we would need more articles to that end. I myself was planning on doing a series examining the impact of the *invernaderos* – that is, plastic greenhouses – and how they were sucking up the limited groundwater and polluting the landscape, but I needed time to get to that and I was mostly too busy in the weeks after our first issue came out.

In fact, I was quite busy when Patrick came in, so I jotted his name down anyway and filed it under 'possible contributor', although I never followed up on it and lost it some time later. This turned out to be a great mistake on my part as I later found out that the man was the author Patrick Whitefield, an esteemed teacher in the field of permaculture, which is the art and science of making human civilisation harmonious with nature. That was a serious miss on my part, but luckily there were plenty of other interesting people in the area with a similar interest.

Two more came in the form of David and Aspen, an English couple who turned up at the office wanting to place an ad. They said they were involved in some kind of land restoration project on their own farm, high up in the hills, and asked me if I wanted to come and write a story about it. This sounded perfect – it would be my first journalistic assignment.

A few days later I was once again driving up dusty tracks in search of somewhere that wasn't easy to find and had no official address. When I did eventually find their farm and got out of the car a largish dog came charging towards me, barking wildly and with its teeth bared. I pulled back in fear, holding up my briefcase as a shield, but just then a familiar smallish woman with a kind face and blue eyes appeared, reprimanding the snarling cur which slunk away guiltily. "I'm so sorry about him," said Aspen, extending a hand in greeting, "we don't get many visitors up here."

David appeared behind her in the doorway and immediately began to take me on a tour of their farm. A former mathematician and computer programmer, David Edge, was a genteel and well-spoken man with an academic's neatly trimmed grey beard, and he had lived at *Semilla Besada* for seven years with Aspen. Their aim was simple: to prove that southern Spain could be turned back into a green paradise, instead of letting it slide into a state of desertification.

One of the first things David showed me was a large mesh-cage compost heap, and I watched as he drew out a length of cane as if he were pulling out a dipstick. "Hmm," he said, "feel that – it's not warm at all." I did as he said and, it was true, it wasn't warm. "That means the heat generating process of decomposition is complete. This compost is ready for use." He replaced the cane and moved onto the next one. David, I soon learnt, knew a lot about compost heaps. The land around his project farm, *Semilla Besada*, perched high up in the hills above Lanjarón, was scattered with them. Most were full of decomposing vegetation but it was hard not to notice a bloodied lamb fleece, thick with black flies. And what on earth was on that one there? "Ah, that's related to the toilet block," David said, ushering me on to admire his squash plants.

We walked around for the best part of an hour, looking at the small paradise these two eco gardeners had created. There were trees weighed down with apples and pears, abundant vegetable gardens and lush green areas filled with grass and wildflowers. I noticed a small hill-like structure, seemingly sculpted from sun-baked mud and pock marked with holes. On closer inspection it turned out to be a specially made rabbit warren. Sure enough, there were fluffy bunnies hopping around and peering out of the holes as if in a pet shop. "Good in stews," said David matter-of-factly.

When the tour had concluded I found myself seated at a heavy wooden table in the cosy kitchen of their farmhouse. I was offered a cinnamon scone, fresh out of the oven, to have with my coffee. "You see," said Aspen, who, like David, was wearing a set of well-worn overalls "we live in a brittle and dry environment and that means it's just not good enough to set it aside and hope it regenerates itself. That approach may work in northern Europe, where it rains a lot and moisture is high, but here in southern Spain the surest way to kill the soil is to leave it alone."

I took a nibble of my scone and considered this. From my briefcase I pulled out a notebook and the little Dictaphone I'd bought for such an occasion as this. Briefly, I wondered who exactly had given me permission to call myself a reporter. I took a gulp of coffee and listened to Aspen as she continued outlining her vision for ecological regeneration.

"What we need up here is more grazing animals – Spain has been abandoned to desert," she continued. "Animals graze the land and their droppings add to the fertility, if it's managed correctly, which is what we are trying to do."

It was an interesting idea and one that is, I suspected, was controversial enough given the high number of vegans in the area. But David and Aspen had conducted numerous experiments with their land, amassing a huge amount of data, much of it written in the paper ledgers and files that piled up on shelves around the small kitchen and the house that they had built.

She went on to explain how she thought bringing in goats, rabbits, donkeys, cows and other plant-nibbling animals was essential in restoring nutrients to the soil, and the devastating impact that emptying the land of people had had on these parts. Cradling his coffee cup, David continued, "Land that is left idle just gets covered in annual plants that desiccate and cause a fire risk. And with no perennial grasses growing, whenever it rains heavily the topsoil just gets washed down the hillside and is lost into the rivers."

It was a gloomy prospect for this area and many other marginalised regions around the Mediterranean. Flick through any newspaper in Andalucía and you'd likely find mention of desertification, climate change and wildfires. Some scientists were saying up a half of Spain could become arid desert this century. Where, centuries ago, there had stood forests rich in wildlife there now lay the familiar yellow hills covered with spiky shrubs and, if you were lucky, the occasional conifer. Dry riverbeds ran through dusty ravines and abandoned farmhouses crumbled back into the earth. It was a familiar enough scene, and in the right light, it could be beautiful in a bleak kind of way. However there was nothing beautiful about the idea of Andalucía becoming a giant dustbowl devoid of topsoil and unable to support anything much larger than a cockroach.

"I used to be a tree man before I came here," said David, perhaps sensing the apocalyptic scene playing out in my mind. "Now I'm more of a grass man in that I realise grasses can be just as important as trees in an environment. Some perennial grasses have root systems going down several metres."

"Look," said Aspen "it's about the very basis of life. The environment has to come top in any decision making process because everything depends on it. If we destroy our ecosystems, then we destroy ourselves."

Theory lesson over we drained our cups and headed out into the garden again to inspect the results of their efforts. What they had created was unlikely to win any prizes at the Chelsea Flower Show, but I was willing to believe that it was probably one of the most biodiverse plots of land in the whole region. Semi-circular beds were demarcated by roof tiles and within them grew a profusion of different crops that David identified one at a time as I scribbled notes and took photos. "No that's not maize, it's sorghum. You can make a kind of porridge from it"; "These are our tomatoes – a rather tatty affair aren't they but they taste great and are packed with nutrients"; "Ah yes, the courgettes. I'd have watered them if I'd known you were going to take pictures." David didn't miss out anything he thought might be of interest. He explained the proximity of some recently planted nettle trees to other crops in terms of their nitrogen fixing roots. He was almost apologetic about growing annual vegetables and described his reservations about using a Rotavator to till the soil, "We thought about getting a mule so as to do it without using fossil fuels, but then the mule would have been consuming energy all year round, even when it wasn't working, so we opted for the machinery."

"You know," said Aspen, "we're practically self-sufficient up here. We live off-grid and make nearly all of our own food and energy, but there's no way anyone could honestly claim to be one hundred percent self-sufficient, after all you can't grow your own car insurance. And so we are forced to earn a bit of cash as well."

When they explained their decisions like this I began to get an inkling of the pragmatism they had embraced in their lives, and how their small-scale solutions were so at odds with the idea that technology or politicians or protesting would save us all. It was pretty clear, when you thought about it, that desertification wasn't going to go away by building more dams or throwing money at the problem. Neither was it clear how better technology could reverse the situation. "We're trying to find out ways to stop it happening at source, that's basically what we're about," said David.

And with that I left them to their composting and data collecting, and drove off up the mountain until *Semilla Besada* was but a small green oasis in a sea of yellow below me. Back at the office I typed up my notes and laid out what would be my first feature article in the newspaper. I called it 'Gardeners of Eden', and I was quite proud of it – this journalism thing was easier than I thought.

- 18 -

A few days after our first issue came out I saw a familiar looking figure walking along on Calle Doctor Fleming with the kind of characteristic jaunty lope that identifies a certain type of Englishmen. A tallish man, with curly greying hair and glasses, there was no doubt that who I was looking at was none other than Chris Stewart, the author of the bestselling *Driving over Lemons*. In his book Stewart detailed his move to La Alpujarra in the 1980s to 'escape Thatcher's Britain' and his subsequent transformation into a penniless hill shepherd. I had read it one miserably grey Christmas Day while living in Denmark and decided more-or-less before I went to bed that night that I too would move to this mythical-sounding place. Luckily for me, Michelle was also up for the idea. And now, here we were. Much had been made of the success of his book and Stewart had become something of a local hero, credited with putting La Alpujarra on the map and initiating Órgiva's rejuvenation. The mayor, it was said, had even talked about erecting a bronze statue in the plaza to the writer, apparently to his horror.

As I passed him, I noticed that the famed writer was eating *churros*, those fried sugary dough sticks that are dunked in hot chocolate for breakfast. There was nothing unusual about this but I couldn't help noticing that they were wrapped in a familiar-looking newspaper with a green masthead.

I went back to the office and told the others who I had just seen and the fact that he was using *The Olive Press* as a grease-absorbing wrapper. Marcus leaped up from his desk and grabbed a copy of *Driving over Lemons* from the office bookshelf. "You know what I'm going to do?" he ranted. "I'm going to carry this book around with me and if I see him in the street I'll rip out a page and wipe my fucking arse with it!"

I never did find out whether Marcus carried out this threat, but the next time I saw Chris Stewart he was drinking from a fountain in Pampaneira. I introduced myself and told him about *The Olive Press*. "Yes, I've seen it," he said. "Good luck with it – other people have tried the same and failed in these parts. It's a tough nut to crack."

He was right, of course. In time he came to write for us, and he could be relied upon to produce thoughtful and very readable articles, mostly about the local environment. Aside from being an international best-selling author, he also reared lambs in the spring and was a member of the local Green Party ("God help Órgiva if he ever gets elected," said his wife). He downplayed the media's constant focus on his being a founding member of the band *Genesis,* preferring instead to talk about his organic farm and literary heroes.

Meeting Chris Stewart got me thinking about writers in Spain, and the idea of a series was hatched. I decided to pen a number of articles about foreign writers, figuring I could use it as an excuse to go off and visit some of the places I wanted to see. First on my list, seeing as it was closest, was the coastal town of Almuñécar, just to the south of La Alpujarra.

The story went that one December day in the 1930s a thin and ragged looking tramp arrived in Almuñécar, which was then still a fishing village. Barely more than a youth with gangly limbs and piercing blue eyes, the seaside outpost represented the end of a long and gruelling walk from Galicia in the north. He was carrying little more than a fiddle. Sensing the gathering clouds of war the young Englishman decided to hole up for the winter and took a position as an odd-job man at one of the village's two hotels down by the beach.

That youth was Laurie Lee, at the time an aspiring poet and writer who had set out on foot from his family home in a Gloucestershire village, a journey described in his memoir *As I Walked Out One Midsummer Morning.*

Laurie Lee, or *El Lorenzo* as the locals came to call him, ended up staying In Almuñécar for much longer than he ever thought he would. At the time it was a down-at-heel fishing village where the fishermen were too poor even to afford boats. Instead they would wade into the surf with nets and try to catch the scattering sardines that flitted around in the shallows.

He describes the listless sense of boredom that perpetually hung over the village and the way the locals would sometimes make their own fun by tying the village idiot to a chair and torturing him. They stretched the poor man's ears and smeared mustard on his face while pouring wine over his head, much to the amusement of the *Guardia Civil* officers, who were just as bored.

The old men of the time were described as being "*small and bony, like dried-up birds, perched moodily around the edge of the sea [who] spent much of the day just staring at their hands and sucking cigarettes.*" Not much seemed to have changed in this respect and I spotted a few old birds sitting on a bench gazing seawards. I approached them and asked if they had any stories about *El Lorenzo*. No, they said, shaking their heads when I showed them a picture of the youthful Lee. One of them thought he could remember a young writer but, on reflection, he thought it had been a German. But then these old men would themselves have been babies at most when Lee was living here.

It was here that Lee had sheltered when the Spanish civil war broke out. Lee recalled vividly the day the war came to town one day in mid-July with the sound of a woman wailing in the street. In those days Almuñécar was solidly communist and red flags hung from everyone's balconies. Peasants, armed with flintlock rifles, would congregate in the plaza outside the town hall to discuss the coming revolution. When war looked inevitable the surrounding countryside was emptied and Almuñécar was filled with men, women, children from the surrounding countryside, along with their farm animals. There was no safety to be had holding out at the family *finca* as the instances of violence began to escalate. Fascist sympathisers, including priests, were rounded up and placed under arrest. The villagers, expecting retribution, waited for the war to come to them and, as Lee put it, *"Fear lay panting in the street like a dog."*

And then it came. A destroyer appeared off the beach one night and probed the village with a spotlight as if selecting a target. The terrified villagers ran down to the beach and stood with their arms raised. The beam was extinguished and the following silence was abruptly broken as the warship sent shells screaming down into the *pueblo*. People fled in terror as houses were razed and trees were blasted to matchwood. When it was all over the searchlight came on again, illuminating the scene of carnage. Lee was present to chronicle what he saw, writing, "In the naked beam of the searchlight we saw them come stumbling up the streets, bent double, crying and moaning, mothers and fathers dragging their children behind them, the old folk tottering and falling down."

The ludicrous truth about what had happened emerged the next morning when the captain of the destroyer sent his apologies, saying he had thought the villagers had been enemy insurgents. It had all been an episode of friendly fire.

Some weeks later another destroyer appeared in the harbour. Although Lee didn't know it at the time this was his taxi home. British Navy personnel stepped ashore to seek out any miscreant British subjects and, as Lee put it *"stop us making fools of ourselves."* And so the young writer was bundled on board and escorted to Gibraltar, leaving him feeling humiliated and with his adventures snuffed out just as they were starting to get interesting. "So it has come – the sudden end to my year's adventure, with the long arm reaching from home."

As I walked around the modern town, I tried to imagine the characters Lee had illustrated in his book such as Jorge, a man who trained a sparrow to steal tiny sips of beer from other men's glasses and deposit it in his own. Or Manolo, the waiter and hard-line communist who enlisted Lee in trips to the mountains of La Alpujarra to carry coded messages about stashes of 'seed potatoes', that is, hand grenades.

It was difficult to imagine Almuñécar as it had been when Lee arrived almost eighty years before. For although the historical core remained intact, it was no longer a village but a large coastal town that has expanded up the nearby hillsides and threatened to merge with Salobreña and La Herradura. The hotel where Lee had once worked had been demolished and the only real reminder that the town was once the haunt of the writer was a small and incongruous monument near the beach.

Despite this, there still remained a certain air of intrigue about the place, and I could well imagine the young Englishman using it as a redoubt in which to hold, dodging the shells raining down on him at the end of his arduous walk from England.

Back in the office it was a great relief to discover that, all in all, people around the region were saying *The Olive Press* was a success, and we received a handful of messages congratulating us on its launch. There was one unfortunate fly in the ointment, and that came in the form of an unlikely coincidence. Our back page columnist John, who was writing under the moniker of a three-legged pig called *The Amputee*, lived in the mountain village of Bubión, where Marcus and Molly also resided. Bubión was a peaceful village of less than three hundred souls, perched high up on the side of the mountain, but it had received a new resident – an Englishman – at around the exact same time our first issue had gone out. The quiet village life was broken when said Englishman announced his arrival in his new mountain idyll by getting furiously drunk in one of the bars and challenging several people to a fight. The locals could not understand this aggressive behaviour, although the man could have been forgiven for feeling testy, as he had recently lost his leg following a motorbike accident and went around on a set of crutches. It seemed he had moved to the village for recuperative purposes and didn't want to be reminded of the fact that his leg had just been cut off in a hospital.

It was only a matter of time before someone erroneously guessed that the new arrival was the anonymous *Amputee,* and slipped him a copy of *The Olive Press,* praising his bravery. The one-legged man, it was reported, didn't react well to the assertion he was a cartoon pig, and when he found out that the editor of this offensive publication lived in the same village, there was talk in the bars of him hunting down Marcus to give him a kicking. On hearing these rumours Marcus was forced to resort to evasive tactics, and took to slinking down back alleys and avoiding certain routes in the village. John, too, was worried about meeting the real amputee and fretted about being done over by the embittered Englishman.

Luckily, the story had a happy ending. When Marcus eventually came face to face with him after weeks of worry, the one-legged man had either forgotten about the affair, or had decided it wasn't worth pursuing, to both Marcus and John's great relief.

I had been having car trouble. The silver Land Rover Freelander I'd brought with me from Denmark didn't seem to have taken to Spain in the same way I had. It had served me well at first; I'd used it to haul all of our stuff on the four thousand mile round-trip from Copenhagen to Órgiva no less than three times, and it had coped admirably with all the dirt tracks, once I'd figured out how to drive it with the four-wheel drive engaged, as well as the indignity of being loaded to the ceiling with newspapers every fortnight and driven all over the province. But now it seemed to be rebelling.

I first started to notice problems when the sunroof began opening and closing at random intervals. This then spread to the back window, which – being an unusual feature of Freelanders – went up and down like a side window at the press of a button. Equally random warnings appeared on the dashboard and the headlights would go on and off while I was driving. Annoyed by all this I took it to a Land Rover service centre in Granada and a technician hooked the car's control centre up to a laptop to see what the problem was. But the car's computer refused to communicate with the man's computer and he shook his head sadly saying it was "speaking a strange language". Unfortunately, Danish fiscal bureaucracy being so strict and unyielding had meant that I was still trying to figure out a way to legally import the car into Spain without being fleeced. The technician said he was unable to help me further, given that the vehicle was still registered in Scandinavia and therefore all output from the computer was in Danish. He replaced all the fuses anyway, either to see if it would help, or to prevent me from leaving without a hefty repair bill. I suspected the latter.

Things improved for a little while until it started playing tricks on me again, this time with the locking mechanism. To start with, it imprisoned me inside one hot day. I'd just parked up in town and when I tried to get out I found all the doors locked. Slightly annoyed at this latest turn of events I attempted to put the key back in the ignition, figuring this might enable me to disable the locks, or at least park in the shade. No, it wasn't having that at all – I couldn't even turn the key. In full sun and with the interior temperature rising fast, the thought crossed my mind that I'd better get this sorted out fast if I didn't want to die an embarrassing death as people walked past with their shopping. Luckily, just as I was thinking this, the doors decided to unlock themselves without me doing anything at all. I breathed a sigh of relief.

Nevertheless, this wasn't the last time it happened and it pulled the trick a couple more times, always letting me out after a few minutes, usually when I had become sweaty and panicky. Perhaps I was imagining things but it seemed like my car was messing with me.

On another occasion, a few weeks later again, the car simply died as I was driving along. This was unfortunate as I was several miles from Órgiva and it was three o'clock in the morning. I'd just picked Michelle's brother, Tonino, up from the airport in Malaga after his flight had been delayed and then diverted from Granada at the last minute. We had been driving along a dark and bendy road when the engine suddenly cut out and the headlights went off, and it was all I could do to coast to the side of the road before the steering wheel locked up. We walked back the rest of the way, pulling luggage behind us, and eventually arrived in Órgiva just before dawn.

A local garage picked the car up the next day, discovering that it was out of fuel – even though the digital fuel gauge showed a quarter of a tank still remained. Was the car now trying to kill me? I began to worry. It was almost as if it had become possessed by some kind of Andalucían *djinn* that had got into its electrical components and was dead set on bumping me off. I mentioned my concerns to a local café owner who considered this possibility with equanimity, suggesting that I got a priest out to perform an exorcism.

And then one day it totally overstepped the line. I drove into town and parked outside Baraka, and then went into the office. When I came back to the car after a day at work the doors were all locked and no amount of pressing on the remote button or turning the key in the door could convince it to let me in. The headlights flashed once or twice and the door locks made a slight sound as though the car was *thinking* about letting me in, but otherwise nothing.

Feeling hot and bothered I made calls to Land Rover and ended up being stuck in a phone tree that concluded at a dead end featuring a robotic voice telling me to bring the car in to my local registered dealer. In Denmark. That evening I had to hitchhike home carrying my briefcase and a bag of shopping, arriving back in Pampaneira in a state of gloom.

When I cadged a lift back down the next day the car was still there and it still wouldn't let me in. But now, when I tried to open the doors the car's stereo started blasting out music so loud it made the car vibrate. It didn't help that it was playing the last CD I'd had on, which was AC/DC, or that the track was *Back in Black*. I was, by now, almost convinced that some form of supernatural entity had taken over the vehicle. To the clientele sitting at tables outside Baraka I must have looked a bit dodgy to say the least, circling the car and trying the door handles, but nobody said anything.

I explained my problem to a local expat mechanic who came out and had a look at the intransigent car. "Nah, it's not a demon, mate," he said, rubbing his chin. "It's just shit British engineering. Your model was the last year before BMW took over making the electrics – it's a common issue."

"What can I do?" I asked. By now I was starting to feel exasperated. Land Rover had sent me an email suggesting I get the car placed on a flat bed truck and driven up to Denmark for them to have a look at it, as if I was a millionaire or something.

"Leave the car for another day or two," advised the mechanic. "It probably thinks it's being stolen, so you just have to wait it out. Its defences will come down eventually."

And so it was a long, hot wait for a bus to take me up the mountain again that evening. Yet on my visit the next day the car was still in no mood to let me in. By now covered in a layer of dust, this time when I went to tried to open the doors the car set off its alarm. The harsh metalling honking seemed to echo off the surrounding mountains, shattering the morning calm. But there was no way for me to turn it off, and after a few sweaty minutes of cursing and pressing buttons I left the car to its little tantrum and slipped away – but not before noticing a few hard stares from customers outside the café.

That night I was unable to stop focusing on this seemingly intractable problem. It was so maddening to see the ignition right there through the window and not be able to put the key in which, I hoped, would permit me to override the systems. By about two o'clock I'd had an idea. I slipped out of bed, tiptoed downstairs and opened the front door. By the light of the moon, I made my way to the storehouse next to the porch where we stored the firewood Julio had brought round. After I'd found what I needed I went back to bed again and slept soundly.

The next morning, after hitching a ride with Marcus and Molly down to Órgiva, I stood beside the car outside Baraka as a few people sipped on their morning *café con leches* and *zumos de naranja*. I focused on the miscreant vehicle and said quietly to it "I'm giving you one last chance, you fucker." My hand was on the driver's door handle and I closed my eyes and gently pulled. Immediately the air was rent with the ear-splitting din of the alarm. People began to look at me – some no doubt were starting to recognise me from previous mornings. So be it. I exhaled and, calmly – for I had practiced this in my mind over and over the night before – put Plan B into action.

If any of the customers had looked up from their coffees at that moment, as I imagine most of them had, they would have a seen a man, wearing dark glasses, place a leather briefcase on the ground and calmly take out a medium length log-splitting axe. They would then have watched as the man stood slightly back from the car and, assuming a pose not dissimilar to an American baseball pitcher taking aim, swing the axe at the driver-side window. The axe would then have bounced back from the toughened safety glass – perhaps the man had not realised how much force was necessary to break it? – before he took a second, more forceful, swing at it. They would have seen the window disintegrate into thousands of tiny pieces while an alarm wailed as if the car itself had been mortally wounded. The man would then have placed the axe back in the briefcase before fumbling with a set of keys. Opening the door and stepping inside the vehicle, the man would have started the engine and driven away at some speed, leaving nothing behind except for some shattered pieces of glass and blessed silence.

Those same observers, in relating this tale, might have learned that a couple of weeks later the man drove the car all the way to Denmark, returning on a plane with a pocket full of cash, and was later overheard in a local bar telling listeners that he would "Never touch a Land Rover again with a barge pole."

- 20 -

"Los Pechos?" giggled Molly when I told her the name of the house we were buying. "Do know what '*los pechos*' means?" She could barely keep a straight face.

"Hmm, no," I admitted.

In straight Spanish, she explained, it literally meant 'the breasts', but the term *pechos* was often was used more crudely. But in the case of the house it simply meant 'the hills', *pecho* being an equivalent word for 'hill' and 'tit' in the Alpujarran argot.

Molly's sniggering grew louder a few days later when she found out that after I had got rid of my unfit-for-purpose Land Rover Freelander I'd gone down to a used car lot in Granada and bought a metallic blue Mitsubishi Pajero. The car had a formidable set of gears that required two gear sticks, and there was a cable winch on the front for unexpected emergencies. I figured I was going to need a robust and reliable vehicle to deal with the rutted track that led up to our new house, as people said it could be a dust bath one day and a mud torrent the next. What's more, the dealer had given it to me for a good price, I thought. In fact, I was quite proud of how I had haggled him down in Spanish.

"You do know what *Pajero* means, don't you?" said Molly, almost bursting with laughter.

"Hmm, no," I admitted, once again. She explained.

Mitsubishi, a Japanese company, had acted in good faith when they named the model after a particular type of South American wildcat that roams the vast cane forests of Argentina, known as the *Paja*. They assumed it would translate well to the European market, but failed to ask any Spaniards what they thought of the name *Pajero*, which doesn't mean 'South American wildcat' it means 'one who masturbates' – i.e. 'wanker'. When Mitsubishi realised their error the name of that model was swiftly withdrawn from the Spanish market, and replaced with the inoffensive 'Shogun' although the old name was still displayed on some of the earlier models, like mine.

"Perhaps that's why it was so cheap," said Molly.

And so, in the space of a month, I had become someone who had bought a house with a sign outside it saying 'the tits' and drove a 'wanker'. Marcus though it was funny, too.

We bought Los Pechos hurriedly as it didn't pay to loiter in a sellers' market. Less than a month later I found myself handing envelopes stuffed with five hundred euro notes to the sellers, of which there were eight parties in total. Some of them had travelled from afar to be in the notary office that morning, the furthest driving down from Barcelona. They all seemed amazed that someone was handing over so much money for a pile of snake-infested outbuildings up a bumpy track on the side of a depopulated hill in an unfashionable part of Spain, and the atmosphere in the *notario* was one of a syndicate lottery win. They counted the money over and over in wonderment and I experienced a frisson of existential panic as I watched them thumb through the piles of crisp purple notes that were both our life savings and a substantial mortgage on top.

The property deeds, as was still common in Andalucía, were frightful and complicated, and it became a condition of the sale that a solicitor was appointed and charged with amalgamating the chaotic mess into a single legal document. For this they would be granted a trust fund, and the process was expected to take several years: without such an arrangement the house would remain unsold and would sink into oblivion on the hillside. Our intention was to sell our house in Pampaneira, which had been our toehold in Spain, and use the proceeds to part finance the extensive renovations needed at Los Pechos. But until the sale happened I'd had to take out a mortgage to finance the gap.

When I'd gone to see him a few weeks prior to all this the bank manager, who was from somewhere 'civilised' in northern Spain and regarded his posting in Órgiva as a hardship, didn't seem all that keen on lending us money. He seemed genuinely puzzled as to why we would want to buy a ramshackle farm property in La Alpujarra when you could get a nice all mod cons newbuild in the suburbs of Granada.

I did my best to explain our reasoning, but I got the impression he remained unconvinced. He shrugged and said "okay" and initiated the mortgage application.

But, for some reason, the paperwork for the mortgage seemed to stop there. Whenever I enquired with the bank manager about its progress he told me in a lackadaisical way that there was some trifling detail that warranted closer inspection, or that he was waiting for authorisation from another office for something. I began to think that he was having second thoughts about lending us the money, voicing my fears to Nikki the estate agent, who knew him quite well.

"Did you take him out for lunch?" she asked, taking a drag on a cigarette.

"Why would I do that?" I asked

"That's how it works. You want things speeded up, you'll have to wine and dine him." She blew smoke out of her nostrils and flicked her long golden locks aside. I just stood there, feeling stupid.

"His favourite restaurant is at the bottom camping, and he loves the trout," she added.

"Thanks," I said. "I'll ask him."

Despite my reservations, I did as she said and asked the bank manager if he fancied a spot of lunch. "That's a great idea, *hombre*," he said, getting up and giving me a pally slap on the back. He didn't seem to need much encouragement, and we were out the door in minutes. After we had eaten, and with a stomach full of *trucha a la plancha* washed down with a nice bottle of white, he invited me into the closed bank during the *siesta* hour.

He sat down at his desk, drew out a pen and asked me what size mortgage we needed. He didn't seem overly bothered about my financial situation. Any analysis would have immediately seen that I was a risky proposition to have on the books: an over-leveraged foreigner starting a business he had no experience in, and who had no other form of income. But sober analyses were conspicuously absent in the heady days of 2006, at the height of a property bubble that saw planeloads of foreigners turn up with bundles of cash on a daily basis [Nikki had told me of one woman, a City banker from London 'in her early twenties' who had turned up and said "I want to buy six properties in the next two days – I don't have time to look at them all so I'll trust your judgement about what's worth buying." Making money in these circumstances was like shooting fish in a barrel.]

As far as the bank manager was concerned, he didn't care if I was not able to demonstrate a steady income – he had seen *The Olive Press* and said he was sure it would do well, "Very professional looking, for something from Órgiva," were his words. In any case, he must have been reasoning, even if it all went wrong and I ended up destitute and broke, he himself would be moving to another branch within a year, as all bank managers in Spain must do to prevent them getting too cosy with local businesses. By then I'd be someone else's problem. So, in the absence of any sober judgement in the bank manager's office, there were instead two tipsy men; one a lender and the other one a borrower. He signed the papers and sent them off to head office, promising the mortgage funds would be in my account within days.

Fast forward a month, on the evening of the sale, when all the paperwork had been sorted out and the sellers had returned to the four corners of Spain with their wads of cash, I drove down to Los Pechos from Pampaneira to have a closer look at the dusty chunk of hillside I had just staked my future on. The car crawled slowly down the suspension-killing track as thorny bushes scraped against the sides. Stars seemed to guide my way on this dark, moonless night and I eventually pulled up outside the house, which was hard to find in the dark, and cut the engine. There was complete silence. Taking a torch, I found my way to the front door. I then took out the key I had earlier been ceremoniously handed and turned it in the lock. The oxide encrusted steel door creaked open and, after hesitating a moment for fear of what I might find within, I stepped inside.

It felt almost as if I were trespassing. My rational mind refused to take in the fact that I now possessed a mountain farmhouse with land. Only a year or so before I had been teaching English classes to disinterested businesspeople in Copenhagen and living in a boxy terraced house next to a main road: oh what a turn life had taken! I moved silently from room to room shining the torch into the dark crevices and catching the quick movement of geckos scrabbling into the bamboo cane on the ceiling. There was a harsh empty echo to my footsteps, and the composite stone floor reflected dimly in the torchlight as I made my way up the stairs and into a small room. I eased open the bolt on another steel door and found myself stepping out onto a small outdoor terrace. Spread out below was the deep velvety blackness of the countryside, pricked here and there by the lights of isolated houses but otherwise dark.

I stood and gazed at the peaceful scene spread out before me. Apart from the football rattle sound of the cicadas and the occasional bark of a campo dog, a faint syncopated drumbeat could be heard rising up from the river valley on the night breeze. The sound was emanating from the encampment of travellers and road warriors at Cigarrones across the river, but at this distance the sound, to my ears, was muffled and soft and it mingled in some peculiar way with the fragrant smell of night jasmine and the starlight.

Returning inside again, my attempts to lock the terrace door failed. The rusty bolt refused to go back into the metal barrel and so I ended up leaving the door ajar, allowing the night-scented to air to enter into the musty interior. I went carefully down the stairs again and looked into the room where the old man had had his bed. It was a relief to see that it was now gone, as were the chunks of meat and the huge pile of almonds that had been upstairs just a few weeks before. There was not a trace of him anywhere.

Despite the old man's absence, I didn't feel as if the place belonged to me in any meaningful way. There was the unmistakable imprint left by the generations that lived there up to that point, as well as a faint feeling of abandonment buildings can possess. What's more there was a chill in the air and, perhaps it was just my imagination, but it felt like the house was watching me; examining me and feeling me out to see if I would make a suitable inhabitant. I wondered if I had made a mistake; whether I'd be able to turn this echoey old shell of a building into a family home. Sure, it could be knocked into shape and, in time, turned into a nice place to raise a family, but for now there was an overwhelming feeling that I didn't belong there, that I was a misplaced person. A shiver ran through me.

I'd had enough of creeping around and made to leave, but just then I froze. There had been the unmistakeable sound of feet in the house. I kept dead still, alert to the slightest sound. My heart thudded dully in my chest and I felt the blood pulsing through veins in my throat, but I heard no further noises. Perhaps the place was haunted, I thought, just like our house in Pampaneira. I moved slowly back into the large room that would one day become our kitchen and that's when I saw him. It was the outline of a small stoop-backed person, silhouetted in the doorframe to the outside. I stopped in my tracks, frozen. I didn't know who it was or what they was doing there, and in the darkness I couldn't even tell if they were facing me or not, but I didn't think they had seen me. There was a faint sound of breathing and I thought I could see a glint where the face should be, as if an eye had caught some light. So there I stood, rigid and hardly daring to breathe.

And then, soundlessly and without a word, the figure turned and left. For some time I stood there in the dark, alert to any sounds that might indicate they were still outside the door. Regaining my composure, I walked outside but there was nobody there. The car sat there, a dark but reassuringly solid mass half-visible beneath an olive tree. I got in it and started the engine. As I drove back home I began to feel sure that it must have been the old man, lingering on like a living ghost for some reason. But if it had been him, what was he doing there? The estate agent said he'd gone to live with relatives in town.

By the time I got back onto the main road and the lights of Pampaneira were floating up ahead in the darkness of the gorge I began to relax again. I even found myself chuckling a little, vowing not to be so easily spooked in future.

- 21 -

It seemed like we should start featuring restaurant reviews in the paper so I asked Vicki if she knew of any good ones. There was one that had just opened, she said, down on the coast at Salobreña, and they were considering advertising with us. Perhaps a trip down there and a favourable review would entice them to take out a longer run of adverts, she reasoned.

I considered this. Weren't restaurant reviews supposed to be conducted in secrecy, with the restaurateur only realising the identity of the shadowy figure who had dined alone when they opened the *Food & Drink* section the following week? Arranging it beforehand with a nudge and a wink and the promise of a free meal seemed a bit like cheating. "But that's what all the other papers do," said Marcus when I aired my thoughts. "We can do anonymous ones when we can afford it."

And so it was arranged that I would have lunch there the next day. I didn't fancy dining alone and Michelle was busy so I took Jasmine, who was three at the time. The drive down to the coast from La Alpujarra was like travelling from one world to the next. I had developed a theory that the extreme windiness of the roads was one of the most effective barriers against the region being ruined by developers. There was no way into La Alpujarra without negotiating at least half an hour of stomach churning turns.

Alas, even then, the Junta de Andalucía was drawing up plans to initiate a road straightening and bridge building programme along the northern flank of the Sierra de la Contraviesa in order to expedite the flow of salad-bearing lorries from Almería to the major motorways running north. And not only that but a large stretch of highway – the *Autovia del Mediterraneo* – was being built with EU money along the southern coast from Malaga, which would connect with another stretch running south from Granada. At times, it seemed like the whole region was crawling with cement trucks and bristling with cranes, while the ceaseless *thud thud thud* of explosives levelled the hills and tamed the terrain for the tarmac rollers.

But on this particular summer day, before the motorway had been built, we whistled south along the old road. It ran beside the trickle of the Guadalfeo River and meandered between the crags of the rocky pass through which the remnants of the Moors had walked, defeated, on their way back to North Africa. It was always a liminal experience heading through the pass. Radio reception would splutter and die, and mobile phones would say 'no signal' as the tall cliffs rose up precipitously on either side. Drivers, seemingly oblivious to danger, would rarely ease off the accelerator and the sharp bends racked up almost daily casualties. The riverbed in certain spots was scattered with smashed trucks and rusting upside-down cars.

Emerging from the shade of this rock cathedral, one was suddenly no longer in the mountains but was instead in the blinding sunlight on the littoral of the Costa Tropical, and everything was different. Moroccans stood beside the roads with stalls selling mangos and avocados, as well as ones less familiar to northern eyes, such as the polygonal milky-fleshed *cherimoyas* and the delicious little bittersweet orange *nispero*s. The fact that this kind of fruit could be grown so easily in this microclimate had led to the tropical moniker, although in later years real estate developers had seized upon it for it paradise associations. Nevertheless, this section of coast had so far survived the over-development of the sixties and seventies. Why this is so was a matter of debate, but it could have something to do with the innate conservatism of Granada Province, compared to nearby Malaga, or its wild-west neighbour on the other side, Almería. The fact that the beaches are mostly pebbly and the annual burn-off of agricultural waste, which clogs the air with acidic smelling smoke for two months of the year, might also have kept the holiday developments away.

Salobreña, where we were to have lunch, was my favourite seaside town. It can be seen from miles away, a shining white hill rising from the coastal plain, crowned with an Arab fortress. Steep streets that are as narrow as a car and deter all but the intrepid, allow the place to retain much of its quirky and organic lack of symmetry. Instead, developers have turned their attention to the base of the hill along the shoreline, although even here it is still mostly taken up with thick plantations of sugar cane. It was in amongst all this shoreline urbanisation that the restaurant was situated, just back from the monkey-run where every weekend young Granadinos would parade in their pimped up Seat Leons, blasting Flamenco music.

I had never written a restaurant review before so I looked at a few others to get an idea of how I should approach it. The owners didn't know this of course, yet it was difficult to pretend to be a gourmet critic accompanied, as I was, by a three-year-old girl. But that didn't matter in the least as I was greeted by Jackie, who herself had a small child with whom Jasmine immediately started to play. We were seated at a table looking out at the sea, which on this day was sparkling and blue, just as the Mediterranean should be. The restaurant was French. After all, what else could it be with a name like *Chez Pierre?*

"My husband, the chef, is the French one," explained Jackie, who was from Scotland. "Maybe you would like to meet him after you have eaten?"

I said I would, and was soon tucking into a starter that, according to the menu, was French *tapas*. Looking more closely at the menu I noticed that it was somewhat quirky. Alongside dishes such as lobster *tajine* and baked oysters, were baked beans on toast and black pudding. When I mentioned this to my hostess she raised a wry eyebrow. "My husband is, uh, well known for being a bit cocky with the menu." I didn't know what she meant by this but all became clear after I had finished my *pot au feu* and we had both polished off a slice of chocolate cake.

I was led into the kitchen to meet the man behind the menu. Pierre was doing all the cooking himself but took off his apron for a few minutes to share a coffee with me at the bar and chat. He had an impish grin and he related his life story to me that, it's fair to say, I had not been expecting in the least. For Pierre Levicky was not *just* another chef – he was a man credited with starting a gastronomic revolution in Britain. He was also a bit of a rogue and risk-taker, it turned out, and the story of his rise and fall was remarkable. In the 1980s, he told me, he had arrived in Scotland with one hundred pounds in his pocket, picking up jobs in restaurants to pay his way. Within a few years he had opened a small bistro of his own in Edinburgh, promising proper French cuisine for the proletariat. Pierre's little restaurant became famous for its *coq au vin* for five pounds, and the clientele sat at rickety wooden tables, while the day's specials were chalked up on blackboards in swirling Gallic handwriting. The look and the concept became a roaring success and Pierre opened up more restaurants that adopted the same theme. Food writers in the broadsheets loved it, heaping praise on Pierre, and setting off a clamour to copy and replicate Pierre's simple style and open up gastronomy to the masses. In fact, it soon became culturally okay in Britain to talk about dining without being accused of snobbishness, and restaurants everywhere began to put up blackboards illustrated with swirly writing and offer posh sounding food at unpretentious prices.

Within a number of years Pierre had built up an empire of over one hundred and forty restaurants in his *Pierre Victoire* chain. Most UK high streets had one, and the groundwork for the phenomenon of gastro pubs had been laid. Pierre, despite his flamboyant jet-set lifestyle, could do no wrong, and the media loved him. But then, in 1998, his chain went spectacularly bust. It was so unexpected that it wrong-footed City investors, who lost fortunes. With six million pounds outstanding, the disgraced entrepreneur jumped in a camper van and fled Britain, leaving behind a lot of open-mouthed investors, a baying pack of journalists and, not least, the tax man.

For two years he and Jackie laid low, living a peripatetic life travelling the back roads of Europe in their camper van. But with next to no money to sustain them, Pierre eventually was forced to eat humble pie and sought work in the kind of Paris restaurants where he'd started out. In this way, over a number of years, they saved up the seed capital to lease a new space and open *Chez Pierre*, where we were now sat. As he finished his coffee he shook my hand saying with a shrug that he had to get back to the kitchen. I cautiously asked him if he was still on the run and he replied that, no, he had learned from his mistakes and was on the straight and narrow having declared bankruptcy and set his affairs in order. Now, aiming to make a comeback, he was in Spain. "Why here?" I asked.

"It's just that kind of place," he said. "Magic can happen here. I really feel that."

We clinked our coffee cups together and wished each other's respective ventures success. I then headed back to the office ready to write my first restaurant 'review'.

- 22 -

Aside from the paper version of *The Olive Press* we also made a digital version. It was early days for the smaller news outlets to have an accompanying website, but we nevertheless figured it was a growing trend and we'd better have a digital presence. Dan, our web designer, made us a landing page and it wasn't long before it was populated with stories. It looked good, but the content management system was slow and buggy and it was slightly laborious uploading articles. What's more, the stats showed that very few people ever clicked on the stories, with perhaps a hundred hits signifying the absolute upper level of interest in any single article. Given that the page cost us money and time, it hardly seemed worth the effort.

That all changed one day when Marcus translated a story he'd found buried in the pages of a local newspaper. I could hear him snorting and chuckling as typed it out. When it was finished he said, "Well *that* was an interesting one."

He emailed it over to me and I read it. It concerned the arrest of a man and woman for a lewd public display one afternoon on a hot Granada pavement. By the time the police arrived a crowd had gathered around the couple, who according to witnesses were 'going at it like rabbits'. Only when the police got them back to the station did they find that the couple was in fact a mother and her son.

It was story that was in shockingly bad taste, but I uploaded it to our website and waited to see if anyone would read it or comment on it. In hindsight, it was probably a poor decision – clearly the perpetrators were either mentally unwell or out of their heads on drugs. Nevertheless, the article was soon noticed, and I watched as the viewing stats began to rise. As a matter of fact, every time I checked the figures, they seemed to have doubled: they were rising exponentially.

"Why's our website not working?" I asked Dan, when I got to work one day.

"Hmm," he replied, bringing up a screen of analytics, "looks like you'll have to buy more bandwidth." He explained that the capacity had been exceeded as people from all over the globe were simultaneously trying to read the '*Mother and Son in Public Sex Romp*' story, and that we'd have to pay the Internet provider for more. The stats indicated that several million people had clicked on it, and media in the United States, India and beyond had picked it up. A flurry of comments and emails followed, with some questioning what kind of a sick society we lived in and others offering mental help. Conservative bloggers picked up on it too, highlighting it as a case of the kind of moral decrepitude that we could all expect from a 'socialist country like Spain', while left wing bloggers decried a lack of government funded healthcare and blamed the incident on capitalism. Numerous porn sites linked to www.theolivepress.es and some people asked us for pictures.

It took a few weeks for the interest in the unsavoury article to die down, but in the process we had gained far more readers. Google even improved our site's ranking of importance, and inducted *The Olive Press* into its list of 'serious' news sources. We had, in effect, been noticed. They say sex sells.

Questionable stories aside, one issue we faced was that the spell-checker software on our computers made it difficult to write articles about the local area, adding numerous errors to the copy before they were (mostly) ironed out by proofreading. It seemed to have issues with place names, and would change Granada to *Granddad*, Bubión to *Bunion*, Pampaneira to *Pampered*, Capileira to *Caterpillar* and Órgiva to *Orgasm*.

But potentially the most embarrassing auto-correction came in a Spanish cookery article, in which the unrecognised word 'aubergine' was changed to 'aborigine' by the American software. Luckily, the error was spotted by Vicki as she proofed the finished article which would have come out as: "Take two plump *aborigines* and slice them into quarters with a sharp knife before removing the skins and rubbing salt into the flesh. Drizzle with olive oil and cook over the open coals with a dash of Tabasco sauce – delicious!"

It was all the luckier that she spotted this clanger, as it would have appeared in our 'Vegetarian Special' issue.

- 23 -

Like being on an island somewhere in the middle of the ocean, living in La Alpujarra could feel a bit stifling after a while. With the vast expanse of Spain spreading out around us, people with itchy feet naturally felt like striking out for a peek beyond the horizon every now and again. Given that I was now working at a newspaper that had a need for feature articles about Spain I had the perfect excuse to launch myself off on any mini adventure that took my fancy. And so I decided to visit the Badlands of Baza.

I had come across an article that concerned an ancient statue of a woman, and nobody seemed to know how old it was. The best guess by archaeologists was about two and a half thousand years, but this was up for debate as nobody could agree which culture had produced the statue. *La Dama de Baza* (the Lady of Baza), as she was called, had been discovered in 1971 and was displayed in the local museum until she was controversially moved to Madrid to undergo 'restoration'. Like many who take off for the capital, *La Dama* was never to return, and to this day the museum in the town of Baza displays a replica version. Reproduction or not I was determined to go and see for myself what all the fuss was about.

Baza is a town to the north of the mountain range that borders La Alpujarra, although people tend to use the term to refer to the entire area in which it is situated. To get to it, one cannot simply drive over the top of the mountains, so a circuitous diversion via Granada was needed. Aside from the statue, the region is famed for its underground cave dwellings, and whole villages can be found carved into the undulating hills of soft rock. My plan was to stay in a cave during this excursion.

Over countless aeons that very same soft rock had given rise to a vast expanse of canyon lands, and these days the dusty hills and plains are speckled with almond trees, and a few olives where there is enough water. Amongst these groves can be found volcanic springs and Neolithic ruins. Sparsely populated, overwhelmingly rural, and almost unknown to tourists, the austere region is often simply called the 'Badlands' on account of its dry terrain and starkly eroded topography. It's the type of place where, if you were to get lost on foot, you could reasonably expect your dusty bones to one day be kicked aside by a passing goatherd.

I put an overnight bag in the car and, along with my daughter Jasmine, headed north. By lunchtime we were floating in the warm waters of a natural hot spring, surrounded on all sides by crenelated chalky-white hills beneath a rain-tormented sky.

Fernando worked in the ticket office of the hot springs of Zujar, which is where we had stopped for a break, and he was eager to practice his English on me. This being the middle of the week in the off season, there weren't all that many other people around to talk to in this desert oasis.

"The earth is fractured here," he said "that is why the waters are so hot. The Romans used to come here and bathe."

"That's fascinating," I said, blinking brackish water out of my eyes as the warmth of the pool seeped into my body.

"And there are dolmens around here – hundreds – perhaps thousands of them!" he enthused. I nodded some more. "Nobody knows how many there are!"

121

Now I had to admit that I had only a shaky idea of what a dolmen was at the time. Nevertheless I did own a copy of Julian Cope's *The Megalithic European,* so I knew he must be talking about the mysterious and ancient stone structures dotted all over Europe. Fernando, who seemed to know a lot about these things, was eager to tell me all about them. This area of northern Granada Province, he said, was filled with prehistoric ruins left over from an ancient culture that had spread throughout Europe and stretched back to before the Bronze Age. This seemed incongruous to me, as the last thing I had expected to find in this dusty and arid part of Spain was a load of stone circles and forgotten passage graves. "Yes, yes!" said Fernando. "People here are not interested in these things, but more and more they are being explored these days."

I pondered what he said as I sat in the thick volcanic water which felt like hot saliva on my skin. Gazing out across the parched desert I could see a dark curtain of rain approached us from the west. Jasmine, three years old and blissfully uninterested in ancient Iberian civilisations, paddled around the steamy pool in her plastic ring with unabashed joy. We had come upon this place in the desert by accident on our way to Baza. Before I'd left I had agreed with Marcus and Molly to scout out distribution points around Guadix, a renaissance architectural gem of a town. Curiosity had caused me to head off the main road and into the interior following signs with ancient dolmens depicted on them. Driving into this empty landscape almost felt like leaving civilisation behind, and I was relieved when we'd eventually come across the little oasis with its café and plastic sun loungers.

The lush surroundings and the natural pools were a blissful reprieve from the heat of the day, but with the rain approaching we decided it was time to move on. We dried off and retreated to the oven-like interior of the car before driving back along the arrow-straight road that had led us in from the A92n. With the windows wide open we soon dried off. Oncoming cars floated like UFOs in the heat wave for minutes at a time and then roared past with only inches to spare on the narrow road. It was a wonder any nearside wing mirrors survive in these parts. I pulled over to take in the view from a vantage point, gazing out across a huge depression of eroded rocks and dry rivers. Stretching into the distance one could only see mile upon mile of curious perky mounds and occasional green patches marking the presence of some spring or natural pool. Vast smooth-sided hills rose up on the horizon like terrestrial gods and it was hard to imagine this landscape had changed much since the appearance of bands of peculiar bipedal apes which would one day take over the world. Locals modestly called their region the 'Cradle of European Humankind'.

Fast-forwarding a few millennia we rolled into modern day Guadix. In the shadow of the dominating cathedral I sipped a cold beer and devour a *tapa*. The afternoon sun had honeyed the sandstone walls of the cathedral and swarms of swallows dipped and wheeled around the baroque architecture. This spot, as was often the case in Spain, was the site of a former a mosque, and before that it had been sacred to people for millennia. I wondered about the people who lived here before the arrival of Christianity and Islam. Surely such a commanding spot in a naturally fertile area would have served as a place of veneration for nature spirits, or maybe it was a confluence of invisible earth energies. Who knew? I asked Jasmine what her opinion was on the matter but she was busy colouring in a cartoon bear and pretended not to hear.

Baza is not all that far away from Guadix along the main road, and so we headed there next. I parked up and strolled to the Plaza Mayor where the attractive sixteenth century church and museum are located. We were the only visitors and, from the curator's obvious delight, possibly the only ones for some time. The statue I had come to see was situated on the top floor and we climbed the marble staircase with a certain sense of anticipation (I had told Jasmine that we were going to see a 'stone lady'). *La Dama* was sitting on a winged throne inside a glass box. I tried to block out the knowledge that she was a reproduction, imagining instead the fantasy of unearthing her in some dry and dusty dolmen. The label above her said she might have been Roman. Or perhaps Visigoth. Or maybe an Iberian Celt or some other culture we don't know much about.

Being of almost life-sized proportions she appears to be of European or North African ethnicity, and has a Victorian 'we are not amused' look on her face. She is, perhaps, a young queen and wears exuberant jewellery and headwear. There is a channel in the side of her throne, so she was possibly a reliquary for ashes or bones. I gazed at her in this exquisite wood-panelled room, trying to imagine the hands that carved her – a futile attempt at connection with a long since extinguished culture.

Our place of accommodation for the night was, fittingly, a cave. A good proportion of the population in the region still lived in subterranean abodes, carved out of the soft mud-like earth like so many termite mounds. Back in Guadix, the upper *barrio* of town was the cave quarter, and that was where our hotel was supposed to be. Talk of troglodytes and cave dwellings has put me in a Tolkeinesque frame of mind, but most of the caves have been extended outwards into the open air and the overall impression was not of subterranea but suburbia – more Surbiton than Hobbiton. I drove around looking for our cave hotel, totally lost due to the absence of street signs, and occasionally stopped to scowl at the map and ask for directions.

Nobody, it seems, has any idea where our cave hotel was. Eventually, way out in the *campo*, we found our lodgings just as the sun was beginning to set over the distant Sierra Nevada. Maria led us to our room, which was a modern cave with a TV and a minibar. Inside it was slightly dank, with the faint suggestion of encroaching mould.

Jasmine fell asleep off more or less immediately and I sat outside on the step with a bottle of *Gran Feudo*, a couple of books on Spain and the emerging stars. We were far enough out of town to allow for a desert silence to surround us and I sat and read until late, drawn in by the fascinating history of Iberia. Not too much is known about the various tribes and races that lived in what is now Spain and Portugal before the arrival of the Phoenicians, who arrived as salt traders from what is now Lebanon. Legend has it that a fantastic Iberian city called Tartarus existed at this time, although no evidence has ever been unearthed to support this. By the time the Romans arrived on the scene the ethnic mix of Andalucía featured Celtic tribes from Central Europe, Greek traders, belligerent Carthaginians and numerous others. There didn't seem to be any evidence of any pan Iberian culture or religion, although there is evidence of bull-worshipping cults as a side effect of settlement by Minotaur-venerating Cretans – the probable origin of Spain's obsession with slaying bulls.

Visiting the Badlands of Baza and seeing the statue had given me ample pause for thought that evening as I sat out under the stars. The region was endowed with standing stones, outcrops, barrows and various Neolithic monuments and yet most of them seemed overlooked. Seeing no value in them, some farmers were even breaking the stones up or using the barrows to store farm machinery. Just to the north of Granada, in Jaén Province, was the Cueva de la Graja, where a cave had been discovered filled with symbolic depictions of a mysterious figure on the rocks similar to others found in Almería Province to the east. Just who painted those symbols and what or who did they represent?

But what was just as interesting, and caught hold of my imagination, was that I was quite possibly looking at a slice of my own origins. A study conducted by Bryan Sykes, a professor of human genetics at Oxford University, found that by examining the mitochondrial DNA of modern Britons, it could be proved that many of us were descended from the ancient peoples of Iberia. These sea-going people had made it to the British Isles around six thousand years ago, where they found a land only recently vacated by the huge ice sheets of the last ice age. They were a small people, only about five feet three in height, and came from the coastal regions of Spain. Could the *Dama de Baza* have been one of these people? This could certainly be an unusual take on why so many modern Britons felt at home in Spain.

- 24 -

Moving from our village house in Pampaneira down to our new abode in Cerro Negro took several months. For a start, there was a lot of work that needed to be done to

126

the farmhouse to make it at least semi-habitable. The main jobs that needed doing were putting wiring in, installing a water system and raising the roof by a few feet so that the almond store could be turned into a bedroom. There were also the not inconsiderable tasks of plastering the interior walls, tiling the floors and shoring up a couple of sagging terraces that looked like they might be about to collapse. The house had somewhere between four and eight bedrooms, depending on where you drew the line between what was a room and what was a ruin. We opted to have four bedrooms done up and one separate *casita*, which would be double as a workshop for Michelle's upholstery workings, as well as a place in which to house the batteries and inverter for the solar system that would power Los Pechos.

Most of the time while the initial work was going on at Los Pechos I would be busy working at the office. I popped in as often as I could to check on progress, and on one such visit I remember seeing fifteen men working around the place doing all manner of jobs. Our poor old farmhouse was taking a fair hammering, with muscular tattooed men using jackhammers to rip up floors and bash down walls, while others were hollowing out channels for electrical conduits and moving materials around in wheelbarrows. I began to feel excited about the prospect of moving in. But, builders being builders, there were unexpected problems and cost overruns. We had a budget to stick to, and it soon became clear that it would run out sooner rather than later. When all was said and done, we squeaked in just above the budget. All of the infrastructure work was done – water, a new roof, heating in the form of a wood burning stove, solar powered electricity and a kitchen – even if the place wasn't exactly luxurious. The rest, I figured, we could do ourselves.

Actually, to say it *wasn't exactly luxurious* is perhaps an understatement. There were piles of rubble everywhere, walls were unrendered, the outside bathroom was barely functional and there was no front door. The whole house looked like it had been ripped apart and not put back together again properly, which was of course exactly what had happened. We moved in anyway. In fact, we didn't have a choice as we needed to sell our Pampaneira house to pay for more work to be done and clear the mortgage. However, being overly sentimental and probably overly optimistic about the ability of *The Olive Press* to provide some form of income, we decided to put off selling the Pampaneira house. We were quite fond of it, despite its haunted status, and opted to rent it out to holidaymakers as a means of getting some cash in.

And so we moved into our half-renovated farmhouse during the hottest months of summer and commenced two years of living in a building site. Despite the mess and the steep learning curve associated with the vagaries of living off grid, I instantly loved living at Los Pechos. What was most pleasing was the sense of peace and quiet and of having so much space around us. In the mornings I would wake up early and sit outside with a cup of tea, watching the light spread across the land as bees visited the flowers around me and birds flitted from tree to tree.

With our own furniture in it the house felt like it belonged to us now. The spooky feeling I had got on that first night when I had come down to inspect it had vanished entirely, with the place was soon filled with music, friends and the squeals of our children running around playing hide and seek. Was this the kind of paradise I had been dreaming about? It certainly felt like it.

But we hadn't moved there just for the pleasant ambience. We wanted to grow as much food as we could from the land and live in a way that would be more resilient to any of the economic or ecological shocks that were by now clearly shambling towards us out of the gloom. The first thing I figured I should do was pick the almonds that hung by the thousand from the trees and littered the hard-baked earth. I had never paid much attention to almonds before, associating them more with marzipan than anything else, but becoming the owner of so many almond trees – or *almendros* – put paid to that. In the spring, when all the work had been going on with the builders, I'd watched the trees burst into blossom. They'd made the farmhouse look as though it were cocooned in frothy pink cotton wool. The smell of the blossom was enough to make you giddy and thousands of bees created a collective almost electric-sounding hum as they flew from flower to flower, extracting nectar.

Some of the bees were truly wild – I had seen their colonies hanging from tall trees – but many of them must have been something to do with our new neighbour Antonio, who kept around a hundred hand-made hives on his land. When we got to know him properly, I joked with him that his bees were stealing all my nectar, but of course they were also pollinating the trees. In any case, Antonio, who was the best neighbour anyone could ever wish for, always gave us plenty of dark sweet honey in the autumn.

Almonds, it turns out, are not nuts but fruits. This is clear when they are growing, as they develop into velvety green fruit with hard, fluffy, cases. In fact they are a kind a peach and what we consider to be the almond nut is in fact the kernel inside the stone. When they are ripe the sun dehydrates the fruit, causing it to harden, curl up and fall off. The remaining kernels are easy to knock down with a long bamboo stick and collect in nets. A good strike can see up to fifty of them knocked off in one whack and it is wise to wear a helmet whilst doing so, we discovered. Once gathered together, the almonds could easily be cracked open with whatever rock was at hand, and one soon learned the exact force needed to crack one open without pulverising the treasure within. Our children could often be found walking around the garden clutching fist-sized rocks and with their arms filled with almonds, figs, lemons and – during the winter season – oranges.

One of the great things about almonds is that they keep for years in this state and, moreover, they come ready-packaged. They are an easily storable form of protein, which is why the Spanish use them in so many dishes, from cooking with rice or roasting, to making almond soup, marzipan or any number of desserts. They are also believed to harbour medicinal properties and some claim that eating them lowers the risk of contracting cancer or suffering a heart attack. This, combined with the fact that the trees can grow in the driest of conditions, goes a long way towards explaining why the almond tree has taken root so well in Spain.

And they taught me something too. One night, standing in the moonlight in the garden, I listened to a wild boar as it chomped its way through a pile of almonds that I had rather ignorantly left on the ground. There were many things to figure out when moving to the Spanish *campo*, and learning not to leave piles of almonds lying around was one of them. The *jabalí* was stood not more than six feet away on the other side of a bush, and it presumably hadn't heard my approach because of the dreadful racket it was making as it munched away at its prize find with its giant gnashers. Local people shot wild boar on sight, but I liked to imagine them as my friendly scavenging neighbours. However, the sound of this beast grinding his way through the stone-hard almonds made me think again. *Jabalis* had been known to kill people by charging at them and thrusting their nicely rounded tusks into their soft bodies. Listening to him, it was hard to believe how powerful their jaws must be to not just break through the tough almond shells but also do so as if they were scoffing a bowl of dry roasted peanuts. The beast on the other side of the bush suddenly stopped munching and began sniffing the air. I held my breath and remained perfectly still. Just then my bristly garden guest let out a deep grunt; it was a grunt so deep and powerful it was like a rumbling from the bowels of some long extinct volcano. It stirred some primal fear deep within me and made the hairs all over my body stand on end. And this is what I learned as I backed away in terror, praying that the dark shadow behind the bush didn't see me: the lesson was that it is probably never a good idea to get too close to a *jabali* in the dark.

- 25 -

I got Paul McGwin's copy just before the issue went to press. Better late than never, I thought, but when I started reading it I realised that perhaps this wasn't the case. Given that the brief we'd given the Vietnam vet was to write about Spanish culture, he'd taken himself off to Granada for the weekend to scout out some of its many treasures. I was expecting an article about the Alhambra, or perhaps the gypsy quarter of Sacromonte, but instead he had filed a typo-strewn six-hundred-word polemic about the instant coffee machine in his hotel. The focus of his article was how the machine had 'stolen' a euro from him. Paul had placed his coin in the machine and pressed the button for a *café con leche*, but had instead been met with a blinking red light and an empty plastic coffee cup. The fact that the duty clerk at reception had seemed indifferent to his plight had only served to add to his growing sense of outrage at the coin-pinching machine, and he had embarked on an angry screed about the comparative superiority of American instant coffee machines over European ones.

"Did he provide any accompanying pictures?" asked Marcus, when I showed him.

"No," I said. "He doesn't have a camera. But we can't publish this anyway, it's irrelevant."

"Irrelevant in *your* opinion," Marcus replied. "But who's to say others won't find it interesting? Culture is subjective, you know. American tourists might be fascinated by it."

"There's a thousand years of history in Granada and some of the most beautiful architecture in Europe. Perhaps he could have written about that," I countered. "But instead he's given me a report about an instant coffee machine that was probably made in China and has nothing to do with Spain."

Marcus thought about this for a moment. "Yes, but the machine serves *Spanish* instant coffee, in *Spain*, and is used by *Spanish* people," he said, logically. "You shouldn't be so elitist and judgemental."

"Hmm," I replied.

That issue's heavily edited culture article, when it was printed, was certainly original, if nothing else. We were still struggling to get decent articles printed, although our writers were, for the most part, doing a good job. Every two weeks there were still those thirty-two blank pages to fill, however, and there will still very little money flowing into *The Olive Press* bank account from advertisers.

"What we should be doing is more advertorials," said Marcus. "We'll write about people if they take out a bunch of adverts with us."

This seemed like a good idea and we asked Vicki to find some potential subjects. She soon came up with a couple who had something to do with polystyrene blocks and were keen for any form of media exposure. To that end I was sent out to go and meet them.

I had to admit that I wasn't prepared for it. No sooner had I stepped out of the car, roadmap still in hand, than a young man with the impressively sized shoulder-mounted television camera was right up in my face. I was in Cacin, hidden away in the countryside near Alhama de Granada and here I was looking down the barrel of a lens. Some hidden instinct told me to pretend it wasn't there: just ignore it and it will go away. I was there to meet Claire and Jamie, and find out what had lured them to this very rural idyll and, more intriguingly, what had persuaded them to allow a film crew to intrude upon their lives.

I stumbled up the path, cameraman in tow, and there was Claire, whom I recognised from a picture she'd emailed to us, extending a welcoming hand and asking me if I'd found their place easily (answer: no – there couldn't be many foreigners choosing to live in such an out of the way location as this). "Yes, fine," I said breezily, my first TV lie. She didn't seem to notice the camera and immediately began taking me on a tour of their house and land. In the garden, I couldn't help noticing a large half-built structure that seemed to be made of giant polystyrene Lego bricks.

Claire stood in front of the idiosyncratic building and began a lengthy explanation of the considerable thermal qualities of insulating concrete formwork. I wasn't sure if this was for the benefit of me or the viewers who may be watching at home. The cameraman moved his lens right up into my face as I nodded and uttered "Uh, huhs," and pretended it wasn't there. Perhaps some explanation is required at this point. Claire and Jamie had recently moved to Spain after watching a TV show about buying property, and they wanted to build their own house. From previous visits they knew it got very hot in the summer as well as cold in the winter, and so they wanted to ensure their house was properly insulated.

They knew of a company in the UK that made polystyrene blocks from which you could easily assemble the shell of a building and then pour concrete between them at the end of the day when the structure was complete. Bingo – an instant house! They were so impressed they bought the company. Well, not quite, but they did decide to become the official Spanish distributors of the product.

In the shade by the main house was a whole gaggle of relatives. Young and old alike mingled by a similarly half-built outdoor kitchen. Jamie stepped forward and shook my hand. "Hold on, I know you from somewhere," I said, looking at his face. There followed a short geographical narrowing down of previous lives, the epicentre of which turned out to be the Saddler's Arms pub in Solihull, where I misspent a portion of my youth. All the while the TV camera was recording our conversation with its all-seeing lens. There was an awkward pause and the cameraman, putting on an eerily flat TV voice, said "Jamie and Claire have invited someone from a local expat newspaper in an effort to drum up interest for their product."

There was another prolonged pause in conversation, which induced the cameraman to hit the stop button. "Hi, sorry about that," he said. "Better to get it, you know, raw."

"Fancy a glass of wine?" said Jamie. "We've been up since the crack of dawn doing the garage in time for the filming," he said, gesturing at the glaring white building at the end of the garden.

He explained that this was to be the last day of filming and all the stops had to be pulled out to ensure various narrative strings were tied together. Christian, the cameraman, would be driving back to an editing suite in London the next day, and he would be taking with him the precious tapes containing eight weeks of filming for *Living in the Sun*. Jamie took me inside the polystyrene garage to show me the finished product. I knocked on the walls; they sounded pretty solid.

"It's really energy-efficient," he enthused. "A single light bulb will heat this space."

Claire walked in added a few more perky comments about the thermal properties of polystyrene. She seemed more relaxed now the camera was off so I asked what had persuaded her to endure trial by television when moving to Spain. "Well," she said "someone nominated us for the series and we agreed to it after thinking things through and deciding the exposure might give our business a boost."

"What do the locals make of you coming here and constructing buildings out of polystyrene? I bet they think you're mad!" I said, half-joking. Claire looked at me, horrified.

There was a click at my ear and the whirring started up again. "Can you just say that again," whispered the cameraman. The heat of the mid afternoon sun and the white wine were not helping my head as I tried to get to grips with this strangely artificial situation. I imagined Nadia Sawalha narrating jauntily over our conversation – a prospect that further impeded my thought processes.

"Er, what makes you think this polystyrene idea will be a success?" I asked ineptly.

"Er, well ... we liked the product before we came out..." Claire said, haltingly. A minute ago we were two grown adults having a normal conversation but being filmed had turned us into numbskulls. I wanted to ask her how she and her family could put up with type of intrusion on a daily basis, but I couldn't because she was on camera and it just wouldn't be fair.

Instead I asked something about whether she thought rural Spanish people, with their conservative tendencies, were likely to buy their polystyrene building products. The camera lens zoomed in on her face even as I was asking. Claire managed a spirited answer (after all, she'd had two months to practice) and I bowed out.

Off camera I asked Jamie how it had been. "You get used to it," was his response. The production company had been filming their whole Spanish adventure to date, including a trip to the town hall to apply for planning permission. I suggested the subsequent approval might have been helped along by the presence of a film crew. "Perhaps," he chuckled, "I don't think they'd ever seen a TV camera round here before."

Later, leaning against a (brick) wall I chatted with the production assistant, a tragically hip Finnish bloke who looked like he had accidentally stepped straight out of London Fashion Week and was wondering how to get back. He also seemed terminally bored and yawned conspicuously several times as I spoke to him. I said there must get hundreds of potential subjects for each series. "Yah, hundreds," he nodded disinterestedly. "Absolutely bloody hundreds."

"And some of them must have some pretty unusual ideas for getting on television?" I ventured.

"Yup. Some of them," he yawned.

136

"And how," I asked, "do you select the ones to appear?"

He turned his expensive shades to me. "Oh, let's just say that if you've got the photogenics then you make the cut. We fill in the rest."

The afternoon rolled on and other guests turned up for the end of filming party. "It's a rap," called Christian and everyone seemed relieved. I imagined they could now simply get on with being themselves again without such media intrusion. Taking my leave, I wondered as I got in the car what angle the producers would decide to take once they had constructed the narrative from the many hours of film that had been gathered. Would they be kind or would they be merciless? Unfavourable comparisons of ancient Rome arose in my head.

- 26 -

When I had written up the advertorial on Claire and Jamie it occurred to me that encouraging people to construct buildings from plastic blocks was probably at odds with the desire for *The Olive Press* to be a 'green' newspaper. "Gotta pay the bills," said Marcus, and of course, he was right.

Still, what I had seen looking down from the summit of Iberia's highest mountain had continued to play on my mind. A whole landscape, known as the Campo de Dalias, had been smothered by plastic. This was what people meant when they talked about '*plasticultura*' an unholy marriage between agriculture and plastic that had transformed parched Almería from dust bowl to salad bowl in a generation. On a small scale, plastic greenhouses could provide gardeners and smallholders with the extra warmth and diffused light necessary to grow produce throughout the winter months; but this was on a distorted and monstrous scale – so gargantuan that it is clearly visible from space. One only needed to look at satellite images, centring on the ghastly expanse of slum-like shacks of El Ejido, to see it. The spread of greenhouses, like some ghastly flaky skin condition, could be seen to be seen eating up the coastal plain and beyond.

But aesthetics aside, the puzzling question remained: why grow anything at all in Almería, which is officially the driest place in Europe? Up until the early 1980s, nothing of any note grew in the area, except for a few cacti and some hardy grasses

It had been technology that had allowed progress to occur in the realm of growing plants where they didn't grow naturally. Advances made within the field of hydroponics – the growing of food with a minimum of organic material and using drip feed irrigation – combined with the large scale drilling of bore holes down into the huge aquifer that lies beneath Andalucía, had permitted a revolution to occur. Diesel pumps bring the subterranean water up to the surface, where it is mixed with chemical fertilizer and drip-fed to the salad crops, which are suspended inside the climate-controlled plastic greenhouses. The fact that Almería receives so much light makes it possible to grow food all year round there, and supplying the supermarkets of Europe with fresh lettuce, cucumbers and tomatoes has become a multi-billion Euro concern.

It had made a lot of people very wealthy in an area that has traditionally been poor. For centuries, the city of Almería was regarded as something of a basket case. Eastward looking, desiccated and poor, the city has had to put up with more than its fair share of misfortune over the ages. The area had always been prone to seismic movements, but the earthquake that hit the city in 1522 came as a triple whammy. The powerful tremor itself levelled buildings, killing thousands and trapping many more in the rubble, but the tragedy was compounded by the fact that it happened during the night, as fire from spilled oil lamps took hold and burned many of the trapped survivors. And then, to add insult to terrible injury, the quake also unleashed a tsunami that swept over the coastal city, drowning many of those who had escaped being crushed or burned.

Three more earthquakes hit Almería within a hundred years and, in 1937, the German navy unleashed a deadly assault, bombing the city mercilessly in a display of strength. In 1966 a US air force B-52 bomber accidentally dropped four nuclear bombs on Almería following a mid-air crash with a refuelling plane. Luckily the bombs failed to detonate, but the incident was hushed up to save face for the US at the height of the Cold War, and avoid tarnishing Spain's nascent tourism industry. The bombs were recovered, including one that fell in the sea, but the area around Palomares is still said to be contaminated with radioactive materials.

So Almeríans couldn't believe their luck when technology, the fall of Franco, and cheap fossil fuel inputs suddenly made it possible for them to transform their economically marginal land into a salad crop growing gold mine. A shocking satellite picture used by Greenpeace shows the 'before and after' transformation of the region between 1974 and 2004. Anyone with a scrap of land had only to hire a drilling rig for a day, erect a metal frame on which to hang the plastic outer shell of a greenhouse, hire a few labourers from one of the local gang lords and sit back to watch the money roll in. Of course, even this basic infrastructure cost money, which is where banks were willing to step in and lend cash to people who up until then didn't even have an account.

But as the *invernaderos* began to spread across the land it soon became apparent that there were not enough people to tend them. The work was hot and dangerous and involved spending all day inside the hot greenhouses in the presence of dangerous chemicals. Understandably, not many of the locals were keen on doing this kind of work, so instead, the workforce poured in from Africa. Mostly illegal, and without paperwork to prove who they were, the workers were ripe for exploitation.

I took a trip down to El Ejido to see for myself what it was like. I saw in the dusty backstreets (in as much as it could be called a street where every building is made of plastic) wandered the sons of Africa, faces angled downwards and quick to melt away whenever I approached. I had heard stories of these people being offered a job in Europe and smuggled over to here in Almería, where they found themselves being forced to work continuously in deplorable conditions. They owed money to their masters for 'rent' – money they would never be able to pay off. If this was not modern day slavery then I didn't know what was.

There wasn't much to see in El Ejido except for the greenhouses and the factories that did the processing and the stockpiling. Here and there, skips were filled with rotting tomatoes, while concrete channels overflowed with all manner of plastic detritus, including empty fertiliser canisters, which would be washed out to sea when the next heavy rains came.

Aside from the shiny new cars and buildings in Almería City I couldn't see much good about the greenhouse industry. Having run out of flat land on which to erect the greenhouses developers were now in the process of levelling hilltops and gouging scoops out of the sides of mountains to make the terrain more amenable. Illegal boreholes were being drilled in the knowledge that the Spanish judicial system had a backlog of many thousands of similar cases. Typically it would be several years before the extractor would be called up to court, by which time the investor would have used his newfound wealth to easily pay off whatever fine he was given. The *Guardia Civil* were powerless to intervene and could, at most, put up some of their plastic tape before going off to investigate the next set of reported violations. Indeed, coming themselves from local families, why would the officers even want to prevent new boreholes being drilled if they brought so much wealth to the area?

The simple truth was that this gold rush wouldn't last for long. It was difficult to picture quite how large the water table is that lies underneath Andalucía, but with Spain's estimated half a million illegal boreholes sucking ever greater quantities of water out at an ever greater rate, it is clear that the water will be gone at some point. Many of the aquifers in coastal areas had already turned to sludge, and others are filling up with salt water as the sea penetrates them far below the surface. In much of Almería the tap water was now undrinkable and you had to buy water in plastic bottles, thus adding to the plastic problem.

Between them, the greenhouse industry and the demand for more golf courses seemed to be out of control. There was a sad irony in the fact that the water was being wasted in the most rapacious manner precisely where it was most needed, with the UN estimating that a single eight-hole golf course in Andalucía needs over two million litres of water a day to keep it green. This wouldn't be so bad if it were located in damp Scotland, where golf was invented, but the tragedy was that the water table under Andalucía is getting lower each year. Politicians and developers were looking at different ways of securing a supply of the magical substance, and pumping water over the hills from La Alpujarra would sate the thirst of the salad barons and the golf course developers, even if the price paid would be a huge one in terms of the loss of wildlife, small scale agriculture and natural beauty.

- 27 -

Making a newspaper wasn't all fun and games. After each edition we faced the daunting prospect of filling yet another one with fresh words and images. And then we'd have to do it all again. Marcus, as ever, was undaunted and immediately set about purchasing local Spanish newspapers and hammered out any news stories he found interesting or were relevant to our area. He and Molly also went off to explore a number of vineyards and write a series of articles about regional wines. I did my best too, gathering together as many general interest articles, opinion pieces and photo features as I could lay my hands on, whatever the quality.

But as challenging as it was to fill up the pages, the real puzzle was how to pay for it all. Since the first issue the number of advertisers had shown steady growth, driven in part by us taking on a number of commission-only sales staff. The best of these was Caroline, who drove around in a thirsty old Mazda and seemed to be able to wring money out of shopkeepers and artisans all over the province. But our other sales staff, on the whole, were learning that it was by no means easy to convince business owners to part with their cash. People who had lived in the area over the years had seen a succession of newspapers come and go and, in general, they wanted to see us still around after a year or two before committing to taking out an advertising contract. So, with only a trickle of money coming in from adverts there was the problem of finding enough money every month to pay for the printers, utilities, rent, writers and distributors – let alone ourselves.

I had read that a new business was like a baby bird learning to fly. It needed to get its wings flapping, even as it rapidly put on weight and faced the prospect of one day having to launch itself out of the nest. And the trick to getting a new business off the ground was to get the income up to a level that covered outgoings before you ran out of seed capital. But that was the problem: our investment capital was running out. Every week it felt as if I had a queue of people standing at my desk while I fished for notes in the moneybox to pay them. If they were salespeople this was okay, as they usually handed over a wad of notes before I handed some back as their commission. Increasingly, however, it seemed that there was a long line of writers asking for money that, sometimes, we didn't have. In fact, it began to feel as if the challenge was to get the baby business to flap its wings fast enough so that it didn't dash itself to bits on the ground below the nest. Yes, we were learning to fly.

"What we need is someone who knows what the fuck they're doing," said Molly, a little too bluntly for my liking. We all knew who she had in mind. Rick, who was still working downstairs for Mel and Nikki, had the gift of the gab and a persistence and professionalism that made him an ideal salesman. Even a casual glance showed that he had ambition running through his veins. He drove a silver Ford Focus and sometimes wore wraparound shades like an American GI. "He'd sort out our mess," opined Molly.

And so we invited him out for a clandestine cup of coffee and put the idea of working for *The Olive Press* to him. Initially Rick seemed happy to agree – anything to escape working for the estate agents, who were hard taskmasters and tight with their commissions.

However, being the kind of hard-nosed salesman we desperately needed, he then arranged another meeting and brought with him a list of conditions we'd have to agree to if we wanted him on board. For a start he wanted his own separate office room, a proper legal employment contract, a salary with commission and a new computer. But one of the biggest demands was that his girlfriend, Jayne – who was also working downstairs – would take over the role of office administrator and receptionist, which Vicki had been doing so well up until then. In return, he said, he would invest some money in the business and work day and night to make it a success.

It was a hard bargain but it didn't seem like we didn't have much of a choice. At the rate we were going we would only have enough cash for a few more issues. And so we agreed, with reservations. It fell to me to let Vicki know that she would no longer be needed. Doing so felt traitorous as she had been key in helping to launch the newspaper, but Rick had his conditions, and replacing Vicki with Jayne was one of them.

Vicki gathered her things together and left the building. Understandably, both she and her husband were not keen on talking to me after that, which was a bit awkward in a small town, especially as our daughters were friends at the same nursery.

When Rick started he spent most of the first day trying to assemble the new flat-pack Ikea desk we had bought for him. A lot of cursing and banging noises came from the office room I'd just vacated, culminating in our new salesperson flying into a rage and kicking a chair across the office. It wasn't an auspicious start. "He's a fookin' nutter," whispered Marcus nervously, perhaps realising Vicki was preferable after all. But Vicki was gone, and in her place sat Jayne, who seemed very happy to have escaped working for Mel and Nikki.

When his desk was finally assembled and he was seated at it, Rick began to cast his eye over our accounts. I'd already provided him with a rough summary of them when we'd been negotiating with him, but he wanted to see the whole lot in detail right down to the last *centimo*. He printed everything off and got out a red pen, staring ponderously at the figures. As he did so he made the occasional tutting noise. Marcus and I sat nearby feeling nervous. It was a bit like having your dirty underwear inspected by a customs official, and Rick would occasionally come over and ask me what so and so figure related to before shaking his head and moving back to his office space.

That evening Rick phoned us all and convened a meeting in the office for the following day. As he spoke his tone of voice was serious and it was clear that he wasn't impressed with our efforts at running a company. The next morning I got the first inkling that things were not going to be pleasant when I walked in and saw Jayne sitting on the sofa dabbing at her eyes with a hankie. "Ah, Jason," he said, "we were just waiting for you." Gingerly, I took a seat on the sofa beside Molly and Marcus.

"Let's get straight to the point," said Rick, striding up and down the room between the facing sofas as if he were the case for the prosecution in a courtroom. "You employed us here on false pretences." He stopped moving abruptly, pivoted on one heel and gave Marcus and I a withering look. We sat with our heads bowed as he continued. "This company, if you can call it that, is up shit creek without a paddle. You've been spending money like idiots and unless we get serious cash flow running this so-called newspaper will be bust within a couple of months, if not sooner. You told us you were breaking even – that was a lie!"

There was a period of guilty silence as myself, Marcus and Molly contemplated the floor tiles and Jayne issued muffled sobs. Zac the husky slunk away and hid under a desk. Marcus raised his face to speak. "But that's why we need your help," he said, a little meekly.

Rick stared at him. "Well, if we'd known the financial hole you were in we wouldn't have quit our shitty-but-safe jobs downstairs. The fact is the pair of you are out of your depth and if this place is going to survive we need to make big changes." I sat there despondently, wondering what big changes he had in mind. "Number one," he began, "writers get paid five cents a word. Whose idea was it to pay them twelve?" Nobody answered. One of the things that Marcus and I had agreed upon from the start as a matter of principle was that writers should get paid a fair amount for their work. Five cents a word sounded like a pittance, and I knew that some of them would not take well to it. "And another thing," Rick continued. "How come you employ an office cleaner? We don't need an office cleaner, we can take it in turns to do it ourselves."

"He's also the gardening writer," I protested. Rick glared at me and continued.

"Sales staff must have their commissions cut. And you two," he said, pointing at me and Marcus, "as company directors, you will not get paid until we break a clear profit. There will be no more buying local newspapers, we need to find a cheaper accountant, the printing contract needs renegotiating, we'll have to slash the print run, and the petty cash is *not* for buying coffees and *bocadillos* with."

To finish off he added that we'd all have to work until late into the evening every day, nobody was to have any time off except for weekends, and treats for Zac were *not* a reasonable business expense. Marcus stood up abruptly, muttered something under his breath and stalked off to his desk where he began to punch at keys on his laptop. Rick raised his eyebrows, walked into his own office and shut the door gently.

That meeting was only the first of many as Rick and Jayne busily organised us in an attempt to put some lift under the wings of the madly flapping *Olive Press*. Progress was monitored and reports were issued on a regular basis as we each went about our respective tasks to try and stop the business failing. Rick cast a critical eye over the newspaper and took an axe to things he called 'dead wood'. Small advertisers were tossed out and the focus was now to be on financial service providers, airlines and the bigger estate agents. Gone were most of the small ads for reflexologists, dog-walking services and aromatherapists with names like Honeysuckle Starchild, and in came big payers with well-designed full page adverts for mortgages, luxury golf resorts and insurance products.

All day long, with his door propped open, Rick's telephone carousing filled the office and Marcus put on his headphones and turned up the volume as he tapped away at the keys. He had refused to budge on the point of not buying Spanish newspapers and seemed to be acquiring more of them than ever. As a matter of fact, they were spilling off his desk and had begun to pile up on the floor. It was almost as if he was building a wall made out of newspapers around him.

And so, with this new dynamic in play, we set about creating our next issue, hoping that Rick would save us.

- 28 -

When Jon Clarke strode into our lives with his over-sized boots I immediately knew that nothing would be the same again. His initial communiqué arrived in the form of an email stating matter-of–factly that he had picked up a copy of *The Olive Press* at Granada Airport and, upon reading it, had been overcome by the feeling that we were in desperate need of his help. He was, he said, a Fleet Street journalist of some standing and now lived in Ronda, several hours' drive to the west of La Alpujarra. He also informed us that he would make his way over to us as a matter of urgency to discuss how he could help us.

I asked Marcus what he made of this and he agreed that it did indeed sound like an intriguing proposition. After all, we had nothing to lose by accepting someone's advice, especially if they were as experienced as this person said he was. We arranged to meet Jon Clarke at a campsite on the outskirts of town a few days later.

It was a warm March day and we waited for him in the shade of an olive tree in the car park. A campsite might seem an odd place to do business but in Órgiva it was considered the place where you took people to discuss important matters. Marcus and I stood there in the heat, not knowing what to expect. The time when Jon Clarke was supposed to arrive came and went, and after half an hour of waiting we repaired to some outdoor tables and quenched our thirst with cold drinks. The warmth of spring was upon us and it wouldn't be long before the din of cicadas would be the constant soundtrack to the days. From the campsite we could see a long way down the Guadalfeo valley in the direction of the coast, and approaching cars could be spotted making their way along a windy ribbon of road. An hour had gone by and we had drained our second glass but there was still no sign of any Fleet Street journalists in the vicinity. "Oh well," said Marcus, and we were about to leave when we saw a dark green car making its way towards us along the road.

Even though the car was far off, I had an intuitive feeling that it was him. Marcus began to fidget and grind at the coins in his trouser pockets with his clenched fists like he always did when he was nervous. Several minutes passed as the green car negotiated the last mile or so of bendy road, went through the short and low tunnel that had only recently sliced the top floor off a hippie bus, and turned left onto the Seven Eye Bridge that spanned the Guadalfeo. The battered old Mazda swung into the campsite carpark and eased into the only available slot, which was marked 'Private: No Parking'.

The door opened and the car's occupant got out. Physically tall, he was wearing a crumpled lightweight cotton jacket, blue jeans and scuffed cowboy boots. He walked over to our table, speaking with some animation into a mobile phone, and remained a few feet away as he continued his conversation, seemingly oblivious to our presence. We sat there in bemused anticipation as he gesticulated and spoke ever louder into the phone. He seemed to be trying to talk over the top of the person on the other end and, although he was speaking Spanish, it was clear that whatever it was they were disagreeing about would not be resolved any time soon. The flow of words coming out of Jon Clarke's mouth suddenly stopped as if cut off by a valve and he began to peer at the mobile phone in the manner of someone diagnosing a technical problem. He put it back to his ear. "Paco ... Paco?" he said, giving the phone a little shake. But wherever Paco had gone to it didn't seem like he was coming back and Jon Clarke gave a small shrug and slipped the phone into his jacket pocket. He turned to us and, pausing for a moment as if changing mode, broke into a wide smile and extended his hand to us. "Sorry I'm late," he said. "These bloody roads. I tell you, it's beautiful around here but there's no way my wife would let me live here – it's far too remote."

We exchanged pleasantries for a few minutes, and spoke about the recent hot weather, as all Brits must. "Are you hungry?" I asked. "The restaurant here is pretty good."

"Starving," he replied. "This one's on me."

I thought I'd better warn him that he was parked in the space normally reserved for the camp site owner, "Oh, I wouldn't park your car there," I said, pointing at the sign.

Jon Clarke gave me a quizzical look. "Don't be soft, man," he said. "This is Spain – I mean, what are they going to do? Anyway, let's get some food and talk business."

Inside, we sat at a table with a view of the mountains. Marcus was interested to know what kind of *tapas* they served in Ronda, where Jon lived. This was the one subject Marcus could talk about non-stop without ever tiring of, and he seemed to be able to remember every dish he had been served on his various excursions to different parts of Spain. In his mind, I imagined, was a map of the country illustrated not by place names and geographical features but by little dishes of savoury morsels. He rated a place on its *tapas* and claimed to have discovered unheard of towns in Jaén Province where the bar snacks were out of this world. It was all the more strange because his strict adherence to vegetarianism must have put at least three quarters of dishes off-limits to him. Nevertheless, he said, he enjoyed watching other people eat the meat dishes, especially Molly.

The three of us ate, making small talk and feeling out each other's positions. The restaurant, like most in Spain, had a tiled floor and heavy wooden furniture with chairs that squeaked loudly when someone stood up. Jon ordered the wine, making a great display of swilling it around in the glass and snorting it several times before sampling it.

"So," said Jon "It's good to be back on the mainland. I just spent two days waiting to spring the Irish PM in the Canaries, and he never even turned up. These stringer jobs can be such bummers can't they?"

Marcus nodded sagely in agreement, as if it were the kind of thing he was also asked to do all the time.

"And then I get back and the builder's gone and put a wall where we didn't want one and I have to tell him to knock it down again and 'no, I'm not paying for your mistakes' was what I said. Don't you just hate dealing with builders?"

I could relate to Jon's frustration with dealing with builders but when it came to talking about being a journalist I had nothing to add. The waiter brought over some plates of ham and olives, and a bowl of *gazpacho* for Marcus "He's the journo, not me," I said, nodding in Marcus's direction.

"Ah," said Jon, focusing on Marcus, "it's good to meet a fellow partner in crime down here." He then embarked on a string of anecdotes that often seemed to start with "When I worked on Fleet Street," or "During my time at the Mail," or "this one time when I was interviewing Mohammed al Fayed..."

Marcus was grinning politely, but I could see the veins on his temple beginning to throb, revealing his inner turmoil. I had encountered those veins on several occasions in the office. Marcus gripped his knife and fork harder and tried to laugh nonchalantly. He tried one of his own anecdotes about the time he'd met Kevin Keegan, but Jon just stared at him nonplussed. "So, which paper was that for?" In the awkward silence I topped up my glass and took another slice of *serrano* ham. "Oh, hold on a minute," said Jon as he scrutinised his buzzing mobile phone before choosing to ignore whoever it was.

"I'm just going to the bathroom," said Marcus.

After the meal Jon lit a cigarette and leaned back in his seat. He seemed to suddenly remember something and reached into a small satchel, fishing out a copy of *The Olive Press* and placing it between us on the table. I noticed it was covered in a red scrawl, like bad homework. Jon leafed through it, breathing smoke out of his nose. "You know, when I first picked this up at the airport I was amazed. And I'm not talking about just thinking 'that's a good idea' and all that – I mean totally amazed. Here, in Spain, was an English newspaper that actually dealt with Spanish things and had the guts to say something about this corruption that is going on everywhere. I mean, I'm an investigative journalist and, I'm sorry if this sounds immodest, but I reckon I'm pretty good at it. Tony King, eh, remember him?" Marcus nodded but I said I didn't. Jon fished in his satchel again and came out with a paperback book: *Costa Killer* by Jon Clarke. I raised my eyebrows. "Serial killer. Nasty piece of work but he's banged up in Malaga now. He'll probably come looking for me when he gets out. But, as I was saying, it's one thing having the guts to write a book like that – and I did help the police with their investigations – but quite another to take on all these corrupt mayors like you two are."

I thought I had better put him right. "Not me," I said, "I'm just the features editor. I cover all the fun stuff."

"Well then," continued Jon, looking at Marcus, "hats off to you sir. You must have *cojones* the size watermelons." Marcus looked petrified for a moment but then decided to roll with the complement.

Jon allowed the image of Marcus with watermelon balls to hang in the air for a few moments before continuing. "But what really impressed me is that you guys are standing up for the environment. This is Spain's first green newspaper. Landmark!" He thwacked the copy on the table with the back of his fingers.

"I don't really like to think of us as being green..." Marcus began, but Jon cut him short.

"Have you heard of Los Merinos? No? Los Merinos is..." he searched for the right words "an abomination on the soul of Spain." He waited for this to sink in. "They're building a golf course on a piece of forest outside Ronda. But it's not just any forest, it's an ancient and protected oak forest that's been there since time immemorial, and they want to cut down the trees and build hundreds of houses and hotels. And you know what? It's illegal! It's illegal at the local council level, illegal at the provincial level, illegal at the autonomous regional level, illegal at the national level, and if that wasn't enough, it's illegal under international law because it's a bloody UNESCO heritage site!"

He was really fired up over this golf course and had to take a swig of water. "That's really awful," was all I could think of saying, but the fact was hardly surprising – dozens, if not hundreds of new golf courses were being planned for the region, and nothing seemed to be able to get in the way of them being constructed, least of all lack of planning permission or water to keep them green.

"Yeah, it's terrible," he continued. "You think it's terrible, I think it's terrible, we can all agree that we think it's terrible. But what about the Spanish authorities, do they think it's terrible? Oh no, they're too busy lining their own pockets most of them. It's easy to buy them off or just tell them there will be construction jobs. To them it's all just progress and money and damn the consequences."

"Yes, they're all corrupt," chimed in Marcus.

"Well," said Jon "that's where we come in."

"We?"

"Yes, we can start a campaign and get the ball rolling on this one. We'll break in and take pictures, expose what they're doing to the world. And we'll get international NGOs on our side, and they'll try to shut us up but we won't take it lying down. Do you guys keep your address a secret? No need to involve our families in all this. I've got a shit hot lawyer and a direct line to every daily editor in London [and with this he tapped his mobile phone]. And we've got Alistair Boyd as well – you know him? – Lord Kilmarnock, Martin Amis's stepfather. He's practically one of my neighbours and he wants to fight them too. This'll be a new dawn for campaigning journalism in Andalucía – we'll show 'em, I've already got a plan of action drawn up."

Marcus and I exchanged a furtive, shocked, glance. It seemed an exciting prospect; the chance to actually make a difference no matter how remote the odds of its success might be. Ever since I had seen the plastic greenhouses I had hoped we could give a voice to Spain's fragile environment, but Jon seemed to be wanting to take this to a whole new level. He looked at us expectantly, an excited are-you-up-for-it look in his eye. As a matter of fact he appeared a bit like an overgrown schoolboy, with his tousled brown hair and the satchel at his side. He might have been proposing breaking into the headmaster's study and photocopying our genitals.

His mobile phone beeped again and he read the message with obvious interest, before pocketing it and taking his jacket from the back of the chair where it had been hanging.

"Anyway boys, think it over and get back to me. But we have to move fast and I've got to head off now. They've got another job for me but I'll be in touch."

We stood up and all agreed it had been an interesting meeting and that we would no doubt enjoy working together in some capacity or other. "Oh," said Jon, as he was about to leave "have a look at this boys." He pushed the much-abused copy of *The Olive Press* over to us. "Believe me, I've worked on the most successful newspapers in Britain and I know what makes them sell. Have a look at my comments and take particular note of what I've written about the headlines. They're too small. What you want is BIG headlines. Nobody's going to pick up a newspaper with timid little headlines like yours. You've got to learn to be more aggressive."

And with that he turned and left. "What do you think?" I said. Marcus was holding the newspaper and staring at the screaming red ink. It pulsated like a slab of meat that was somehow still alive.

"Nimby," he said quietly. "Upper class fookin' nimby."

Outside I saw the battered green Mazda pull away, with Jon already talking into the mobile phone clamped between his shoulder and cheek.

I looked back at Marcus. "Did he pay his bill?"

Living in the dust and rubble at home at the same time as trying to grow *The Olive Press* was a daily challenge, so we decided to get away from it all one weekend and remind ourselves why we had moved to Spain in the first place. What's more, it was my birthday and I'd promised the rest of the family a treat. We'd never been to Cabo do Gata, a couple of hours along the coast to the east, but it was said to be one of the last unspoiled coasts of Spain.

The drive took us over the almond covered Sierra de la Contraviesa and down to the coastal littoral. We then passed through the dispiriting plastic wastelands of the Campo de Dalias, and soon after this the natural park of Cabo de Gata appeared suddenly. The approach road ran through a flat plain populated by desiccated century plants, appearing like some kind of primeval skeletal forest. We drove past these alien sentinels in the gathering gloom of the downpour-to-come as black clouds hung over nearby hills, ready to drop their load. Soon we found ourselves travelling into an arena of darkly rounded hills dotted with old-style wooden windmills. Awakening children stirred in the back and eyed this peculiar new landscape with caution, perhaps wondering if this was some kind of Teletubbies-induced dream.

Our hotel was an old ranch, transformed into a series of low-rise individual rooms sitting on the edge of the desert. If it seemed familiar it was because it had been used as a set in the film *A Fistful of Dollars* – the bit right at the start where Clint Eastwood rides up on his horse. There were courtyards spartanly decorated with cacti and refulgent desert flowers and, to the delight of our daughters, a paddock held several young foals. Figures wearing jodhpurs and cowboy hats strode authoritatively around, reminding me that Spain never ceased to amaze in it diversity from one region to the next. "On Sunday we have a confirmation party with two hundred guests," the receptionist informed me as she cast an eye over my frayed t-shirt and shorts. "It is a black tie event."

Not long afterwards we found ourselves standing on a wide stretch of sandy beach with the late afternoon sun illuminating the spiny foliage along the barren shore. As we stood and watched, a nearby hill that was shaped like a volcano appeared to be erupting. But it wasn't lava or sulphurous fumes pouring out of it, it was goats. At first there were just a few of them, barely visible as white specks. But then more and more came. The tide lapped against the beach and the sun sank lower in the west as the faint sound of the approaching caprine horde carried on the breeze. They came in waves, spilling recklessly down the sides of the volcano-like hill, each one a pure blank dot on a grey-green canvas.

The rain had arrived the previous evening; a whole year's worth in one day, according to reports. Here, said to be the driest, most parched spot in all of mainland Europe, vast puddles reflected the retreating clouds. The sun-hardened earth seemed unsure about this sudden abundance of water and, for the time being, denied it entry. Perhaps the goats could sense lush green shoots lurking below the surface and were coming to devour them.

Some of the goats were getting close now. Jasmine eyed them nervously and reached for my hand, while Sofia gurgled and flapped from her pushchair. Gushing from the cone, as if summoned forth from some mythic subterranean realm, the albino army drew ever closer, prancing and scampering to a dongle chorus of copper bells. I could see now that these were no ordinary goats.

157

Their huge bodies were supported by powerful legs and great, gnarled horns topped ancient-looking faces set with pink eyes. As they neared they showed no sign of slowing. Jasmine gripped my hand harder. "Let's go," I said, gathering the children.

Stomachs began to rumble and we made our way into San José, the nearby resort town. Set around a sandy bay, San José exhibits a style of North African architecture common to the region, with domed houses featuring icing-on-the-cake render and soft lines clamouring up the hills for views of the azure blue sea. Lower down, at beach level, the scene was kiss-me-quick holiday resort meets Woodstock '69 as barefoot peddlers of ethnic jewellery called out in French, and waiters stood outside their pizzerias fish restaurants trying to entice you inside. A paella price war was underway with eateries displaying their latest offers on blackboards, hoping to hook the tourists as they promenaded along the beachfront.

The town was abuzz with the newly arrived, and Nippy little city cars bearing Almería number plates fought for parking spaces. From them emerged weekend-happy revellers, as well as families piled up with cooler boxes, suitcases and inflatable crocodiles. "People are drawn here for the feeling of freedom here," said the old woman who was serving us fresh seafood in the restaurant we had picked. "There is nowhere else in Spain like here." I gazed out of the window at a posse of scabby and underweight wharf cats sitting beside a pile of crab pots and awaiting the return of the fishermen. A curious feeling of déjà vu came over me; this place reminded me of somewhere.

Over the next three days we explored the area and took things easy. With its wide sandy beaches and uncluttered shoreline, the cape was holding out valiantly against the encroaching spew of concrete and plastic which smothered most of the Mediterranean coast of Spain. Cabo de Gata, meaning 'Hilly Cape', is a rocky peninsula that ends in a point with a lonely lighthouse. Just out to sea lies the *Arrecife de las Sirenas* – the 'Reef of the Mermaids' – and looking out at it from a rugged cliff top it wasn't too hard to imagine the sound of splintering hulls and the wails of shipwrecked sailors in times gone by. These sandy beaches and rocky coves were said to have been used by wreckers and smugglers. A jolly eyepatch-wearing plastic pirate advertising cheap sangria outside a restaurant only added to my growing fantasy.

The next day we drove out to the village of Las Negras, passing through several hamlets along the route. Bright red poppies filled the plains between the hills and unfamiliar looking birds darted from the roadside at our approach. Stopping off at the dusty village of Rodalquilar I took a stroll around the church under the heavy mid-afternoon sun. The place appeared to be deserted, and not just because of the hour. Dozens of newly built houses had been abandoned, each having fallen into a premature state of decay. Perhaps this was one of the battlefield fronts in the war against illegal developments Marcus had been writing articles about. Only recently, I recalled, a giant hotel had been provocatively put up on the Cabo de Gata shoreline. The local government had subsequently requisitioned it and there were plans to blow it up with dynamite it as a warning to other would-be illegal developers. I got back in the car and we drove for several kilometres more down to where the road ends abruptly at Las Negras.

Our guidebook used the word 'sinister' to describe Las Negras. As far as I could see though, there was no reason this should be so. After all, it was just a pretty little seaside town with the requisite number of craft shops, cafés and crooked little houses. There were wooden fishing boats drawn up on the sand and salty old men of the sea sitting and repairing their nets.

As I parked the car I noticed a man with 1970s *Chips* style sunglasses eyeing our arrival. A cheaply erected sign above the stool on which he sat advertised the construction of an *urbanizacion*. He lit a cigarette and crossed one leg over the other, revealing calf-high cowboy boots. "You buy house from me," he shouted over. It sounded like an order and I shook my head. 'Ach,' he spat, and turned away.

Back at the hotel the confirmation party that the receptionist had told me about was in full swing. The car park was full of expensive new cars – mostly black – and well-fed children frolicked under the watchful eyes of their immaculately attired parents. A violin was playing somewhere and waiters walked to and fro with silver trays of drinks and canapés. This hotel might have been where The Man With No Name shot a gang of *Rojos*, but now it looked more like a set from *The Godfather*. It was a very hot day and so I wandered over to the reassuring coolness of the pool and slumped onto a lounger with a glass of cold beer. The sun was just beginning to set behind the baked hills and I watched as the sky started to bruise purple as dusk approached. Distant jets taking off from Almería Airport rose silently into the darkening sky like little silver darts. I closed my eyes and let my mind float away. Falling towards sleep, goats turned into sheep, paella to pasties. Cabo de Gata was such a confusing place. Was I in Spain, or was it the Mexico of the Spaghetti Westerns. The Berber architecture, the Italian pizzerias and the French jewellery stalls all swirled in my mind, and as I drifted off my subconscious mind made the connection it had been trying to tell its conscious half about, and there arose in my hypnagogic state childhood memories of mackerels and mermaids, shipwrecks and smugglers, and of small crabs in rock pools in distant … Cornwall.

- 30 -

It wasn't long after we had first met him that Jon Clarke decided to pay us another visit. Marcus was mysteriously absent that day, so it fell to me to meet up with him in the town's pizzeria. It had a splendid garden filled with orange trees and the pizzas were all handmade. Jon sat down and, just as he had done when we first met him, pulled out the latest copy of *The Olive Press* from his leather case, slapping it on the table between us. I couldn't fail to notice that – once again – it was covered in more red ink and scribbles.

"The newspaper is great," he started out. This sounded positive to me, but I suspected he might have more to say. "In fact I've been kicking myself that I didn't think of doing something like this to start with."

"*But*," he continued. There was always going to be a *but*, "you chaps are still not bold enough with your headlines!"

I squinted at the paper to see what he meant. "Exactly," he exclaimed. "You can hardly see them. They need to be at least three times bigger and in bold caps. Do you actually want people to pick this up? It doesn't look like it."

I agreed that they could do with being a bit bigger, said I'd discuss it with Marcus. Jon started flicking through the pages. "And your captions. You need to work on them too. It's no good just writing some words under the pictures, you need to tell readers what they are *supposed to think* about it."

Nodding, I took a sip of the wine the waitress had just brought over.

"Look, I worked for the *Daily Mail* – the most successful newspaper in Britain – so I know a thing or two about what makes a hit and what makes a miss. Tiny headlines and weak captions look like failure to me. You see this caption?"

I looked at the paper. It was a story about a local girl who had been injured by a wild boar charging at her during a *fiesta*. There was a stock photo of a boar and a caption that read "The girl sustained injuries in the attack."

"That's so weak," said Jon, bashing his palm down on the much-abused newspaper. "Want to know how I would do it?"

"Go on," I said.

"The headline would be "**BEAUTY SAVAGED BY BEAST – VILLAGE IN SHOCK**" It would be in 72 Times font bold caps and underneath there would be close-up pictures of her injuries. Was the boar hunted down afterwards? Yes, it was, so I'd have pictures of men with guns. If they'd got it I'd have a picture of a wild boar hanging from a hook and dripping blood. If they *hadn't* got it I'd have a close-up of some snarling teeth and "**WANTED: HELLBEAST ON THE LOOSE**" plastered across it sideways."

"Hmm," I said, taking another sip. I could get where Jon was coming from. It had never occurred to us to try and manipulate people in this way, and we'd assumed that just printing the news should have been enough. I said as such.

"Look, I used to work for the *Daily Mail,*" he repeated, "I know what makes a successful paper, and I tell you, you're going about it all wrong."

The pizzas arrived and we ate them, with Jon flicking through *The Olive Press* and making comments.

"Who's this Lisa woman?" he said between chomps. "She writes like a commie. Better watch her, she'll start putting subversive messages in that'll put off the advertisers. And Vernon, your property writer? His articles are about two thousand words long. You're not paying him by the word are you?"

I nodded guiltily.

"He's taking you lot for a ride! What about this bloke Zenon Zappa whose photos you keep using? That's obviously not his real name is it? I sincerely hope you are not paying him anything at all – they're *rubbish*. It should be enough for him just to see his weird name in print without expecting any money for it. Bloody snappers – give a monkey a camera and it'd probably do a better job than half of them. And what about this *Amputee* person? He's not actually had any limbs cut off has he? No? Good. Anyway, he's great – probably one of the best things in there. Your stuff about solar panels and plastic greenhouses is good too. I like that, there's plenty of potential in all that green stuff."

We went through the whole newspaper in this way. By the time we'd finished, Jon had demolished *The Olive Press*, making it seem like the most inept attempt at a newspaper in the history of mankind.

"But don't mind me," he concluded, holding a glass and about to take a sip. "I might have two decades' experience on Fleet Street and have worked for some of the most successful publications in Britain, but it's up to you guys whether or not you use me or not."

I nodded. I could see where he was going with this.

"So, anyway, I've been thinking."

"Uhuh."

"I'm willing to make you chaps an offer regarding the newspaper. I'm thinking of setting up my own version. We can collaborate, sharing stories and pictures and the like. I'll provide you with editorial guidance and stories from my end of Andalucía, and we can split the costs and profits."

"What profits?" I asked.

"Oh, don't worry," said Jon, "they'll come rolling in soon enough. Don't forget, I know what success looks like, I used to work for the *Daily* …"

"Yes, I know," I interrupted. "But I can tell you right away that there's no chance at all Marcus will agree to you making changes to *The Olive Press.*"

"Who's talking about *The Olive Press*?" said Jon, taking a sip of Rioja. He held his glass up to the sun and contemplated it. "I've got my own version planned out."

"Oh really? What will it be called?"

Jon put his glass down and looked at me. "*The Wine Press*," he said. "It'll be like *The Olive Press*, but with a red colour scheme rather than green. People will love it."

- 31 -

Rick's draconian changes were producing results. Almost as soon as he started the money began to roll in, and for the first month since we launched we didn't lose thousands of euros. He spent all day with his phone clamped to his ear cold-calling people and businesses the length and breadth of Andalucía. He somehow even managed to convince Spanish businesses to take a punt on *The Olive Press*, even though his Spanish was pretty limited. We had to hand it to him – Rick had saved us from financial ruin. But, of course, there was a price attached to the increased money flow. Some of the advertisers were unhappy about the articles we were printing about local government corruption and illegal golf courses. They said we were making it hard for them to sell their lifestyle products and asked us to tone it down a bit. We were, they said, frightening off the expats – and one must never frighten off the expats.

In fact, a growing chorus of advertisers started to complain that our stories of plastic greenhouses, desertification and municipal double-dealing were completely putting people off from living in the area and driving potential settlers away to other regions. Some former distribution points refused to have our newspaper on display and others revealed to Rick that they simply binned it the moment our distributor walked out of the door.

"Has the world ended yet?" sneered an Internet café owner down on the coast one day when I tried to give him a pile of our latest issue. On the cover was a picture of some plastic greenhouses near Cabo de Gata with piles of rotting tomatoes littering the foreground underneath the headline **"TOXIC PLASTIC NIGHTMARE THREATENS NATIONAL PARK** (we had taken Jon's advice and gone with bigger headlines). "We don't want that crap here," he said, pushing the newspapers back in my direction.

Advertising issues aside, we began to hear more and more from Jon Clarke as he moved ahead with his *Wine Press* newspaper. It seemed he was still working as a stringer for various London based newspapers, such as *The Sun* and the *Daily Mail*, meaning they would also send him out to cover stories when they needed a pair of boots on the ground.

A couple of times he made the long drive from Ronda over to La Alpujarra for a catch-up, usually stopping off at one or more restaurants *en route* to add to a fine dining guide he was putting together. Whenever he came over we'd all end up going out for lunch somewhere and talking about *The Olive Press* and how his own version was progressing.

It was on one of these visits that saw him come into the office in Órgiva having returned recently from Praia da Luz in Portugal. He'd been there reporting on the disappearance of the three-year-old girl Madeleine McCann, who had vanished without trace from her bedroom while her parents had dinner at a nearby restaurant. In his role as a stringer Jon had been called up by the *Daily Mail* and told to get to the scene as fast as he could. The Algarve was easily reachable from where he lived in Ronda, meaning that he was able to get there ahead of the rest of the press pack. At that point, neither he nor us realised what a big story it would become, even though it was already making headlines in Britain and elsewhere, but Jon was insistent that we should make it our main news story for our next issue.

"What do you think happened?" I asked him, thinking that he might have some insight as he said he was the first international journalist on the scene.

"Snatched by a paedophile," he said. "No doubt about it, he got in through the window."

"Hardly surprising," said Marcus, "they're all over the place."

And so, when it came out, the entire front page was a photograph of the missing child that people could tear off and stick in their windows. A lot of readers were upset about the case and we got messages from all over, with one woman demanding that we drop everything and go out searching for the girl right there and then. The fact was, however, that Maddie had disappeared almost four hundred miles from Órgiva – so it would have been a bit like searching in Inverness for a child that had disappeared in Maidstone.

It was clear from incidents like this that Jon could bring a lot of value to us. For a start, he was actually getting out there and reporting on the news rather than just translating articles from local media. He'd already begun to put together his own newspaper, and was eager to cooperate ever more closely with us. Rick was keen on this and began talking about the benefits of economies of scale and the possibilities of getting more advertising in, but Marcus and Molly were harder to convince and tended to disappear whenever Jon turned up. But Jon had some good ideas about how we could engage the readers more, and he thought we should expand the distribution to encompass more of the coastal communities. Given our problems engaging different types of reader, however, I couldn't see how this could be done without annoying one group or other.

Part of the reason we were coming up against people who didn't like the newspaper was because it had never been conceived with them in mind. La Alpujarra, as I saw it, was a small enclave that attracted a certain type of down-to-earth person. Those hills were populated with folks who wanted more than anything to get away from the celebrity and gossip obsessed culture they'd just escaped from. What's more, they tended to be the type of people who blended into the scenery and did not feel compelled to make everything seem 'like home' – indeed, many of them had more or less renounced their own national backgrounds and all the associated cultural baggage. But what was happening was that the larger advertisers, who were now keeping us afloat, were demanding that we saturate the coastal areas where the market was much bigger and the readers wealthier. Indeed, some of them wanted to be completely disassociated from down-at-heel Órgiva and all that the place represented to them, with one advertiser saying: "I'll happily pay more if you *don't* hand it out there."

The dynamic was becoming clearer: the costs of producing a newspaper were too high to allow us to only focus on people living in an economically weak area. The smallholders, healers, artists and other anarchic riffraff who defied categorisation, might have started out as our core readership, but they simply didn't have the money to support a printed newspaper, even if they would happily pick up a copy for free.

Some of the larger advertisers that Rick had hauled in, and who we now depended upon to meet our costs, were refusing to extend their contracts unless the news stories we printed were either positive, or at least inoffensive. The target customer of these companies was someone who played golf, lived in a villa and was doing well from the property speculation bubble.

And so these two groups of readers – barefoot, *Om*-chanting yoga teachers on the one hand, and caddy pulling gold chain wearing expats on the other – were diametric opposites of one another, making the task of putting together a newspaper that pleased everyone all but impossible. Of course, you couldn't generalise too much and there were plenty of wealthy folks living in La Alpujarra, just as there were a few flower children living in tepees along the coast. Nevertheless there was an almost audible ripping noise as *The Olive Press* began to be pulled in two different directions. As the old aphorism goes, if you chase two rabbits you catch none.

It was not just commercial concerns doing the pulling. From the start Marcus had been lukewarm about the issues I wanted to highlight and was dismissive of the paper having a local and environmental focus. To that end, he and Molly started to talk about making an offshoot glossy magazine featuring many of the top eateries and luxury food producers of the wider province – all reviewed and written up, of course, by themselves. Any talk on my part about protecting ecosystems and highlighting the menace of the plastic greenhouses was met, increasingly, with perplexed looks. This was, of course, an arrangement without a future.

- 32 -

When I went to see a man and his wife at a remote house in the Contraviesa mountains one night for a new feature, they promised to take me on a trip through the galaxy. It took a while to find the place amongst the almond covered hills but when I rounded the crest of a hilly track at dusk and looked down on the remodelled farmhouse there was no doubt that I had found the right place: a giant telescope protruded from a fibre glass dome built into the roof of the otherwise conventional Alpujarran dwelling.

Paul Downing greeted me wearing a floppy bush hat and holding a glass of red wine. "I told you you'd find it eventually," he said, as the cooling car engine ticked in the late evening heat. I'd been told to come as late as possible, but not before it got so dark that I wouldn't be able to find the place. He led me inside and introduced me to his wife Liz, who had dinner waiting for us. As I sat down to eat, Paul and Liz told me all about their passion for the stars. They had been involved with astrophotography for many years, flitting between three home bases in England, Spain and Texas. They had picked La Alpujarra as the place to build their observatory because of the lack of light pollution combined with the dry air and altitude. "Look at a night time image of Western Europe and you'll notice that the

169

area we're in now is a large black hole," said Paul. "We like black holes – that's why we're here."

After dinner I was led up onto the roof and into the dome I had seen earlier, from which an eerie red light spilled out. Inside it was like being in a small control room, lit by an infrared bulb. "Our eyes will take at least twenty minutes to adjust to night vision," Paul explained as he flicked switches and fired up a bank of laptops. "Tonight we're going to be photographing a distant Messier object which means I'm going to have to freeze the chips."

I had no idea what he was talking about, although having young children meant I was familiar with messy objects and frozen chips, and said so. Paul rolled his eyes at my weak pun, which he'd probably heard a thousand times before, and explained that a Messier Object was something – be it a galaxy, cluster of stars or other astronomical object – first categorised by the 18th century French stargazer Charles Messier. Being rather far away, with the distance being measured in light years, the photographic subjects were incredibly faint. So faint, in fact, that the exposure time for the photograph ran to hours, during which time the telescope had to stay perfectly still and focused on this distant object. Of course, over this duration the earth itself moves, meaning that the telescope also has to counterbalance it otherwise the resulting photo would just be a blur. This was achieved with the aid of Paul's laptops and a set of minute gears in the telescope mount that could keep the lens trained perfectly on the same patch of sky for hours at a time. Static electricity in the computer's circuitry presented another problem, Paul explained, as even one tiny flash of static on the computer chips could end up looking like a star on the final image. A star where it shouldn't be would cause confusion among the world's serious astronomers and so to get around this the microchips had to be cooled to almost minus two hundred degrees Celsius before work could begin. At this ultra-low temperature, even static electricity keels over and dies.

To view these distant nebulae and galaxies Paul used his impressive-looking 16-inch truss scope with a quantum scientific imaging camera mounted in the observatory on the roof of his farmhouse. We went inside and sat down – I imagined this is what it felt like to sit in a tank turret. Paul flicked a switch and a small light came on, illuminating the interior with an eerie red light. "The red light won't ruin our night vision," he said as he booted up the laptops and flicked more switches. There was the sound of a small compressor as the microchip freezing process began, followed by the whirring of small gears as the telescope repositioned itself. Paul led me outside again onto the flat roof.

"It'll be twenty minutes before our night vision kicks in – make sure you don't look at any light in the meantime, even a distant motorbike headlight in the hills." Liz had by now joined us, and was lying on a sun lounger facing upwards. "These are our observation loungers," said Paul. "They're very useful for not getting a crick in your neck." I lay down on one and stared up at the heavens. "Give it a few minutes and then it'll be like 'pop'," said Paul. I wasn't sure what he was talking about but soon enough it became clear in more ways than one. After no more than a quarter of an hour my eyes seemed to suddenly flip over into a completely different mode. Where before there had been hundreds of stars there were now thousands, if not millions.

"Whoa," I said, "I feel like I'm in outer space."

"Yes, it's awesome, isn't it?" said Liz.

And it *was* awesome. I was lying there feeling like I was floating within the Milky Way, which – of course – I was (as we all are). The sky was so dark and the stars so clear it was quite literally breathtaking. The points of light were arrayed so clearly and the surrounding countryside was so peaceful and quiet it was entirely possible to feel and imagine that I was floating free of Planet Earth and drifting off into the dark realms of the cosmos. The experience was nothing short of ecstatic.

"I wish more people could experience this," said Liz, in a quiet voice, "but the light pollution around cities means that only a few are able to."

I gazed into the inky depths of space, mesmerised. It was not at all still, as one might expect, but was a bit like staring into a rock pool and watching as things flitted here and there. "Mostly it's just bits of dust and rock," said Paul, "but that's a satellite over there, and we might see the International Space Station later on."

The couple of astronomers pointed out various planets and star systems to me as I continued to gaze in awe, already wondering how much a telescope might cost and whether I could buy one in Spain. Paul showed me cluster of stars using a smaller scope that was mounted to the roof. "That's the Pleiades," he said, "also known as the Seven Sisters, it's the closest major cluster to us at only about four hundred and forty light years – you can even see it with the naked eye."

"Tonight's perfect for viewing," chipped in Liz, "there's no moon to muck up the sky with light – *moon* is a four letter word to us."

"*Full moon* is two four letter words," added Paul. "But tonight we're going to photograph something a lot further away than the Pleiades, which are almost in our back yard."

"What are you thinking?" asked Liz.

172

"I'm thinking Messier 13," he replied, adding for my benefit, "globular cluster of half a million stars about twenty five thousand light years away."

Paul got up and led me inside the observatory once again. By now the chips were properly cooled and the laptops were humming away. He tapped on a keyboard and brought up a range of targets. Then, typing in some coordinates, the scope began to turn and point at a patch of sky. "Here it is," said Paul, showing me something on a screen. It was a cluster of stars, looking like something between an explosion in a sci-fi film and a Jackson Pollock painting. "Also known as the Great Globular Cluster, it should take about an hour to get the image and then another hour to pick up the colours." I watched as he plotted in some more coordinates and set up the imaging software. After a couple of minutes he was done. "That's it," he said. "All that's left to do is leave it alone and go and have a glass of wine."

We went out again and gazed at the stars. Every now and again a shooting star would streak across the sky; they were remarkably frequent when everything was so high-res and sharp. By about 2am I felt that I might fall asleep and drift off into outer space if I lay on my back any longer. It had been a remarkable evening and I thanked Paul and Liz for their hospitality as they showed me back downstairs. The harsh light in the kitchen was almost blinding in its intensity compared to the soft starlight I had become used to over the preceding hours. We said goodbye and I drove back over the silent hills to Órgiva and Cerro Negro. Never, in all my life had I ever felt so … earthbound.

- 33 -

As our first anniversary came and went I continued to write more articles about people who I thought were making a difference. I met with farmers protesting against the ongoing issue of water theft by corporations, guerrilla tree planters restoring the local environment, and even a young English boy who was growing up as a shepherd in the hills. I also tried to keep the writers on side, many of whom were annoyed at their lowered rate of pay and the general direction the paper seemed to be taking. Probably the most 'professional' regular writer we had was a man called Bob Maddox. Marcus had somehow brought him into the paper and maintained all correspondence with him. Bob, as far as I could make out because I never met him, was a retired geography teacher and lived in the village of Yegen, where the English writer Gerald Brenan had once lived. I asked Marcus what Bob was like. "How should I know?" was his reply. "I've never seen or spoken to him. Apparently he looks like Mick Hucknall."

This was a trait of Marcus: an unwillingness to communicate with anyone except by email. We sat with our backs to each other in the office, communicating in this way. It had all started when Rick and I had agreed that something needed to be said about the raft of bad news stories he was churning out. There was nothing wrong *per se* with bad news, after all newspapers thrive on it. But some people had cheekily started calling our newspaper *The Olive dePress* and one reader told me it gave her nightmares every time she picked it up. This wasn't surprising. It was becoming increasingly common that an issue would feature a shocking image on the cover, such as the mangled corpse of a horse, and follow with stories of rape, murder, corruption, horrific car accidents and abuse. To someone turning up in the area for the first time and picking up a copy it must have seemed as if they had landed in some nightmarish dystopia and that the easy-going nature and friendly countenances of the locals was merely a mask for their true devilish nature.

Everyone agreed that it had gone too far, so we decided to hold a meeting with Marcus and ask him – not for the first time – to introduce more balance into the news mix. I even found a couple of 'nice' stories from local media, such as the Science Museum in Granada opening a new exhibition, and another about a local child winning a gymnastics prize abroad.

Predictably, Marcus found the suggestion deeply problematic, and rushed into the bathroom, emerging some ten minutes later, still angry. The bathroom had become his place of refuge whenever anyone wanted to speak to him directly, and we could often hear him in there, washing his hands as if they were covered in oil. Rick and Jayne wondered if perhaps all the dismal news stories he was contemplating were getting to him. But any attempt to talk to him about anything important resulted in his locking himself in the toilet or rushing out of the office on some 'urgent' errand from which he would not return until later when we had all gone. Molly, who had by now quit downstairs and was working alongside Jayne, was apologetic, explaining that her husband was highly-strung on account of his deep intellect and sensitivity.

But Rick and Jayne were not pacified by Molly's explanation. They worried that it was only a question of time before the newspaper was boycotted all over the region. It had already been banned from the Alhambra on account of our front-page story about the staff ripping off visitors and watching porn on the CCTV monitors. Next it was disallowed in the tourist offices in Granada and Lanjarón, and I found out that they were throwing away copies in bulk when I peered inside a paper recycling bin next to their office one day. It was pretty obvious why: we were putting people off coming there.

More weeks passed in this uneasy state of impasse and the situation in the office was becoming unbearable, with even casual visitors noticing the cut-the-air-with-a-knife tension. Vernon Grant, our property and travel writer, scented blood and suggested that we might like someone with 'a bit of maturity' to take over the news editing. Vernon, a TV producer who claimed to be a good friend of Jimmy Savile, and had been responsible for inflicting Robert Kilroy Silk on the world, thought that maybe Marcus and I should have our heads banged together. "*Nobody* wants to read the kind of crap you're printing," he said. "You're biting that hand that feeds you," he added, in response to an editorial I had written criticising Ryanair. Loathe as I was to give in to Rick, with his demands for even more commercial articles about property, tax and legal affairs (which he could then use to leverage high-spending advertisers into place) I had to concede that this was preferable to what the newspaper was already becoming.

Something would have to give and, quite frankly, I wasn't looking forward to it.

- 34 -

There had been an unfortunate incident with a retired English couple living nearby who'd noticed cracks appearing in the lounge ceiling one afternoon as they entertained friends. Mere moments later the entire roof caved in on top of the guests, who had been sitting on the sofa drinking tea, killing them outright. In this particular instance it had been shoddy workmanship that had been to blame. The concrete in the roof, when it was analysed in a lab, was found to have been mixed in too dilute a form and could have collapsed at any time. The only minor consolation was that the husband had left the room moments before because he thought he had heard a rat upstairs and his wife was able to dive out of the way just in time, although the guests hadn't been so lucky.

I had reason to believe that a similar thing could happen in the little outbuilding at Los Pechos that was both a spare bedroom and a study in which my book collection and computer were housed. The beams in the casita were filled with *carcoma* grubs, and we didn't seem to be able to get rid of them. Whenever I sat at my desk underneath them I found it hard to concentrate, with even the slightest cracking noise seeing me worry the beams were about to give way.

Once an infestation takes hold, which it inevitably will unless the beams have been pre-soaked in insecticide, radical measures are needed to stop it. The tell-tale scratching sound was the first sign, and on closer inspection I noticed a few tiny holes in the beams. Over the course of months the sound become a chorus of gnawing and I would often enter to find my computer keyboard coated with fine orange dust and the black crumbs of maggot excrement. Spraying didn't help, and people advised other methods of dealing with the unwelcome guests. Locals painted a regular application of diesel onto their beams, and Antonio swore by it. This was fine if you didn't mind your house smelling like a petrol station. And I was loathe to employ a fumigator as I had read that the formaldehyde they used could linger on for years and posed a health threat.

A safer way to kill them, I learned, was to deprive them of oxygen. With that in mind I devised a way of burning up all the oxygen in the room and leaving them to suffocate. I didn't like killing things, but they were on a suicide mission anyway and would probably die in any case if the ceiling collapsed on them. Sealing all the doors, I placed the red-hot coals of a barbeque in a pan in the middle of the floor and lit a candle as a form of miners' canary, before retreating and sealing the door. A few hours later I returned to find the room devoid of oxygen, with the candle having gone out and the coals only half-combusted. But the *carcomas* were more alive than ever and seemed to be enjoying the added warmth, munching twice as fast as normal.

Given this failure, I cast around for other methods of halting the little menaces. Heat, it turned out, could be the answer. An organic pest controller advised its use as a means of killing the grubs, which cannot maintain their own body temperature and simply expire when exposed to a steady heat of sixty degrees Centigrade or more. Clearing out the room once again and sealing all the windows, I hired an industrial space heater from a shop in Motril and lugged it back in our trailer. The fearsome-looking machine took the form of a small petrol-burning jet engine – not dissimilar to those used in hot air balloons – and I angled it through an open door, sealing the remaining gap so there would be no escape for the heat. I lit the jet, which roared into life, and stood back. I might have said something like "Enjoy your sauna," to the maggoty little critters that were threatening to cause the roof to cave in, I can't remember.

A thermometer placed inside the window showed me how hot it was getting inside as the jet roared and I imagined the white grubs starting to perspire inside their wooden cocoons. Perhaps they would be looking at one another for assurance as the sweat formed on their miniscule brows and they took a brief break from destroying my property. I watched as the internal temperature got as high as eighty – feeling sure that the grubs would soon be dropping out of the woodwork like little steamed dumplings.

Alas, this extreme, costly and somewhat madcap solution was soon to join a growing list of failures. Before long, the flame that had been erupting from the burner began to sputter and wilt and instead of fire a thick black smoke began pumping out. I turned it off quickly, but not before every surface in the room had been coated in an oily black film that would take weeks to remove and required two new coats of paint on the walls. Science had never been my strong point, and I hadn't factored in that the oxygen-depleted air would cripple the combustion effect and cause the fuel to be only half-burned. Embarrassingly, my neighbour Antonio, having spotted the dense black smoke erupting from my house, came running up with a bucket of water. "*¡Ay, caramba!*" he exclaimed when he saw the industrial heater and me standing beside it, before shaking his head and walking away.

The grubs, under their slimy black coating, were happier than ever, and continued to munch away at the beams with added gusto. The problem was never solved, and eventually the whole roof had to be replaced, along with new beams installed. Carcomas 1 – Humans 0.

- 35 -

That the *Guardia Civil* – Spain's *other* police force – treated foreigners around Órgiva with suspicion was a widely acknowledged fact. The force, which was a

179

leftover relic from the days of Franco's military police, seemed an anomaly in a rapidly modernising country. Many asked what exactly their purpose was. With their green uniforms and holstered pistols, you were most likely to encounter them in one of three situations. The most common reason for engaging with them was as the driver of a car, as the *Guardia* had maintained the habit of setting up roadblocks and randomly flagging down motorists to demand paperwork. Whether they issued you with a fine or not was a matter of whim, it seemed, and they could always find something out of order with your vehicle or paperwork if they so desired. On the other hand, around Órgiva at least, they would often let off even the most inebriated of drivers and only ever seemed to bother shaking down hippies coming out of Cigarrones or Beneficio in order to confiscate their drugs.

The second most likely place to meet a *Guardia* officer was in your local café. Here they usually enjoyed a privileged place at the bar where they sipped coffee and smoked cigarettes. But the third – and most unwelcome – place to meet them was on your doorstep. After local authorities had caught on that they could earn considerable sums of money by levying charges for renovation permits, planning rules were tightened to the extent that you could barely lay a kitchen tile without a sheaf of paperwork needing to be paid for and rubber-stamped at the town hall. Of course, most people wouldn't bother with this, but renovation being such a popular pastime for cash-laden foreigners it made them easy targets for the snooping eye of the law. The *Guardia* seemed to enjoy sniffing out suspect home renovators and they carried bright orange crime-scene style tape in their cars to put around anything they suspected was illegal or without a permit.

I, like most other people, paid for building permits for the larger aspects of our renovation, and hoped for the best when it came to the smaller jobs. One of the builders doing the interior renovation for us at Los Pechos said he had a novel technique for dealing with snooping *Guardia* patrols. Wearing nothing under his work overalls, he and his day labourers were able to lay down their work tools at the slightest sign of trouble and get butt naked in under thirty seconds. He reported that not once had *Guardia* officers taken up his offer to come in for a cup of tea having been greeted at a remote farmhouse by a bunch of sweaty naked Englishmen. He employed a similar hack with his car, decking out the interior with crucifixes and pictures of the local saint in an ostentatiously pious display that would always impress the *Guardia's* conservative Catholic sensibilities. The fact that his tax might be out of date, one taillight was out and he was speeding would therefore be overlooked hurrying, as he was, to attend Mass where his sick mother waited.

The fact of the matter was that the provincial *Guardia* simply didn't know how to deal with foreigners, although they always seemed to suspect us of unfathomable crimes. An illustration of this was the story of a well-liked Belgian man, who had been throwing a dinner party for friends at his *cortijo*. After dinner the man had risen to his feet to propose a toast and promptly dropped dead, wine glass still in hand. When the *Guardia* arrived, alerted by the distressed friends, they took one look at the scene, noting how there was a well-fed elderly man lying on the floor next to the dinner table, and in a leap of logic that Inspector Clouseau would be proud of decided that what they were looking at was a potential murder scene. The dead man's body was left in place while investigations were carried out and his friends and neighbours were taken in for questioning. A chalk outline was drawn around where the body had fallen and, only when a post-mortem revealed he had died from a heart attack were the guests were finally let off the hook and permitted to arrange a funeral.

Apart from such seemingly inept behaviour, there was also the widespread suspicion that the *Guardia* treated foreign expats like cash machines. A friend had received a speeding ticket in the post and a fine of one hundred and fifty euros for supposedly driving at ninety kilometres an hour outside the hamlet of Tíjola. The fine arrived with a brief explanation that officers had secretly clocked him driving at this excessive speed at some unspecified time on some unspecified date. The friend was outraged and stormed into the *Guardia's* fortress-like garrison to demand the fine be retracted.

In most cases it was enough to complain about parking or speeding fines to get them retracted, however this time the officers would not budge. Okay, said the friend, he would pay the fine on one condition: that the officers try to recreate the supposed crime. My friend knew that he had them on this one, firstly because his battered old car had a top speed of considerably less than ninety kilometres an hour, and secondly because the road was so bendy and full of switchbacks in that area that to drive at that speed would have been suicidal. The officers admitted defeat at this point claiming 'faulty equipment' and offered to reduce the fine to fifty euros with a caution, which the friend begrudgingly accepted. In cases such as this, it was a good idea to treat the *Guardia* with a certain amount of caution and display respect when they seemed willing to compromise – if you rubbed them up the wrong way they could make your life a misery.

- 36 -

The next time Jon Clarke paid us a visit it was almost like fate had orchestrated events to coincide with his arrival. I was working alone in the office and had been receiving a steady stream of visitors all day. The first had been a man who'd written a pamphlet outlining a way modern social ills could be eliminated by analysing the strange electromagnetic life forces that surrounded people's bodies. I thanked him and promised to read it when I got a chance.

My subsequent visitor was someone wishing to make a complaint about a classified advert for his car repair service we had failed to run. I didn't recognise the man and had no clue about the advert in question as normally Jayne or Molly dealt with such things. But he was adamant that he had been promised it would be in the last issue and claimed that, as a result of its omission, he had lost a good amount of business. He was, in fact, very unhappy. Dressed all in motorbike leathers and being possessed of a large physical presence, I wasn't about to argue with him and fished about in the petty cash tin for the amount he said he was owed. [A year later this same man, on being thrown out of a bar in the early hours for being drunk and disorderly, had returned in a pickup truck and rammed it through the front of the establishment, whereupon he proceeded to keep the customers hostage until the police arrived and arrested him – so perhaps it was a good thing I hadn't argued with him over the sum of a few euros.]

Lunchtime came and went and I waded through my emails with a *jamon* sandwich on the desk beside me. I was trying to negotiate the republication of an article written by the American journalist Alan Weisman. The article in question, a lengthy essay about the pagan basis of the carnival celebrations in Galicia, had caught my interest years before. I was keen to offer the article to our readers and had got in touch with the author. At first he was circumspect and wanted to see a copy of the paper, which I duly put in an envelope and sent to him in Texas. Having met with his guarded approval we were now onto discussing prices. I had no idea what someone who wrote for *Harper's* and the *New York Times* might expect to be paid, and when he mentioned how much he had originally been commissioned to write the article I had to tell him that such a sum represented several months' running costs for our paper and would be out of the question. I suggested a price a fraction of the amount he had mentioned (it was, after all, a reprint) and to my complete surprise he agreed.

Flushed with the feeling of success, I spent most of the afternoon laying out the article, which was entitled *The Sacred and the Profane of Spanish Carnaval*. It was strange the way things worked, I thought to myself as I adjusted the line indents and resized the images. I must have read the article years before, but it had made some kind of subconscious impression on me. Had I not read it, I would probably never have become interested in Spain, as up until then I had thought the country was just package tours to beach resorts where donkeys wore *sombreros* and sunburned holidaymakers sang *Viva España* until the *sangria* ran out. Thus, I likely would not have been sat here in an office in a peculiar little town in Andalucía and *The Olive Press* would not have existed. I wondered whether Weisman's article had caused one reality to branch off from another for me, and whether there was some alternate universe where the me who hadn't read the article was working in an underground carpark in Birmingham or delivering pizzas on a moped in Auckland.

The doorbell interrupted my nebulous train of thought again. This time it was the owner of the local stationers, a small overly polite man with oily slicked back hair. He handed me a reminder note about an outstanding sum on our account before backing out of the door in a flourish of bows and smiles and I went back to my thoughts again, wondering what weird turn life would take next. I didn't need to wait long to find out.

No sooner had the stationer left than the doorbell rang one more time. I had a lot of work to get through before Jon was due to arrive and wished that Molly or Jayne were there to deal with all these interruptions. But everyone else in the office had been struck down by a virulent strain of the flu which had been ripping its way through the foreign population (and avoiding the locals – it was the literal opposite of the 'Spanish flu') – leaving them incapacitated for up to two weeks at a time. I'd had it myself and could attest to its ferocity, so I wasn't too surprised to find myself alone in the office on that day. I opened the door and Jake, one of our distributors, burst through it and made for the sofa where he sat panting and groaning like a wounded animal. I stared at him, not really knowing what to say. He was covered in dirt and looked like he'd been dragged down a *barranco* backwards. "What the hell happened?" I asked. I hoped he hadn't had some kind of accident while delivering newspapers; insurance was one luxury we couldn't afford.

He continued breathing heavily for a moment and then, eyes aflame, he let loose. "That cow!" he said. "She's out to get me. She thinks she can just walk all over people and get away with it. She's destroying my life! Everything I've worked for is ruined!"

"Whoa," I said, trying to make sense of what he was saying. "Who are you talking about?"

Jake jumped up off the sofa and began pacing around the office, rigid with anger. "Five years I spent building that house. Five years! I put everything I had into it. I worked on it day and night and put all my money into it. All my money! And I built it all with my own hands." Jake held up both hands to illustrate the point. I tried not to look at the cruel deformation that had left him with only two fingers on one of them. He was livid.

"But what's happened to your house? And who are you talking about?"

He fixed me with his red-rimmed eyes, and when he next spoke his voice had dropped in tone almost to a growl. "Margaret Moran. Have you heard of her? Margaret fucking Moran. The bane of my life."

I confessed that I'd never heard of her. Why should I have?

"She's a politician. A Labour MP. *My* MP back in England, as it happens. I moved here to Spain to escape her kind of scum but she's following me. She's got it in for me, she's trying to destroy me." With that he sank down on the sofa again and began to sob. After a moment he looked up, the dust on his face now muddied by the tracks of his tears. "She's cut me off from my house. Stuck a note on my motorbike telling me I can't access my own land even though it's a public right of way."

"So?" I said. "Can't you just ignore it? Anyway, what's a Labour MP doing here in Spain?"

Jake took a shuddering deep breath and composed himself. "I can't, you don't understand. She's got heavies down there. A paid mob. That path is a public right of way, has been for centuries. It's not just me, there are several of us cut off now. She says she doesn't want anyone walking near her property so she's building a wall or something to keep us out."

A dispute between neighbours was what it seemed like. I sympathised with Jake; after all, I knew both him and his wife reasonably well. They had two children, with another on the way, and we'd been giving him free adverts in the paper for his mini-digger service in return for some distribution work.

A thought occurred to me. "How do you know it was her that wrote the note? Maybe it was just one of the *campesinos*, God knows enough of them have got it in for foreigners."

"Oh yeah?" he said "and where would a *campesino* get hold of some House of Commons headed notepaper and learn to write in English?"

This sounded too incredible to be true. "What, so she's writing messages ordering you off your own property in a foreign country on House of Commons notepaper?"

"Yep," replied Jake, dejectedly.

Another thought occurred to me. "Have you got the note?"

"No, no, I didn't think," he said. "I've been there all night playing cat and mouse with her goons. There's a bunch of us. The rest are down there now, we've got her place surrounded and she's too afraid to come out. We'll do whatever's necessary," he added, a touch menacingly. "I just came here to tell you. You've got to alert people. Get a reporter and a photographer down there. I've got a feeling this is going to kick off. If I'm going to hell I'm going to drag her down with me."

Jake left, but not before I'd made him promise to get the note and keep hold of it. After he'd gone I found myself walking around the office, trying to get a grip on the situation. I wondered what I was going to do. *A sitting Labour MP – here in the Alpujarras!* I sat down at my computer and Googled Margaret Moran. A picture of her came up on the screen revealing a short, middle-aged woman with dark brown hair. She was mentioned in several newspaper articles which all referred to her close links with Tony Blair and his New Labour ideology, meaning she was a 'Blair babe'. Glancing at the stories, it seemed she had been the subject of a tabloid exposé over her astronomical office stationery expenses. *Oh boy*, I thought.

Right then, as if on cue, Jon Clarke rang the doorbell. I let him in and he flopped down on the sofa, shedding his journalistic appendages (laptop, camera, file bursting with papers). He looked exhausted and was red in the face. After he had caught his breath he explained he had used the opportunity of being in the area to 'research' some restaurants for his fine dining guide. To that end he'd eaten lunch at two separate gourmet restaurants, one after the other, with the number of courses he'd consumed running into double digits.

When he had sufficiently recovered he looked around the office. "Where are the others?" he asked. "They're not avoiding me are they? What about Marcus?" I explained about the flu and he gave me a hard look. "A good journalist should be able to work even though he's sick. What's Marcus's number? We need him down here now." I explained that Marcus didn't possess a phone and that he'd have to call Molly if he wanted to get in touch with him. I added that it likely wasn't a good idea as it was already late afternoon, and being at work was probably the last thing Marcus wanted to think about. "Nonsense," said Jon. "I need to speak to him, get him down here and working on that story about the Mayor in Armillo. It's important."

"Jon," I said, "something has come up and I think it might be important. There's a standoff going on up near the hill where I live that I think we should follow up on it."

"How so?"

I explained what had happened, how Jake had turned up dishevelled in the office claiming Margaret Moran had cut off the road. Jon went completely still as I told him what was occurring. It was as if he was stunned. "You mean to tell me Margaret Moran, the *Blair Babe,* is *here?*" he stuttered.

"Yes," I replied. "Just up the road near Chris Stewart's house."

"Who else knows about this? Have you told anyone?"

"No, just you," I said.

Jon started at me as if in disbelief. "We've got to get onto this immediately, there isn't a moment to lose."

I found myself rushing out of the office as Jon flew down the stairs. He had his phone out and was demanding to know Molly's number. We got to the street outside and he leaned against his illegally parked car as he summoned Marcus to the telephone. I could almost hear Marcus protesting as Jon barked at him. "I don't *care* how sick you are, mate, you'll get over it. What you'll never get over is missing a story like this. How soon can you be down here? What - three *hours?* That's not good enough. Twenty minutes and we're leaving without you. Alright, half an hour. This is an exclusive, mate! What do you *mean* you can't drive? You're joking, right? I've never heard of a journalist who couldn't drive. Look, if you don't come down now I'm going to come up the mountain and drag you out of bed."

He hung up the phone and gave me a quizzical look. "This could be big," he said. "What arrogance! Preaching socialism in England and then coming down here and acting all lord-of-the-manner over the locals. What's his number?"

"Huh?" I said.

"Jack, or whatever his name is. Your man, the distributor." I looked at my own phone and read out the number as Jon tapped it into his. After a few moments it connected and Jon swung into professional mode. Speaking calmly, he asked Jake where he was and what the current situation was with the supposed standoff and the groups of thugs. "U-huh, u-huh' he was saying as he wrote notes in shorthand on a pad atop his car roof. They spoke for some time and at each moment when the conversation seemed to be drawing to a close Jon would ease it back onto a new course with a "I just have one final question and then I'll let you go" or a "Listen I'll do everything I can to get this out" and the occasional reassurance "Yeah, don't worry, I'm on *your* side."

By the time he had finished talking, Molly had turned up and dropped Marcus off. He looked more peeved than sick, and was wearing a large woolly scarf wrapped around his throat. "About time," said Jon, stepping into his car. "Get in, the pair of you."

"No, wait," I said "the tracks are too rough for this up there. We'll need to go in mine." And so the three of us climbed into my car and set off for the valley running to the east of Cerro Negro where, if Jake was to be believed, a British politician was in some kind of Mexican standoff with several locals, including Jake.

The road, although potholed in places, was fine until we reached the hamlet of Tíjola, a strung out collection of whitewashed houses almost at river level, where it narrowed considerably. One of the houses belonged to our former employee Vicki, and she was sitting in her garden with her daughter beside a large lemon tree (which every year spilled its fruit onto the road and was said to be the very tree which, by his own account, was behind the title of Chris Stewart's book *Driving Over*

Lemons) and I waved as we motored past, driving over the lemons. Vicki returned a puzzled frown, as if the sight of the three of us tearing off in the direction of the hermitage at Padré Eterno simply *could not* bode well. After another mile the road turned into a rough track as it veered off uphill to the left and passed by some abandoned ruins.

Jon was taking charge of the situation, fiddling with his camera and issuing orders. "Jason, you're the photographer and the driver. I want you to take pictures of the house from every angle and keep the car outside with the engine running while Marcus and I go inside. Also, if anyone has a pop at us or you see any of the locals getting beaten up you need to get pictures, understand?" I nodded. Marcus gave a squeak of protest from the back. "How come I have to go in? I'm not well, can't I stay in the car?"

"No," said Jon sternly. "You are the editor of the newspaper; she needs to know that we're not just some Mickey Mouse bunch of hacks sent up from the coast."

"But," Jon added "don't open your mouth unless she asks you a question. Keep quiet and let me do the talking. Make sure you record everything too – you *do* have a recorder on you don't you?"

All this sounded fine but there was just one problem at this stage: we had very little idea of where her house was located. After a few brief forays down blind tracks, and one occasion where we ended up at a remote *cortijo* whose owner looked startled to have visitors, I began to worry about the failing light. Already the sun was beginning to sink and much of the valley was entering into deep shade. This wasn't good if we wanted to photograph – or even find – the place. Also, where were all the gangs of thugs we had been warned about? "I thought you said you knew where it was," said Jon, impatiently.

Presently, and not a moment too soon given the fading light, we saw a small group of men loitering by the side of the track. I pulled up and Jon leaned out of the window. "*Hombres*," he addressed them in his Spanish, which was pretty good, "we are journalists seeking the house of the *ingles* Magrethe Moran, can you tell us where it is?" The men looked at each other, one of them spat into the dust and turned away. Jon continued, "We hear there is some trouble here. We are looking for her house." Again they looked at each other and one of them replied "The house of the English woman?" Yes, we all replied. The man gave a shrug and indicated we needed to turn left down the track they were stood at the mouth of. "But you are forbidden," he added, half-heartedly, "we are told to stop visitors." So, these were the 'thugs'. They didn't look very vicious. "*Hombres*," continued Jon, "we are respected journalists sent from Seville, we must speak to the *señora* as a matter of urgency." Again the men looked at each other, but this seemed to have done it and, with a shrug, one of them pointed to a flat-roofed Cortijo a bit further down the valley. "*Casa de la inglesa*," he said simply, stepping aside.

When I pulled up outside the house my mouth was dry. "Remember," said Jon, "keep the engine running and turn the car around so we can get out of here fast if we need to. We don't know what kind of protection she's got in there." Marcus and Jon got out of the car and I watched them walk to the front door and knock on it. The door opened, spilling out warm light, and a short exchange took place between Jon and the short woman who had opened the door to him. A moment later the three of them stepped inside and the door was shut. I turned the car around and sat there with my hands on the steering wheel with the engine running. I tried to imagine what was going on inside. Perhaps there would be arguing, with accusations and rebuttals flying around, as Moran's protectors stood on a hair trigger, ready to eject the unwelcome guests. Did Tony Blair's ministers have police protection? I had no idea.

One of the men from the road had walked down to the house and he was now sitting on a mini digger next to a mud embankment and smoking a cigarette. Perhaps this was the right of way that was being disputed. I looked around in the trees and bushes, wondering if some of the protestors might be hiding out until nightfall. I remembered Jake's words: "It could kick off at any moment." Time passed. I looked at my watch: they had been in there for twenty minutes. I cut the engine, after all there was no point wasting petrol. I waited some more and turned on the radio. Spanish pop music spilled out. It was a breathless blend of squeaky feminine voices and a plaintive *crie de coeur* set to a techno beat. When it finished another song just like it came on. Then another. Presently I noticed the man on the mini digger tapping his foot, so I turned the volume knob clockwise a few degrees for his benefit and he gave me a half-salute.

More time passed and my phone rang. It was Michelle wondering what time I'd be home for dinner. She'd been looking after the kids all day and was tired and wanted me to come home and put them to bed. The electricity had gone off and she couldn't get the generator started and she was fed up. I explained to her that I was staking out an MP's house, possibly for some kind of world exclusive story, but she wasn't impressed and told me to go inside and ask them to hurry up. Impossible, I told her. Didn't she realise this was important? "And reading a bedtime story for your daughters isn't?" she said before hanging up.

An hour went by and darkness fell. The man on the mini digger had also grown bored and gone home. I got out and stretched my legs, breathing in the cool night air laced with the aromas of the wild herbs that grew in such abundance on those hills. Remembering suddenly that I should have taken some pictures, I went back and got my camera, setting it up on a rock to steady it as I took some shots of the house without a flash. But the pictures didn't come out well, they were just smeared blazes of light on a matt black background. Useless. I went back and sat in the car. Hunger was beginning to bite and I entertained the idea that maybe I *should* go and tell them to hurry up. Vaguely, I wondered if they had been tied up back-to-back or something.

Almost two hours had passed when the door of the farmhouse opened again and Jon and Marcus stepped out into the night. I started the car engine, but they were not running away from the house, they were walking slowly.

"What the hell happened?" I said, half annoyed, but also eager to hear what had gone down.

"Sorry about that," said Jon "we got invited in for a cup of tea. And she had something medicinal for Marcus's flu. Turned out she had some really great wines in her cellar, and she knows a thing or two about the vineyards round here."

"She rustled up a decent bit of *tapas* too," croaked Marcus.

"We totally forgot about you out here," said Jon. "You should have just come in."

"Now you tell me," I said, pulling away from the house and starting to drive back in the direction of Órgiva.

"Nice woman," said Jon, and Marcus nodded in agreement. "It's actually her brother's house. She explained the whole conflict thing with Jack, or whatever his name is. To be honest, it's *her* I feel sorry for, I mean it's her family's home and it's private property, so why shouldn't they be able to cut off the track if she's being bullied by them? Your man, she said, is a bit of an anarchist. It's like the Wild West round here, she says. People just don't respect the rule of law."

We drove on in silence for a while. So, it was nothing more than a storm in a teacup. But it was true that the area *did* have some things in common with the Wild West, so maybe she had a point. I'd drop the two of them off in Órgiva then go home to my dinner and to read a story to the kids.

Suddenly Jon startled me, shouting, "Shit!"

"What is it?" I said, stepping on the brake. I thought an animal had run out in front of the car.

"Don't you see what she's done?" he said. "What did I say Marcus? I said don't look into her eyes. She's gone and charmed us. Taken us in, told us her sob story and what did we do but swallow it hook line and sinker? How could I be so *stupid*! You did record everything, didn't you?" He reached into his pocket and pulled out his phone. "Just pull over here will you." I did as he asked and he stepped out. Leaning against a tree he connected with a newspaper in London. "Yeah, give me the news desk," he said. "This is Jon Clarke. I've got a story for you. Are you ready for this? You'll love it."

When he'd finished speaking I drove on to Órgiva and parked outside the office. We got out and Marcus made his apologies, starting to walk off in the direction of the bus stop. "Where do you think you're going?" Jon called out. "We've got a very busy evening ahead of us."

Marcus turned back and gave him a withering look. "Too ill," he groaned.

"Nonsense, come back here." Said Jon. "You *do* have a coffee machine, don't you?"

When we finally finished the story on Margaret Moran and Jon had sent it through to London, making sure *The Sun* cited the source of the story as *The Olive Press*, it was far too late for him to drive back to Ronda so I asked him if we wanted to stay over at Los Pechos. As we got back I was surprised to find Michelle was still up. She was standing in the doorway, illuminated by candle light with her arms folded.

"What's he doing here?" she said in a low voice, eyeing Jon suspiciously.

"We had to get the story done … he has nowhere to sleep."

Michelle weighed this up. It had been a long evening for her – she'd had to deal with two fractious children and no electricity. I was supposed to have been back in time for dinner, bringing some groceries with me, but instead it was nearly midnight.

"Hiya, beautiful evening isn't it?" grinned Jon, trying to turn on the charm. It didn't work, and slid off Michelle like a fried egg off a non-stick frying pan. She gave me a hard look and led me into the kitchen.

"If you want him to sleep here he'll have to go in the *casita*. He's not coming in the house."

"The *casita*? But … the *carcomas*," I said. The beams in the little outbuilding were still shot through with wood-munching parasites after my failed attempts to get rid of them. "What if a beam falls on him in the night?" I whispered.

"Well," said Michelle, "then you'll have something to write about, won't you?"

I didn't like this – I knew the universe seemed to have a wicked sense of irony, and I didn't want to tempt it.

"I'll sleep wherever, guys," said Jon cheerily, poking his head in. "Just give me a bed and I'll be out in minutes, I'm that tired."

Luckily, for all of us, no beams fell down during the night, but when he emerged the next morning Jon was bleary-eyed and said he hadn't been able to sleep much. "There was a bloody munching sound in there," he said. "I swear it got louder and louder. All night it went on – it took me ages to fall asleep, and when I woke up I was covered in sawdust. You want to get that seen to."

- 37 -

When summer came and the heat in Granada became unbearable, the inhabitants headed *en masse* for the coast. Salobreña, which for the rest of the year is somnolent, became a seething mass of sizzling flesh with cars lining up bumper to bumper along the seafront. They came to lie on the beach and frolic in the refreshing water, but in recent years going to the beach was not what it used to be for these urban escapees, with many not daring to go in the water at all. The reason for their fear: jellyfish. *Pelagia noctiluca* – this was the Latin name for the purplish lumps of jelly that had started to appear *en masse* along the coast. One theory as to why they had become so prevalent focused on the fact that more and more of Andalucía's rivers were being used for agriculture, meaning that the seas around the coast were now saltier, a condition favoured by the pelagic pests. However, there may have been a wider cause, as these jellyfish had proliferated across the world's oceans in recent years, wiping out fish farms and choking the propellers of ships.

Whatever was causing the jellyfish to multiply; it seemed to me they represented an abundance of sorts. One solution to this problem might be to eat them. After all, you could buy packets of dried jellyfish in Asian shops and I had heard that the flesh, while bland, was like a form of marine tofu and was a good medium for retaining added flavour. I emailed a man called Fergus the Forager, who had become well known in Britain for eating things most would not consider food. Rumour had it that he could rustle up a dish of pan-braised squirrels or roasted roadkill fox without batting an eyelid. When I asked him about jellyfish Fergus was of the opinion that they were certainly edible, but advised removing the stinging tentacles first. Furthermore he suggested they should be purified in fresh water and then dried in the sun.

"You're not serious are you?" said Molly, unable to hide the tone of revulsion in her voice.

"Why not?" I replied. "Perhaps if more people ate jellyfish instead of cows and pigs there would be fewer problems in the world."

"I don't believe you. You'd never eat a jellyfish."

But I did.

I harvested a suitable specimen from the beach at Motril and brought it back to Los Pechos. Having put on rubber gloves, I chopped off the tentacles, rubbed the remaining blob with salt and dried it out atop an unlit barbecue for a couple of days. In the full sun it wasn't long before the gelatinous corpse began to shrivel up and take on the appearance of transparent rubber. When it was time to cook it, I rehydrated it in fresh water and cut it into thin strips that were then blanched and marinated in soy sauce with olive oil and chilli. Finally I fried them with some vegetables and rice and invited some people over for a tasting.

As it turned out nobody could make it, so I had to sample my organic free-range jellyfish alone, although the kids were all too happy to watch me. The consistency was as one might expect – rubbery – and overall it wasn't an unpleasant experience. With the right marketing it could catch on.

In the next edition of the *Food and Drink* section of *The Olive Press* I detailed my findings, writing an article entitled *Why Not Eat Jellyfish?* The piece generated two email responses. One was from a man who said it was irresponsible to encourage people to eat something with stinging tentacles, and the other was from a vegan woman who said jellyfish were sentient beings with feelings and had a right to remain uneaten.

"I don't think you're going to convince many people on that one," said Molly. I had to admit that she was probably right.

But I was enjoying writing about food, and by that point had been to several restaurants to do write-ups, including a new one in Órgiva that was causing excitement called El Limonero, set up by a friendly Canadian man called Wes. According to local chatter, El Limonero's opening, along with a fancy café called Café Libertad, and another one called the Willendorf, this was a sign that Órgiva was 'on the up'.

"There's another new restaurant that wants a review doing," said Molly. "Thing is, it's curry and we don't like curry so you'd better go."

I didn't need any more encouragement than this. "Where is it?" I asked

"Out in the sticks, somewhere beyond Baza. It's in a cave. It's actually called The Curry Cave."

This sounded intriguing so I arranged an evening visit the next Friday. Heading out of La Alpujarra and north to Granada, I turned east onto the A-92, which winds through the sparsely populated *altiplano* with the snow-capped peaks of the Sierra Nevada visible to the south. The village where the restaurant was located was barely on the map, but I eventually pulled up outside The Curry Cave as the stars shone brightly above.

The first thing I noticed about The Curry Cave was that it was not a cave. In fact, it was a regular square building situated up against a hill. Inside, I was met by the English owners, Ian and Tracy, who had sunk their life savings into opening an Indian restaurant in a dusty village in the middle of nowhere among a population of fiercely conservative rural Spaniards.

"It's a bit of a gamble," they giggled. "But we felt we had to do it. After all, everyone loves a good curry don't they?"

I looked around at the restaurant. It was a little stark but pleasant enough, with new tables and chairs and a fresh paintjob. In the centre of the room stood some stainless steel serving receptacles with the handles of metal spoons poking out of them. "It's a buffet," explained Ian. "We're hoping the locals will be tempted to try it out."

Looking around, I didn't see any of the locals trying it out. In fact, the only customers were a couple sat silently in a corner nursing glasses of wine and looking like they had stumbled into The Curry Cave by accident.

"Which bit is the cave?" I asked.

"It's over there, that alcove area," said Tracy. "Technically it's not a cave, but two of the walls are bare rock, so in a way it's a partial cave."

I was given a plate onto which I spooned some rice and curry, with a couple of poppadums and some naan bread. It was pretty good, and I hadn't eaten curry for a long time. As I ate I chatted with the owners, who were keen to impress on me their credentials as curry-lovers. "We think Spain is ready for curry," they said.

The next week, back in the office, Molly asked me how my visit went. I told her about the trip, and about how the food was nice but admitted that I had reservations it would catch on.

"Oh well," she said. "You'd better make it a glowing review as they seem like good-paying advertisers."

"Don't worry," she added, "I doubt anyone will actually go and visit to see if you are right or not."

And she was correct; The Curry Cave went out of business a short while later.

- 38 -

One morning our salesman Rick appeared in the office sporting some fresh injuries on his face and neck. He was in a state of some agitation and shock, as was Jayne, and when they explained what had happened it was little wonder. It turned out they had been attacked by their elderly neighbours in Soportújar following a dispute over the placement of a small concrete step Rick had built outside his home. Leaving for work that morning, the octogenarian neighbours had rushed out to shower Rick with invective, calling him a 'foreign devil', and things like that.

When Rick had protested the old man pounced on him, knocking him to the ground and pinning him there. Rick had avoided fighting back too strenuously for fear of injuring the frail old man, and it was at this point the man's wife, a cackling geriatric by all accounts, had flown at Rick and started bashing him with a broomstick. Tossing this aside she then leapt onto our star salesman and sunk her teeth into his throat as he flailed helplessly on the asphalt. Jayne had rushed out to see what all the noise was about and discovered her husband screaming in terror with a chubby elderly woman's jaws clamped onto his throat. In the ensuing melee Rick sustained several further bites as he eventually struggled free and escaped.

He was furious. When Jayne had finished bathing his wounds he immediately drove to the police station in Órgiva to issue an official denouncement and get a doctor to take photographs of his wounds. Later, during a phone call, when I told Jon about what had happened he immediately saw the potential for a story. "Can you get some photos of the woman? What about Rick, is he still bleeding? Get some close-ups."

"He's still a bit upset," I said.

"It's not every day a great story falls into your lap," he replied. "I can see the headline now – **'Old Bat BITES Expat'**"

"Give him time to recover and he might be more amenable," I counselled.

But Rick was having none of it and didn't want to be the centre of attention. It was understandable; no self-respecting healthy male in his mid-thirties would want to admit to being savaged by a pensioner. In the end, Jon did manage to wring a story out of it with Rick's guarded approval, but the incident was much toned down and buried inside the paper. In any case, it was hardly the kind of thing to promote harmony in the region between expats and locals.

Nevertheless, according to residents, the biting incident was the most noteworthy thing to have happened for years in the sleepy village of Soportújar. What's more, the villagers were sympathetic to Rick and united in favour of locking up the attackers and throwing away the key.

Speaking of bites, I'd been writing a series of articles about the dangerous animals and bugs that one was likely to encounter in Spain. I'd done one about the horrible centipedes called *scolopendras*, which would often hide in boots or bed clothing and could pack a powerful bite. I'd also done one on snakes and another on poisonous caterpillars, but what I was really keen to do was add more destinations to my itinerary for my *Writers in Spain* series. These were towns and cities where foreign writers had lived, and I wanted to visit them so I could see the places that they had made so familiar through their words. I also wanted to understand the connection with Spain they had felt and why, in some cases, they had even been willing to fight wars on her soil.

But where to pick? George Orwell's Catalonia was too far away and Norman Lewis's fishing village Faro, of which he wrote in *Voices of the Old Sea*, no longer existed since it was literally buried under a new sea of concrete on what is now the Costa Brava.

Hemingway's Ronda was at least within striking distance, while closer to home there was Gerald Brenan's Yegen and Washington Irving's Granada. And then there was the legendary adventurer and early Hispanophile, George Borrow, a nineteenth century Norfolk man who claimed to speak twenty languages, walked sixty miles a day and could drink a pint of rum down in one. The rambunctious Borrow travelled around Spain as a Bible salesman, banging on people's doors late at night and demanding to be accommodated. His book *The Bible in Spain* became a classic and is still worth a read as a first-hand account of the original loud-mouthed Brit abroad, although for my purposes there was no single place particularly associated with him.

But all these writers were dead and gone. Perhaps, I figured, I should start out with the living ones … and I knew exactly where I could find one of them.

One Friday morning I found myself driving through what seemed like the largest olive grove on earth. I was in Jaén province, just to the north of Granada, where some sixty-six million olive trees stretched to every horizon. Sitting in the passenger seat was the travel writer and art historian Michael Jacobs. He was a bit tired from a late night at an art exhibition in Malaga the previous evening and was eager to get home. Home, in his case was Frailes, a typical Jaénese village of sixteen hundred souls in the Sierra Sur Mountains. "I've got to let the dog out," he fretted, "the housekeeper's there but the poor chap will be wondering where I've got to."

The rendezvous had been a synchronicity of sorts. Having just turned the final page of Jacobs' book *The Factory of Light* I fired off an email to Jon saying I was going to try and track down Michael Jacobs for the next writer feature. Jon, meanwhile, a hundred miles from home, was apparently already *with* the author in a tiny village of no significance in the back of beyond. In fact, Jacobs was sitting at the next table in the village's only restaurant and the two had struck up a conversation, even though they didn't know one another. We agreed what an odd coincidence this was.

And now here I was, a week later, with the writer sat beside me wearing a crumpled suit as we hurtled along a tarmac road that ran like a black ribbon through the olivescape. It might have been a weird coincidence that had led to this meeting, but I soon learned that Jacobs' life seemed to be ruled by strange coincidence and serendipities. In fact, to him, this kind of thing was the norm, and he almost took it for granted. That's how he had ended up in Jaén in the first place. It was, bizarrely, in a Slovakian police station that he first heard about an obscure slightly run-down village from a pair of agitated Australian pensioners who were preparing for

Armageddon. They claimed the village was associated with mysterious saint-like figure who performed miracles and cured the sick.

Spooling forward a few years, Michael Jacobs had then found himself billeted in the 'only remaining holiday rental in Andalucía' one hot summer – in the very village the octogenarian doomers had been speaking of: Frailes. Something aligned in the stars and from that moment on, his and the village's fates had been interminably intertwined. We rounded a bend and Frailes came into view as a small town of white houses with red roof tiles nestled in the folds of the surrounding hills. "I don't want to sound like a crackpot," he cautioned, "but I'm convinced there's something supernatural about this place."

We pulled up in a small plaza at the foot of a craggy inland cliff and got out of the car. Arriving in Frailes after reading *The Factory of Light* was akin to arriving on the set of a film, but with the mind-bending reality that the characters were real and could be seen going about their daily business. A scruffy door seemed to lead into solid rock at the foot of the cliff and Michael casually stepped up and opened it, gesturing for me to follow. Stepping inside we entered a dingy, limestone cave filled with old men sat at square wooden tables playing backgammon, and I realised that this was the mysterious cave tavern which saw much of the 'action' in the story.

People in the smoke-filled cave bar greeted Michael as we entered, and a few strode over to shake his hand before getting back to their games. We ordered coffee and sat at a table in a hollowed out alcove. Michael rubbed his eyes and sipped his *café con leche*. Since he had written those lines a few years ago he had become one of the cave bar's fixtures. And having just finished a heavyweight translation from Spanish of a popular guidebook, he said he was now free to continue writing up his next travel adventure. It was about a journey along the length of the Andes undertaken the previous year – some of it with his friend Chris Stewart [later published with the title *Andes*]. "At one point we were trapped in a revolutionary Bolivia," he said matter-of-factly as he sipped his coffee. "I almost got blown up by a mortar, you know. I was with the FARC guerrillas. Nice people, most of them."

Out on the streets of Frailes again and it was market day. Fraileros greeted Michael and stopped for a chat with him every few yards and I wondered how he ever managed to get any work done in such a convivial place. He took me next to the house of his friend, Manolo (better known as 'El Sereno' in his books), a sprightly eighty-three year-old who plays a leading role in *The Factory of Light*, just as he does in village life. El Sereno was famed for, amongst other things, building and operating the smallest and noisiest mechanical olive press in the world. His extraordinary character quickly became apparent as I was whisked around his house to be given a guided tour of the many peculiarities that lay within.

The house was situated at the centre of the village next to the church on a rocky outcrop with commanding views. "Look, look," he said as I was shown around a large garden featuring a shed that used to be Michael's study when he first arrived in Frailes. He had started off renting a room above the noisy village nightclub, and needed somewhere with a bit of peace and quiet at the time. In the kitchen I found myself being kissed on each cheek by a diminutive elf-like old lady who, it was explained, was El Sereno's remaining living sister.

The mini olive press was in a small room off the kitchen that might normally be reserved for a larder. El Sereno demonstrated how it worked, and the contraption gave off a tremendous racket that left my ears ringing for minutes afterwards. When it was done he collected the oil into a small bottle and pushed it into my hands. I was now the owner of some of the locally coveted *Serenolivo* olive oil.

"Jason has made an olive press too," said Michael to his elderly friend with a grin, but his is made of ink and paper.

El Sereno eyed me momentarily and said "Ah, yes, but I bet mine is smaller and noisier."

"Only just," I replied.

We traipsed upstairs, our guide chattering all the way and pointing out a number of extraordinary certificates and letters that lined the walls, such as one from the ex-mayor of London, Ken Livingston. "Manolo knows *everyone*," whispered Michael. In the library my host showed me his huge collection of books written about Spain in recent years, each one with a personal inscription to the old man from the author. Next up for inspection was the ornate guest bedroom. "This is where the legendary actress Sara Montiel stayed when she visited," he said, motioning towards a voluptuous mahogany bed. "And this," he said pushing open what appeared to be a secret panel leading to a luxurious *en suite* bathroom, "is where she became stuck and I had to leap through the window to rescue her." I had to hand it to him, Manolo appeared to be one of the most well-connected people in Spain, which was all the more remarkable for the fact that he himself was basically nothing more than an olive farmer, and had rarely even left his home village, somehow convincing all these intellectuals, artists and celebrities to come and stay with him.

After the tour we headed up to Michael's house, which was a restored farmhouse on a rise towards the edge of the village. Over sherry and a *tapa* of *remojón de naranja* (juicy orange slices with fig bread, drizzled with olive oil), prepared by my host (who, on account of his cooking skills, was a confirmed Knight of the Pythonesque *Very Illustrious and Noble Order of the Wooden Spoon* – one of Spain's leading gastronomic 'brotherhoods') talk turned to writers, and in particular people who have written about Spain. Michael, it turned out, was a great admirer of Norman Lewis who could write 'without ego', and had met him once. But it was the early British adventurers to Spain such as George Borrow and Richard Ford who were of the most interest to him. He said he missed the genre of 'opinionated guidebooks' such as had been written by Ford – although in my reckoning Michael's own guidebook *Andalucía* was an indispensable tome and I rarely ventured out without it.

We got onto talking about his latest book, and how he fitted into village life since making the place semi-famous. *The Factory of Light* tells the peculiar story of how Michael came to discover and live in Frailes. In it, he first arrives on a metaphysical hunch and finds himself drawn into a slightly arcane world of revered *custodios* (roughly translated as guardian angels) and discovers he can seemingly perform minor miracles, such as making it rain every time he sings loudly in Italian. Living in a rented room above the village nightclub, the dismal *Discoteca Oh!,* he discovers an abandoned Franco-era cinema and sets in motion its reanimation. The story climaxes in a gala evening at which the sex-icon Sara Montiel – who became stuck in Manolo's house – is coaxed from Madrid to appear at a screening of the revered 1957 romantic movie *El Último Cuplé* (called *The Last Torch Song* in English) which, according to El Sereno, had led the cinema aisles to "flow with rivers of semen" when it was originally shown. A Hollywood director gets to hear about it and the whole increasingly chaotic affair is made into a *Buena Vista Social Club* style documentary, bringing fame, if not fortune, to the village.

Michael led me on a walk to the cinema (the eponymous *Factory of Light*) but unfortunately it was all locked up and he didn't know where the key holder was. Like a lot of places in Frailes, there was nothing outwardly special about it and you could have mistaken it for a nondescript house. We walked back down to Bar La Cueva for an afternoon coffee. Standing at the bar were some more of Michael's friends, in this case Merce and Manolo Caño, with whom Michael chatted in his faultless Spanish.

El Sereno appeared again, stuffing my hands with more gifts, in addition to the olive oil, fig bread and books he had already given me. I took a picture of the two of them in the cave, but the light was appalling and El Sereno kept unintentionally pulling faces. "The camera doesn't agree with me," he said.

Before I left I asked Michael what the attraction has been of Andalucía to so many British writers down the years. He replied after a moment of consideration. "Spain has the effect of liberating us and bringing us out of our shells." He added, "Mostly we're just a bunch of slightly shy romantics."

"Which book are you most proud of writing? I asked

"*Between Hopes and Memories: Spanish Journey*," he replied without hesitation. "It was me writing at my best, I thought, but it bombed." He shrugged. "You can't make people like your work, but that's no reason not to do it anyway."

And with that I bade them both farewell and left the gloom of the cave for the harsh brilliance of the Jaén light.

Visiting Michael Jacobs in Jaén – the Saudi Arabia of olive oil – reminded me that we should be earning something from producing our own olives. We had about thirty olive trees, ranging in size from large bushes, to towering gnarled specimens. Most people in the region kept their trees small, trimming them each year and burning all the cuttings. This kept them to a manageable size for when it came to the winter picking season, but many of our trees, were huge or in difficult to reach spots such as the sides of embankments between terraces. To get the fruit you had to spread out nylon nets and bash the branches with a long wooden pole. The olives, ripe and black, would come raining down, completely missing the net more often than not. It could be tough work and to reach the upper branches I would need to climb a ladder and sometimes stand on tiptoe. After several days of this it became hard to fall asleep at night, as whenever I shut my eyes all I could see were branches, heavily laden with the dark purple and black fruit that seemed to invite being whacked with a stick like some kind of organic hyper-real computer game.

The olives that didn't land in the net needed to be picked up by hand. This is where those wild plants became really inconvenient as, whereas most of the locals had made every effort to eliminate virtually any life form other than the olive trees from the landscape, my patch was covered with wild herbs and flowering plants. Those vistas of olive trees stretching to the horizon, such as the ones painted by Van Gogh, might evoke feelings of rural tranquillity in some sun-splashed Mediterranean idyll, but ecologically speaking they were a monoculture that squeezed out other life. Surely there must be some kind of middle ground, perhaps where other plants were allowed to thrive between the olives?

Once the olives were picked and stored in breathable sacks – sacks that seemed to fill up incredibly slowly – they were ready to be taken to the olive press. I once made the mistake of storing my freshly picked olives in polythene sacks, only to discover a few days later that they had turned into an evil-smelling mouldy black pulp. Luckily, the operators at the olive press didn't care one bit about this and tossed the porridgey mess into the mix anyway. Each sack weighed a good fifty kilos and I lugged them into the trailer that was hitched to the back of the old workhorse Mitsubishi. I drove down to the olive mill on the outskirts of Órgiva, once or twice giving our neighbour Antonio a lift with a load of his olives as a return favour for plying us with dozens of avocados, green beans and apples throughout the year.

Unlike me, Antonio was a *real* olive farmer who relied on it for a living. With two daughters, one of whom had just started at university In Granada, there was a lot of pressure on him to support the family. Each year, to bring in his olive harvest, he worked four months of twelve-hour days, seven days a week. Yet each year the amount of money his harvest fetched seemed to become smaller and smaller, with the price of olives being set far away by men in suits in financial institutions. He worked out that he was being paid just over a euro an hour for his work, making me wonder about those foreigners who wanted to get into olive farming as a serious venture and whether they'd thought the whole thing through. But Antonio was stoic about all this and although I felt sorry for him receiving so little I also felt that he'd be alright in the long run. He was born on the hill, and for reasons that I couldn't quite fathom, had been kept alive as a baby by suckling on a goat. He'd grown up on the hill, married another hill girl, and now had his own house on the hill, which he had built 'in a week' with the help of a dozen relatives. He had goats, partridges, chickens and a hundred beehives, and he occasionally bagged a wild boar with his gun. The annual olive harvest might not bring in much cash, but at least they had plenty of food and a small army of relatives to help them out if things got tough. When I thought about it, Antonio was probably richer than almost anyone I knew, but in ways that many wouldn't understand.

Most foreigners in the area didn't bother picking their olives, to the chagrin of the locals, simply letting them fall on the ground and desiccate. But those who wanted to take the plunge risked facing public humiliation at the mill where the fruits were pressed for their oil, and I was no exception in this regard. No local farmer worth his salt would permit space to be wasted in their vehicles, meaning cars, vans and light trucks were often overburdened, the suspension almost sitting the axles. These overburdened cars and trailers would queue up outside the gates of the olive press, as getting there early was essential if you didn't want to face a long wait. When the gates swung open and the machinery clattered to life each farmer took it in turn to drive into the compound and execute a tight several-pointed turn, usually with a trailer on the back, to reverse onto a metal grilled area where the olives could be unloaded and poured directly into a hopper below ground level. The sniggering admonishment of a row of wall-sitting farmers, as well as the impatient horn blaring of those behind in the line awaited anyone who couldn't execute this manoeuvre correctly. Once you had got into position an inspector would then come and look at your olives to make sure they passed muster. When I first went there I wasn't sure what criteria they were looking for, as others were tipping sacks in that seemed to be filled more with sticks and leaves than olives. Some, apparently, even tipped in the previous year's olives, which by now had mummified into hard black stones.

But once you had tipped in all your olives, you could watch as they danced and jiggled on a vibrating rack as a huge industrial blower blasted away all the leaves, twigs and bits of desiccated goat turd. This would explain people not bothering to get rid of all the surplus twigs and leaves, and what remained was automatically weighed. A few minutes would then pass as the fruits of your labour could be seen hurtling along conveyor belts and being shot out of spouts while the ground shook with the tremendous metal thudding of the press hammering the oil out of the fruit, which emerged as a jet of golden liquid that went straight into a large storage tank. Moments later a man with a pencil behind his ear would fill out a scrap of paper entitling you to an amount of oil to be picked up the following day, and you would then have to move you vehicle sharpish to allow the next in line to get into position. I found the whole process a bit nerve-wracking and it was a relief when it was all over.

- 40 -

Renovations continued slowly at Los Pechos. Our electricity supply from the solar panels was stable, but we were still having problems with the water. As it stood, we had a water supply in the form of a watercourse and there were complex rules governing the amount of water we could take from it and when we could do so. Luckily, we didn't have much land compared to many of the farmers who surrounded us, so we could get by on a lot less water. But it wasn't the water supply that was a problem; it was what was in it.

Anyone who has not lived in a remote area in an arid location can have little idea of the difficulties involved in getting clean water to come out of a tap. In our case, it would take a small book to go into all the details. The very short version is that we had rights to several minutes' water flow per week from a watercourse, aka *acequia* – those ancient feats of engineering that had permitted the successful spread of agriculture around La Alpujarra – coming down the mountain and crossing our land. The *acequia* system, fed by underground springs and snowpack melt, was strictly controlled by a committee which enforced the local water rights. In a physical sense, the water distribution was directed through numerous gates and channels, some of which involved no more than shifting large stones into place to divert the flow. There was a timetable for water allocation, and sometimes it would come in the middle of the night and you'd have to jump out of bed and run around opening up valves with a torch between your teeth.

The water delivered to Los Pechos had started out at the top of Mulhacén in the form of snow and rain, and then channelled down the hillsides in rivers and *acequias*. By the time it got to our place in the lower foothills, it had flowed along miles of open channels, and had also passed through several villages on the way down, not all of which treated their sewage. So it was no surprise that when anyone drank from this 'stream' they ran the risk of falling ill with gastroenteritis. But people didn't drink from irrigation streams, they drank from springs. In fact, the very presence of these springs would probably have dictated the original location of the homesteads on our hill.

We didn't have a spring, but our neighbours Antonio and Paquita did, and they didn't mind us wheeling a barrow over to their land and filling up our large plastic containers. Nevertheless, we needed clean water not just to drink but also to shower in and wash our clothes. As one neighbour asked us pointedly when I said I wasn't fussy about *overly* clean water to shower in, "How do you know there isn't a dead animal in the *acequia* just up above your place? Do you really want to smell of rotting sheep juice?"

He had a point, but we didn't want to use chlorine. Put too much in the supply and it can have undesired effects. One of the builders working on making us a water tank found this out to his detriment after his blonde hair turned green following a shower in over-chlorinated water. Equally, if you put too little in the pathogens will survive. This is the reason why we opted to use the ozone water treatment, which eventually turned out to be more of a problem than a solution on account of it using too much electricity and breaking down too frequently.

But even before we got to the purification stage we had to remove all the other things from the water. If the watercourse had been dry for a few days, when the water came it would bring with it a tide of mud, leaves and dried olives, along with whatever else it had picked up. All this needed filtering out and we did this via a collection of tanks arranged on the terraces so that with every stage the water passed through it became a step closer to being clean. Finally, before it went into the ozone tank, which contained an expensive bit of kit shipped over from America, it passed through a porous charcoal filter, which needed cleaning and replacing quite often.

All of this effort to get half decent water running out of the taps was another reminder of the level of utility that we used to in our everyday lives. And there were times when the water never turned up at all and our new ten thousand-litre tank on the top terrace began to look perilously empty. On such occasions I would have to make a trip up the hill to find out what was wrong. With a mattock slung over my shoulder I would walk uphill for about twenty minutes until I got to a small stony field. Trekking across this I would head for the thorny hedge on the far side and find a small gap to squeeze through. Inside was a green tunnel comprised of spiky bushes, through which ran one of the main waterways that wound its way down the hill.

On these excursions it helped to bring along a machete to slash away any tendrils that hung down as you followed the course of the stream. Often it wouldn't be a stream at all, merely a muddy path pockmarked with the footprints of the wild boar which hung out there at night. In these instances, the fact that it was a muddy rather than dry path meant that someone had diverted the water closer to the source, cutting off the branch line that led down to Los Pechos. Walking up it, stooped low to avoid scratching my head on the spiky roof and hacking away at the dangling vines, I would reach the branch point. You could hear it gushing away before you got anywhere near it – always a pleasant sound if you were worried about not having enough water. There was a sluice crudely comprised of a number of large stones, with a particularly large one blocking the gate to our channel. To divert the flow it was a simple case of moving the stone to one side and letting the muddy water pour into my channel. But before I did this I would have to set about the muddy stream bed with my mattock, tossing any big stones and sticks to the side and smoothing it out in readiness for the torrent. This wasn't just to expedite the flow of water, it was also out of politeness and a duty to our neighbours who relied on the maintenance of the channels. They would do the same thing, and once a year we would form into a working party and spend a day digging out any channels that had become silted up, as well as hacking back the ever encroaching brambles, fig and pomegranate bushes.

Pulling the stone aside and letting the water cascade through the sluice was the fun part. I would then have to run back down the tunnel before the water caught up with me and then, if I wished, follow its progress all the way back to my house, pushing aside any build-ups of leaves and sticks as it went. Usually, by the time I arrived home, I would be covered in mud and sweat and my arms would be bleeding from the brambles. Secretly though, I enjoyed fixing the acequia, it was like being a small boy again. Don't think I wasn't ever tempted to bring along a toy boat with me …

So, after the snows had melted, the water would pass across dozens of properties and through numerous diverters before getting to our patch of land. It would then be filtered three times, have ozone blasted through it, get pumped from the tank to the house. Some of it would end up in the toilet. From the toilet, the sewage went about five yards down a sloping pipe into … where exactly? I dug a big hole to find out and discovered that the pipe didn't lead anywhere: it simply seeped into a clod of dark, smelly earth. That explained the worsening stink we had been experiencing; sewage had been backing up the pipe until it was almost at the house.

Someone advised us to flush a bag of building lime down the toilet, as this was a powerful sewage-eating compound that would get through it in no time. This didn't sound very eco-friendly though, so I looked at other solutions. It seemed more logical to build a tank where sewage could be digested and returned to the soil.

The time-honoured Andalucían method of dealing with sewage was remarkably simple and obvious if you knew what you were looking at. Gaze at any old farmhouse on a slope and more often than not there will be a patch of prickly pear cactus, which the Spanish call *chumba*, growing directly beneath it. The reason for this was that the prickly pear, not to put too fine a point on it, eats shit. A remarkably adaptable plant, the *optunia dillenii* came from the Americas and was probably brought back by the sixteenth century Spanish explorers. They must have noticed Native Americans using the cactus to convert human waste into fodder and human food (the 'pears' are sweet and refreshing once you have removed the spikes) and it quickly spread around the Mediterranean basin.

If I had doubted that this was true I had an experience that would teach me a lesson I wouldn't forget. Our particular *chumba* patch was wild and unruly and I decided to get rid of the main plant in favour of building said sewage digestion tank. The tank, I figured, would then supply cleanish water to some of the orange trees on the lower terraces. But first, the *chumba* had to go. I took out my chainsaw and began to tackle the immense trunk, which was so old it had effectively become wood. The blade of the saw bit into it easily and I was about halfway through when a horrible smell began to emanate from the wound I was inflicting. I shifted my position to approach from a different angle and no sooner had I started to cut again than the blade hit the soft core of the giant cactus. What happened next was not pleasant, and I found myself splattered from head to waist with a vile-smelling orange-brown slime, the likes of which I had not smelled since I'd fallen into a ditch in New Delhi some years before. It took at least two showers to get rid of the stink, scrubbing my body all over with soap. And the chainsaw, which had sucked some of this unique 'juice' into its innards, forever kicked out the foul smell whenever I started it up, necessitating the use not just of ear defenders but also nose plugs.

- 41 -

One day I got an email from the former drummer of the legendary band Judas Priest. It turned out that he'd retired from the heavy metal scene and settled in La Alpujarra to teach skiing. As such, he offered me an exclusive interview in exchange for some free publicity for his business. I jumped at the chance.

The rock icon turned up in the office a few days later. He was a wearing a leather jacket, and had a shaved head and a firm handshake. Oddly, I thought, he had a quiet demeanour and it was difficult to imagine him pounding the skins in front of a crowd of thousands as Rob Halford screamed out the lines of *Painkiller*. I got him a cup of coffee and sat down on the sofa opposite with my notepad and pen. Nobody else in the office was paying much attention to us, although Marcus did wander over after a while and listen in, but smiled and got up again a few minutes later. I was hoping to hear some tales about life on the road with one of the world's greatest heavy metal outfits, and I imagined he had quite a few tales of mayhem and hedonistic behaviour to divulge. But he didn't seem keen on sharing his stories, and although he obliged with a few minor anecdotes about drumming he always steered the conversation back to his skiing business.

When he left the office I went over to my desk and wrote out an article about being visited by a metalhead.

What a great job I had! I had never interviewed a rock star before, or dreamed that I would ever get the chance to do so.

The article appeared in the paper the following week, and soon after the office received an email from a concerned woman who claimed to be connected with my interviewee. It was not easy to read it.

"You do realise he has nothing to do with Judas Priest?" it read. "Don't you so-called journalists bother checking anything, or do you just believe whatever anyone tells you?" As I read on I probably went a little pale. The word 'fantasist' cropped up more than once. Over the next few days there were more messages along the same lines from other people who knew him. The bit about him working as a ski guide turned out to be true.

"He didn't fool me," Marcus smirked. "When you've been doing this a while you'll realise how many loonies there are out there." I had to admit that it was a bit embarrassing.

Although the various newsworthy goings-on around our small region of La Alpujarra could be comedic, this wasn't always the case in the wider Granada area. I flinched when reports of yet another car accident came in, and it often seemed to be children who were the casualties. So many lives were being cut short by the kind of idiotic bravado shown by young men in high-powered cars. Often, it was drivers overtaking on blind bends who caused the most serious accidents. Perhaps a part of the discomfort arose from being familiar with the roads and the accident hotspots, and knowing that it could easily have been your own family in the wrong place at the wrong time. The sides of the roads in these spots were adorned with small shrines marking where the victims, sometimes entire families, had been wiped out. I could count on several fingers the number of times I'd seen the fatal aftermaths of crashes around the region since we'd moved there.

But one particular vehicle-related tragedy was too close for comfort. It had been late at night when a young woman pulled off the road in her camper van outside the Beneficio 'Rainbow Gathering' commune, at the very same spot I had dropped the hitchhiker when I first arrived in the region. Along with a female friend, she had driven all the way from Italy, and sleeping peacefully in the back was her eighteen-month-old daughter. Perhaps deciding to wait until daylight before attempting the unlit and bumpy track that led up to the commune, the young mother had decided to call it a night and parked up by the road. What happened next, nobody could be sure, but police later reported that a fire had ripped through the van with incredible ferocity, claiming the lives of both the woman's young child and her friend. The young woman herself was rushed to hospital but died the next day from her burns.

At this point, terrible as it may sound, it was just another tragic story to add to the pile of tragic stories that often filled our 'news in brief' clippings. But the everyday horror of this particular case was brought home to me when I was walking around the outskirts of the village of Tablones and I saw the ill-fated camper van dumped on a piece of weed-strewn wasteland. The local police never did bother too much with the kind of foreigners who turned up in battered buses and vans, adopting a 'live and let die' attitude towards them. In this case they had towed the van away out of sight and dumped it, which was how I found it. Looking inside immediately brought the last moments of those people into sharp focus. Bits of the yellow foam mattress on which the baby had burned were still there, as were scorched pieces of clothing that appeared to have been ripped off in distress. Worse still were all the toys that were still scattered around inside the van and a still-open children's storybook that I imagined the mother might have been reading to her child before the fire took hold. An exploded gas canister, peeled open like an over-ripe pomegranate, lay amongst the detritus on the floor.

It was a sad scene, and it took a long time to get it out of my head.

- 42 -

It had been eighteen months since the first issue, and in some ways we were doing well. Our print run continued to rise and the big map of Andalucía on our wall now had numerous coloured pins in it. They stretched as far as Cabo de Gata in Almería in one direction, and Nerja, at the eastern edge of the Costa del Sol in the other. Our website was doing well, getting thousands of unique visits every day, and we were sometimes mentioned in other media around the world. Jon Clarke had given us a shot of energy, and his version of the newspaper was providing synergy to the project. All this was going well, but the situation in the office hadn't improved.

I went for a long walk, taking a circuitous route out of Órgiva back up to our house, which was still in a state of major disrepair. I was worried. Despite the many advances the newspaper had made and all the hard work we had put in I had still not managed to earn a single cent from it. In fact, as we'd become bigger the costs had mounted, and every month my bank balance was shrinking as we tried to live off the few savings we had left. As a business, we might not have dashed ourselves on the rocks when we jumped off the cliff, but we were hovering right above them, wings flapping wildly. I wondered, not for the first time, whether it had been a mistake to start up a newspaper. It had eaten tens of thousands of euros from my pocket, as well as from Marcus and Molly's, and now Rick's.

Summer had come and gone, giving way to cooler nights and the prospect of roast chestnuts and hot chocolate – always my favourite time of year. At the same time the sight of the mountains and clear blue sky should have been enough to lighten even the blackest of moods, and yet I couldn't shake off my negative thoughts and the fears that lay below them. The bottom line was that I had a mortgage to pay, a family to support, a ruined house to renovate and a newspaper to co-run. I had been working flat-out on juggling these things, and yet I have failed to earn anything since I'd moved to Spain. At this rate, I doubted we would have enough money to live off for more than a few months. What's more, we had kicked the hornet's nest by writing the story about the MP Margaret Moran, and she was now threatening to sue us, saying we had made the whole story up.

The miserable sense of foreboding in the office was dragging me down. Marcus no longer spoke to me at all, even though we sat only a few feet apart. Instead, I was sending my articles through to Jon's *'Olive Press West'* newspaper, and he was publishing them. Was this really why I had moved to Spain? I called Rick and told him we needed to have a private chat. "Come up to our house this evening," he said.

When I arrived at Rick and Jayne's village house they invited me in warmly. We drank some of Rick's homemade wine and sat on the veranda looking out over the Sierra de Lujar as the sun set. "What's to be done?" asked Rick. I swallowed; this wasn't going to be easy.

"We have to put a stop to Marcus's negative attitude otherwise we won't have any readers left. If he won't agree then we should ask him to step down, I say."

"But what about Molly?" asked Rick, "She's good on sales and her Spanish is excellent."

We sat there in gloomy silence for a while, pondering. I couldn't see a way of including Molly in the mix if Marcus was gone, which inevitably he would be if Rick and I insisted he changed his news articles. We couldn't expect Molly to hang around if Marcus was gone, and in any case he was one of the company directors and owned half the shares. We talked about different ways to try and goad Marcus into making a better balance of news stories, but the bottom line was that he and I were joint partners in the enterprise and it wouldn't be easy getting him to change his ways.

"And Jon Clarke," said Rick," where does he fit into all this?"

By then we'd come to a formal agreement with Jon that permitted him to use stories from *The Olive Press*, and in return he supplied us with stories from his part of Spain, many of which featured his ongoing battle against the illegal Los Merinos golf course megaproject. But Jon's bombastic character jarred with Marcus's, and it was obvious to both Rick and I that there could be no close cooperation between the two. "Jon knows what he is doing," I said, "but I don't think Marcus would ever take marching orders from him."

"And what about you?" asked Rick quietly.

"Me?" I said. "What about me?"

Rick considered his words carefully. "Well, have you thought that the problems might be at least partly coming from you? I mean, it *was* Marcus and Molly's dream to start a newspaper, they had wanted to do it even before you turned up."

Rick was right, of course. Pride had prevented me from seeing this simple fact. It was like a cold slap across the face as this new way of seeing things dawned on me. I remembered back to the time when Molly had excitedly told me how she and Marcus wanted to run a little newspaper in their village, and how this simple dream had somehow given rise to a publication that had got too big for its boots. How arrogant had I been to impose myself on them? Me, with no newspaper experience to speak of, waltzing in and launching us all on an ill though-out venture that was now threatening to fall apart at the seams, taking our savings with it. When viewed in this manner I suddenly saw myself as an interloper: it was *me* being unreasonable, not them. Perhaps Marcus had been trying his best to drive me away for this very reason.

Still, a fragment of pride surfaced within me.

"They'd never had done it if it wasn't for me," I said. "Marcus would still be walking around in the hills while Molly struggled to sell houses, earning pennies while Mel and Nikki took the lion's share."

Rick considered this, nodding. "And you, Jason, what would you be doing?"

I thought for a while. What *would* I be doing? I really didn't know. *The Olive Press* had so consumed me that I hadn't considered what I might have been doing otherwise. I had lived and breathed it since its inception, and it was tearing me apart. "I don't know," I replied, "maybe running that café we dreamed about, the one where we would grow our own fresh produce and have shelves of books and where the coffee would be the best in the region."

"Hmm," said Rick, ever the businessman, "that could work. Let me know if you ever get round to it and need investment advice."

"But I don't *want* it to work," I said, "I want *The Olive Press* to work." And that was the truth of the matter.

We carried on talking like this for a while. By the time I left it was late at night and nothing had really been accomplished. Regrettably, I'd had to leave with an ultimatum: Rick and Jayne would have to back either Marcus or myself for full editorial control. They said they would have to think about it for a while. I had come to like and respect Rick; he was a man of action rather than words, and I figured he'd see sense and find a pragmatic solution to our impasse.

The next day I slunk into work and sat, as usual, with my back to Marcus as he typed on his laptop without acknowledging me. Dan, a quiet soul, was the third person in the room, and together we formed a silent, motionless outward-facing triangle, like some kind of modern art installation representing emotionally repressed Englishmen. Zac the husky sat on the sofa – he was now living with Marcus and Molly, who'd taken a shine to him after taking him on some of their long walks.

A week later I walked into work and the two office couples were sat on the sofas with the faded relics of smiles on their faces as though I'd suddenly interrupted a good laugh. Marcus and Molly were on one side, facing Rick and Jayne on the other. The mood was uncomfortable, but not in the old way. Something had changed. "We've had a great idea," said Jayne, breaking the silence. "A property web portal that can piggyback off *The Olive Press* brand. We think it'll be the cash engine we're looking for, and in any case we're already licensed property dealers, it says so on the company deeds."

Rick carried on. "We need to take our brand up-market, so Marcus and Molly will be focusing on the wine and fine dining scene in Andalucía – it's a lucrative growth area that we really should be cashing in on if we're serious about expanding."

I looked at them all and they all looked back at me, but not in an approval-seeking way. There was resolve in their faces, as if I was a problem that needed to be dealt with. "I see," was all I could manage, and even that stuck in my throat.

Later, Rick came up to me when we were on our own and the others had gone out for lunch. "Sorry Jase," he said, putting a hand on my shoulder. "We had a meeting with Marcus and Molly and they turned out to be more amenable than we thought. It's Marcus's experience that we need to make this venture work, so he'll have full editorial control from now on – it's what he wanted. Understand that this isn't anything personal."

"I'm sorry too," I said.

Before the others got back from lunch I had packed up the things from my desk. There was no point hanging around.

- 43 -

"You did *what?*" said a shocked Jon down the phone from Ronda. "You can't leave Marcus in charge, he'll make all the readers commit suicide. And Rick, he'll turn the paper into a corporate press release. I've invested a lot of money and effort in this. I might have to speak to my lawyer about it."

I got a similar call from Rick. "You can't just leave the office like that, you're a Director." It was amusing to be called a 'director' given that the average corner shop probably had a greater cash flow than *The Olive Press*. But

Rick had assigned us all titles and given us business cards – he himself was Sales Director.

"Sorry Rick but I've got to earn money somehow and I can't afford to waste more time sitting in an office with a bunch of people squabbling over a project that's going nowhere."

The result of the conversation, and several more like it, was an agreement that I would continue to carry out some of my duties at the newspaper, but that I would voluntarily give up any control I had over any decision-making processes. Instead, I'd write more feature articles about local environmental heroes and writers, and would do the fortnightly distribution runs along the coast and in Granada. This suited me fine as it meant I'd finally be getting paid for something.

Leaving the office, if not the newspaper, was a great relief and I immediately felt my energy levels rising again. Now I would be able to devote myself to working on the house instead of paying someone else to do it. I also wanted us to become more self-sufficient and figured that with enough hard work Los Pechos could probably provide for a good proportion of our own food and winter fuel.

How should I approach this, I wondered. Now that I was no longer working in the office I had time to throw myself into the various building jobs that needed doing, as well as getting to grips with the land itself. One of the first things I did was call David and Aspen, the couple who had been running their farm as a research station high up above Lanjarón. They offered the service of documenting all the plant species on my land and analysing the soil type to see what would grow well there. They turned up a few days later in their Land Rover, and I watched them stride around the land in their overalls, bending over and photographing even the most innocuous looking weed as Aspen scribbled away on a clipboard, her grey hair done up in a bun. They produced a report for me that gave me an idea about what would grow well there and what would grow not so well. I got to work planting almost immediately, going into town and purchasing a number of fruit trees that I dotted around the land in places I thought they would do well.

One of the attractions of La Alpujarra was that the landscape was still eminently comprehensible. It was possible to stand on a hillside and look out at the physical furniture of the landscape and make sense of it. The white cubes of farmhouses dotted around were visible enough, as were the swathes of the olive groves, the dark lines of the waterways providing melt water to the farms and the roads running to the olive presses where the fruits of months of hard labour would be transformed into liquid gold. If you had a good pair of binoculars you could even make out the individual figures at work in the landscape. There is Antonio ploughing his fields with his new Rotavator, or the goatherd walking along the riverbank with his flock. It was a landscape that had changed little over the centuries and, as such, provided those of us who had just blown in from the wider world with a tantalising look at what our ancestors would have taken for granted – a comprehensible rural scene.

Of course, there were many modern features in this landscape too, such as the high tension power lines draped across the hills and the giant communications masts sitting atop the Sierra de Lujar like a crown of thorns, but the basic cohesiveness of the environment and man's place within it was still easy to relate to and could be read like a book. Our land amounted to only a couple of acres. This wasn't much, but I wanted to get the most out of it without using any artificial chemicals and by employing permaculture principles. The aim was to grow things that we could eat or sell, while still leaving plenty for the birds, insects and other residents of this small patch of hillside. Given that the land was irrigated by the *acequia* system, our land was a small oasis in an otherwise parched and thirsty landscape. I felt we had a duty to look after it and keep it that way, and hopefully make it even richer in life. It was already a haven for birds.

As a bonus, living on the side of a mountain meant that our couple of acres' plot was actually a fair bit bigger. This was because we had the sloping banks between the terraces to grow stuff on as well. Grapes seemed to do particularly well on these slopes. Most of our plot had been planted up with the traditional regional cash crops – olives, almonds and oranges – but there was also space for a couple of sizeable vegetable plots amongst the trees. Almonds and olives didn't require much water, but citrus trees dis, and so I had to decide whether I really wanted so many orange and lemon trees.

To my inexpert eye the land looked to be good condition when we took it over. The terraces had all been neatly ploughed, the olive trees pruned to perfection and the orange trees laden with thousands of healthy looking orbs. Individual trees and bushes were watered by a system of snaking plastic hoses that provided drip feed irrigation in a neatly laid out network. We actually had two separate pieces of land, with a parcel comprising about forty percent of it over on the other side of a track that led past the house. But this extra parcel of land, which was cut into four terraces, was bone dry and had no irrigation at all set up. Despite this, a range of almond and olive trees thrived there, as well as several giant and spiky *aloe vera* plants and a wild quince bush. Our extra plot of land was neatly ploughed when we took it over, revealing the soil to be reddish and rich looking.

But this neat-looking condition of the land wasn't to last long. Following the first spring rains I discovered that Spanish weeds grew at an astonishing speed. Pretty soon our whole plot was a riot of colour and lush, almost jungle-like vegetation, most of it spiky. Dandelions quickly dispersed floating seeds all over the place and the mere act of walking around and brushing against them caused clouds of them to rise up. I took to stalking the land with a flexible cane, dinging the heads off the dandelions before they seeded. But they were hydra-like, and if you cut off one head at least two more sprang up from the ground nearby in its place. And some of the plants grew alarmingly fast; especially one that looked like some kind of wild geranium, which reached at least six feet tall. Wild artichokes also loomed large and filled the air with their seeds, but they had beautiful purple flowers so I let them be. I loved the colour, just as I loved to watch the bees collect pollen from the drooping heads of the poppies and the almond blossom. But at the same time I didn't want the land to get out of control so quickly, and some days it seemed like all I did was walk about whacking and killing plants. I cleared the paths, at least, permitting the wildflowers to live in peace under the trees and across the terraces.

These wild plants were only doing their job of restoring balance to the land. After all, our plot had been wrested from its wild state and given over to trees that would bear money-earning fruit. If left to its own devices I'm sure the land would have preferred to return itself to a state of wild exuberance, covered in thorny bushes, deep rooted grasses and decorated with wildflowers. Most of the trees on it were not even Spanish natives, with the almonds originating in South Asia and the citrus trees stretching their roots back to ancient China. In fact, the only trees that could be said to be native to the

Mediterranean region in any way were the olives, which have been in the region since time immemorial, the very word 'olive' meaning 'oil' in ancient Greek.

True enough, the moment we took our eyes off the land and concentrated on improving the house, nature returned it to its exuberant wild state. And once the first spring had passed and the powerful rays of the sun replaced the rains, all of the formerly lush vegetation turned to crispy bone-dry stems. Our neighbour Antonio came and wagged his finger at me, saying I had created a fire hazard. Just one spark, he said, would turn the land into an inferno, which would spread to neighbouring properties before the fire helicopter could douse the flames.

I began to see what a steep learning curve lay ahead of me. People newly arrived from more temperate climes could not rely on their knowledge of gardening and growing plants to see them through. The conditions around the rim of the Mediterranean were so harsh that an entirely new set of rules applies. For a start, water had to be treasured as though it is liquid gold – and not just the flowing water, but patches of damp as well. My early experiments with compost heaps met with failure because they became so hot in the direct sun that even the microbial life forms within them – which are a pretty tough lot – died. That's when I learned they needed shade and the addition of water to stay alive throughout the hot summer months.

I also discovered that compost heaps don't like citrus fruit. We had ten trees for eating oranges, three Seville oranges, three lemons, two grapefruits, and a few tangerine and kumquat trees. Between them they produced an awful lot of fruit, most of which wasted. Why was it wasted? Simply put, because there was too much supply and not enough demand. The orange trees had gone in, we figured, about ten to fifteen years before, in a time when the price the buyer got for the fruit made it worthwhile to plant them. But, as with any cash crop, the risk was that the bottom could fall out of the market, and by 2007 they were almost worthless. In fact, we *could* have driven down to the big buyers on the coast with our crop of oranges, which all had to be neatly packed in trays, but we would have received less money for them than we would have spent on petrol to get there.

This was a terrible shame because they were the best oranges I had ever tasted. We valiantly tried to eat, drink and give away as many as we could, and I was forever thrusting oranges and lemons into people's hands whether they wanted them or not. Each morning throughout the winter (when the oranges first ripen), spring and early summer, I would fill a basket with oranges, still cool from the night, and take them back to the kitchen where I would press them for their juice. During times when we were low on drinking water we would rely on orange juice instead. Our Vitamin C levels must have gone off the scale. The giant lemons too, were particularly appetising and great lemonade could be made from them, albeit with the addition of plenty of sugar. Some of these lemons grew to monster proportions and looked like huge, knobbly rugby balls hanging in the trees. They achieved this impressive girth without the addition of any fertiliser other than compost, wood ash and whatever nourishment the nitrogen-fixing weeds had added to the soil.

But it wasn't usually the lemons people remarked upon when I showed them around the land, it was the grapefruit. There was one tree down the end of a thin terrace that was perpetually boggy due to the run-off from the pond-like irrigation pool that we shared with a neighbour. It had probably been planted as some kind of bet-hedging experiment because, on the whole, Spanish people were not keen on eating grapefruit. But that single tree produced several hundred very large fruits every year that turned out to be much in demand by the expat population. The health food store in town, Camac, eagerly bought whatever grapefruit I produced.

We tried a lot of other things to get through our citrus surplus, from making orange marmalade to selling rum and lemon shots to ravers at the annual Dragonfest festival across the river in Cigarrones, but we never came close to even getting though a quarter of what we produced. Given their lack of compostability, the best thing to do with the 'waste' citrus was to let them fall and rot where they were. The summer sun soon turned them into tough husks that crunched into a powder when you stood on them. In this way I drew solace from the fact that I was recycling the nutrients back into the soil to feed the trees for another year, and that all had not been wasted.

People said I should sell some of our excess produce to an organic cooperative that had sprung up in town. This sounded like a great idea to me, even if our land wasn't officially designated as organic, so I decided to pay them a visit. The cooperative was housed in a converted nursery opposite the school in town, so I went down to go and meet with its initiator, who was happy for me to write an article about him.

Alberto Hortelano, who with his bushy beard looked not unlike a revolutionary, was sitting behind his desk when I went in. He called me over and pointed a pen at an image on a computer screen that showed children digging in a vegetable garden. "Look," he said. "Children are the beginning of change. If we get them involved with organic agriculture they will go home and tell their parents about the benefits." Alberto's cooperative, called Las Torcas, supported local organic farmers by offering them a fair price for their produce.

I sat down and got out my pen and notepad. "You want a coffee?" he said.

We chatted for quite a while. Alberto was proud of the progress Las Torcas had achieved and in the past year alone his ecological food cooperative had begun to supply chemical-free produce to three coastal schools and an old people's home. They had also opened two shops, one in Órgiva and the other in Almuñécar, giving farmers a market for their food.

"This is becoming really big now," he said. "A few years ago interest in ecologically produced food was confined to a few enthusiasts but today many more people are interested." I looked around at the kindergarten office, the walls of which were plastered with flowcharts, diagrams of organisational affiliations and posters in several languages. Outside, in what was a former play area, boxes of grapes and lettuce were piled up on a table next to a large pair of scales.

"This is our business arm," explained Alberto. The other arm, he said was a foundation set up to provide education and workshops from their base in Velez de Benaudalla. He had needed to adopt a dual approach to change the mindset of local farmers, who had been fed fifty years of advice that amounted to 'use more chemicals'. The result of all this advice was denuded soils, indebted farmers and inferior produce. He wanted to change all that.

The door opened and a woman walked in and introduced herself as Raquel, Alberto's wife. As we talked she continued to take notes of the stock and shuffled cardboard boxes of fruit and vegetables around. "Anyone can join *Las Torcas*," continued Alberto, "as long as they are certified as organic producers and are ecological in their outlook."

Like any talk about growing things in the region the conversation soon turned to the subject of water. Alberto was concerned there may not be enough of it the following summer because of the poor winter precipitation. Some farmers, he said, were even considering not planting in the spring. "What kind of trees do you have?" he asked. When I said 'citrus' he sucked his breath in through his teeth. "Thirsty," he said. "You might want to consider getting rid of a few of them."

But Alberto was passionate about La Alpujarra and said he was actively working to create an Alpujarra 'brand' of organic produce that would be known everywhere as a byword for high quality. "It's to do with the soils around here, and the spring water. It creates a superior product that is recognisably different."

"But what of the price?" I asked, as all journalists are supposed to ask every time the word 'organic' is mentioned, "Isn't organic food more expensive than intensively grown food?" Alberto agreed that this could sometimes be the case but was scathing of those who inflated their prices purely because of the organic label.

"Of course, our costs are greater. Production levels are lower because we don't use chemical fertiliser. Our fertiliser arrives as truckloads of sheep droppings, and everything is done by hand. But – and this is crucial – you will get five times more nutrients kilo for kilo if you eat our ecological food rather than the crap they grow in the plastic greenhouses."

I couldn't disagree with him, I had seen the way they grew tomatoes in the coastal greenhouses, without the aid of soil. The end product was a roundish red object that *looked* like a tomato, but could only ever be a synthetic cocktail of its inputs: air, water, chemical fertilisers and a bit of DNA from the seed it had grown from.

The phone rang and Alberto seemed not to hear it until his wife shouted at from the room next door. Clearly he was fired up over the very thought of *plasticultura* and its destructive nature. He answered the phone, and as he spoke some of the other workers trooped in and out of the office carrying boxes overflowing with colourful fruits.

It was an industrious scene and Alberto was a busy man. He had his work cut out, trying to convince farmers to change their mind about how they produced food, but he seemed to be making great progress. I wished him luck and left him to it.

"Come back if you want to get your organic certificate," he said. "I can help you with the paperwork, it is not difficult." I said I would.

- 44 -

To get by in La Alpujarra you needed to know something about building. Property was cheap, even by Spanish standards, but more often than not you would be buying something that needed a lot of repairs. Often, the local standard of building left much to be desired, with the old time-tested methods of construction having been mostly abandoned. Foreigners, however, usually wanted to live in something that approximated the traditional vernacular architecture of the region, even though this could cost extra. And if you couldn't afford to hire a builder you had to do the next best thing and become one yourself.

When times were good, most of the local foreign builders were too busy to help you out with any small-scale building work. They were in great demand and were able to command a good price for their services. A curious quirk of logic meant that the majority of them ended up living in semi-ruined dwellings, or in caravans parked outside mounds of stone that would one day rise again to be a building. Being builders, of course, they would buy the cheapest properties with a view to rebuilding them. However, during the boom years, they would feel compelled to take on a punishing work schedule for clients, meaning they never had any time to complete their own projects. And during periods when the work dried up, they invariably had no money to spend on materials for their home projects. It was a catch-22 situation, and the wives and girlfriends of builders, often with young kids, were the ones who had to put up with the frustration of living in unsatisfactory conditions and houses that never seemed to get properly built.

Our house was no different, and whatever time off I'd had from the newspaper was invariably used up trying to keep the land moist, the trees alive, the olives picked and the weeds down. Because of this, Los Pechos – if I was honest – with its crooked chimneys, sagging roofs and walls where the render had fallen off looked like a rural slum. I was forever trying to get more work done on it, but there just never seemed to be enough time.

One day, Michelle decided she's had enough of my prevarication and announced that she was going to learn to be a builder herself. She had heard about a female empowerment programme called *Building for Women* run by a Welsh woman who raised llamas on the lower slopes of the Contraviesa. The woman was known as Lizzie the Llama.

Thus enrolled, Michelle would disappear every Saturday, returning home in the late afternoon covered in dust and full of ideas about remodelling Los Pechos. On these days I usually took the opportunity to take the kids somewhere, or get them helping out on the land. Everyone was happy with this arrangement, and after the building course had been running for a few weeks Lizzie invited me to come along and have a look around in the hope that I might get her efforts at female empowerment mentioned in *The Olive Press*. I didn't need to be asked twice, and took the opportunity the following weekend.

It was certainly an unusual scene when I got there. One of the first things I saw was a woman walking past me with a bucket of what looked like wet cement balanced on her head. Elsewhere, women pushed barrows around, slathered cement onto mud bricks and dug foundation trenches with mattocks. Amongst them, llamas grazed on bits of greenery, and the pastoral yet industrious vignette possessed a vaguely surreal feeling as if I were in a dream. None of the she-builders wolf-whistled at me, but one did notice my presence and pointed me out to Lizzie, who came over and shook my hand.

"That's not cement," said Lizzie, seeing me staring at the woman with the bucket on her head, "it's lime." This natural product possessed few of the dubious qualities of modern concrete, she explained, which can keep its form for centuries and usually ends up as an unsightly heap of rubble. "Natural buildings held together with mud and lime decay far more naturally – and what was good enough for the builders of ancient Rome is good enough for us. When I'm dead and gone and my body has returned to the earth, I want my house to do the same."

I stayed for a while, taking photos of the women mixing lime, transporting it in buckets and using it to build walls. It was clear that women were more careful builders than men, and the ambience was peaceful and contemplative, in comparison with the raucous din and macho energy of building sites featuring men. In fact, the sight made me wonder if women weren't actually more suited to building things than men. Perhaps, in a different reality, the men could stay at home and create things in the kitchen instead?

Michelle picked up the skills quickly and it wasn't long before she was rendering walls and even building one at Los Pechos. I, meanwhile, improved my kitchen skills.

- 45 -

That the hills and valleys of La Alpujarra were packed with misfits of one sort or another was no secret. The region had been a place of refuge ever since the Moors had sought to escape persecution by the Christians. Even when the war-weary Gerald Brenan turned up in Yegen in 1919, the sound of exploding shells ringing in his ears, he found a Scotsman had already beaten him to it and was known as a local oddity on account of his red hair and 'peculiar' whisky-drinking ways. A more recent arrival was the actress Margaret Nolan, better known as Dink in the James Bond film *Goldfinger,* who suffered an on-screen death by gold paint. She had thrown in her lot in London after having appeared in a run of *Carry On* films, and moved to a remote farmhouse at the eastern end of La Alpujarra, Here, she had settled into life as an artist, organic gardener and occasional host of full-moon parties.

She wasn't unusual by local standards. Many of the more recent arrivals were therapists and gardeners of one sort or another. Some therapists had reached the conclusion that the patient who needed some work done on them was the one looking back at them in the mirror. "Just spit around here and it'll probably land on a therapist," said Richard Harvey, a 'spiritual psychotherapist' who occasionally wrote for *The Olive Press* and was himself living in the hills near Cáñar. There were plenty of people seeking out such help, often turning up for a therapeutic break at one of the various retreats in the area. You often saw them walking in groups along the road near the holistic therapy centre called *Cortijo Romero* on the outskirts of Órgiva. They usually looked a bit dazed, as if they'd been pulled from their normal everyday lives and thrown into an alien environment. But I could see the value in coming to a place like La Alpujarra following a traumatic episode in one's life, or if one simply felt lost and in need of a bit of guidance, and I'd heard people speak about a special kind of magic the area possessed which gave visitors a feeling of wellbeing and calm. One of my neighbours, a salt-of-the-earth fellow who had spent too long as a white van driver in London went even further, claiming that he sometimes saw a physical manifestation of energy emanating from the Sierra de Lújar on certain afternoons. "I know that sounds a bit odd," he added a little self-consciously, "but the eyes don't lie."

I tried to get in touch with Margaret Nolan one day to see if she was willing to be interviewed. But she was cautious about talking to anyone, preferring instead the peace and quiet of her farmhouse in the anonymous Spanish hills. "What do you want to know?" she asked.

"Erm, I don't know," I said, a bit flustered that I was speaking to a screen goddess. "Just about your life in La Alpujarra."

"Well," she said crisply "I don't really see why anyone would be interested in that. People come here to get away from things, which is precisely what I did. Now if you don't mind, I have things to be getting on with."

"Oh," I said, somewhat downcast. And that was the end of that. I still had a lot to learn about this journalism thing ... but at least I'd got to speak to Dink; how many people could say that?

We had another neighbour on Cerro Negro, an old Danish lady who was the most un-Danish Dane I'd ever met. Gitte picked me up in her little car one day as I was walking into town, my own car being out of action. "Hop in," she said, pulling up beside me. "I'm just driving into town to stock up on feed for my horses." Gitte lived about a ten-minute drive up Cerro Negro from my house. At eighty-four, she was still going strong, and lived alone in a farmhouse with only horses for company. "A couple of years back my house was destroyed in a mudslide," she said casually, "and one of those horrible lifestyle magazine came out from Denmark and interviewed me, twisting all the facts and getting everything wrong."

I was astonished when she told me this because I had seen the article she was talking about. My mother-in-law had clipped it out and given it to us as a none-too-subtle way of saying that moving to Spain was potentially dangerous. At the time I had laughed, pointing out the odds of something similar happening to us must be a million to one. And yet here I was, sitting next to the very same old lady whose house had been destroyed on the very same hill I now lived on. "Obviously I wasn't seriously hurt in the disaster," she said, "but I didn't have any insurance and so I was without a house for a while."

I asked her how it was that she now seemed to have her house back. "Oh, everyone chipped in and rebuilt it for me," she said. "That's what people are like here. Generous. If you'd have lived here when it happened *you'd* have helped me out too. Of course, that doesn't chime with the Danish society; we think that we have the best country in the world, which is probably why the article came out all wrong. I could never go back and live *there* again."

On the way back one of the tyres developed a puncture. In a flash, Gitte jumped out and began to crack the wheel nuts with a hand wrench. "Wait, let me help you with that," I said, realising the absurdity of the situation.

"Don't worry, young man, I didn't make it this far without being a tough old bird, you know. If you want to do something useful you can shift those bags of feed in the boot and dig out the jack."

I did as she asked and watched in awe as the little old lady jacked the car off the ground and changed the wheel while I stood by twiddling my thumbs. It's a good thing nobody happened to pass by at that moment and see the two of us.

- 46 -

Despite our best efforts to make ends meet our finances continued to cause concern. In our eagerness to get the basic infrastructure of Los Pechos functional there had been various cost overruns and unexpected expenditures. It was clear we needed a fresh source of income if we were to survive in Spain, and so I began to cast around for new ways to earn a living.

I'd stepped up my distribution runs for *The Olive Press* and continued to write articles and restaurant reviews for scraps of cash from the office kitty, but the promise of a steady income eluded me. The Pampaneira house was for sale, but so far there had been no interest in it. Michelle, aware that the bank had just put up interest rates on our mortgage, began to grow worried. She was running a small upholstery service which re-covered people's old furniture and made fitted curtains, as well as working as a cleaner at some holiday apartments in Órgiva.

One morning after the school rush she was having coffee in town with some of the other mothers, and she mentioned to her friend Rebecca that we were looking for work. Rebecca said that her husband Leon needed some extra hands, and that she'd ask him when she saw him later. Leon was a builder with a good reputation for quality and honesty. Three years previously, he and Rebecca had abandoned their respective lives of bar owner and sales executive and fled the UK in a beat-up Land Rover. They'd hit the southern coast of Spain and could go no further when, with no money in their pockets, Rebecca turned to Leon and delivered the news that she was pregnant. Leon had had to work as a builder to earn money, quickly becoming his own boss, and they lived a semi-nomadic life moving from house to house, sometimes housesitting, sometimes renting. In due course baby Noah was born, and the pair married in a hand fasting ceremony in a forest up in the high Alpujarra. Their story was not untypical of many people who had come to live in the area.

Leon, who was of a spiritual bent, possessed an eye for natural form and had developed a knack for building things that looked seamless and organic. His creations were all sinuous curves and shapely symmetry, and he incorporated natural materials such as wood and stone wherever he could. It turned out that he was currently contracted on a large renovation job down on the coast that was due to last for the next six months, and – yes –

he needed a labourer to shift rubble and mix cement. The message was conveyed to me that I should turn up in the Metal Bar at a quarter to seven the next Monday morning.

Although I was grateful for the offer, I was in truth full of trepidation. I had never worked on a building site before and wondered whether I would fit in. Nevertheless, the following Monday, I turned up at dawn at the Bar Ruta de la Plata – aka the Metal Bar – so-called because it had been the last stop on the road for miners as they began the long march up to the mountains to dig for silver and lead ore. It was an unpretentious hangout on the outskirts of Órgiva, and the walls were covered with the mounted heads of animals that had been shot by the trigger-happy owner. It was also the place where day labourers waited to see if anyone needed any jobbers for the day ahead. Wearing my most worn out clothes, and with a packed lunch and water bottle in my bag, I stood outside the bar and awaited Leon nervously. Soon enough a tatty white van turned up with four builders and a dog in it. It stopped and the door opened for me to get in. I'd barely met Leon before then, but he introduced me to the driver, Jim, a carpenter, and José, an intense-looking Mexican gentleman with a neat side parting. Another figure, asleep in the back and with a baseball cap pulled down over his face was César, a young Romanian who'd been up partying all night and needed some extra sleep.

Leon himself was tanned and lean, with shoulder length wavy brown hair and a beard to match. His name, which means *lion* in Spanish, might have been a source of amusement to Spaniards, but there was nothing particularly lion-like about Leon. Far from being ferocious, one immediately got a sense of peace in his presence, and he had a reputation as a clear-sighted idealist. It was clear to anyone who met Leon that he was a peaceful man of principle, but neither would he take any shit from anyone.

Jim, whose van we were in, was nothing like Leon. For a start he was more heavily built and had a stoic look about him. Jim liked rollups and *Alhambra* lager – evidenced by the many empty bottles rolling around in the back – and with his sunburned arms and Anglo Saxon complexion he looked like the archetypal 'British builder in Spain'. When I got to know him better, I discovered Jim possessed a generous and modest nature, underscored by an Eeeyorish sense of humour. In the back of the van was a bundle of straggly fur, which in due course I learned was Jim's dog, Herbie. Jim had found Herbie as a puppy wandering the hot streets alone, and now the two were inseparable.

In time, I would come to regard Leon and Jim as a fine couple of friends, each with his own qualities and always willing to help out. But for now they were strangers, and I sat in the back seat of the car feeling tired and a bit nervous. We set off for the coast, and nobody spoke a word as we wound our way down the long bendy road that was the umbilical cord connecting La Alpujarra to the wider world. At Almuñécar Jim pulled the van up in front of a café and we all piled out. César awoke, yawned, and looked at me in a surprised manner before holding out a hand and introducing himself.

The woman who owned the café greeted the builders as if they were her own sons, pulling out chairs for us. She immediately put cups of hot frothy coffee in front of us, and it wasn't long before she came over with hot *tostadas* slathered with fresh tomato and covered in slabs of cured ham, all drizzled in olive oil. Once the coffee had been served and slurped, everyone ordered another one and, by the time we left half an hour later, we were all wide-awake and chatting freely. This, I was to find out, would be my morning ritual for the next few months.

When we arrived at the building site, which was situated on a hill next to a tropical fruit plantation, Leon led me over to a huge pile of rubble that was the remains of a demolished building. "I want you to move this rubble over there," he said, pointing to a large hole at the other end of the site. "Here, wear these gloves."

It took me three days to move it, and when I'd finished I was promoted to the position of cement mixer. Leon and his team were building a large annexe to a villa, which had been constructed atop a concrete irrigation tank. It was situated on a hill overlooking the picturesque crescent bay of La Herradura, and the beautiful hazy blue sea spread out below us. We were working in the garden, and although it was a building site flower bushes and citrus trees nevertheless surrounded us.

I had never used a cement mixer before and when I asked César to show me he thought I was kidding him. "In Romania," he told me, one eyebrow arched, "we learn use cement mixer in kindergarten." But once he had adjusted to the fact that his fellow peon was more used to pushing pens than wheelbarrows he gave me a crash course in the art of mixing concrete. In this matter he regarded himself as a connoisseur, and would cock his head next to the machine in order to discern whether the mixture of cement, water, sand and gravel was in perfect harmony simply by the sound it made as it swished around in the drum. Occasionally he would dip a finger in and regard the residue the way a confectioner might examine the consistency of chocolate. When he saw me try the same thing he pulled my arm away. "*Never* put hand in mixer like me," he warned, waving a cement-encrusted digit at me. "I expert. You not."

It was several days before I became proficient at making concrete, but there was satisfaction in striving to achieve the prefect mix. Too much sand made it dry and crumbly, too much water and it turned to sludge. Too much cement powder was a waste that had Leon tutting at me, while not enough mixing led to weak concrete. I stood with a shovel between two great piles of sand and gravel, counting as I scooped up the materials, occasionally blasting a shot of water into the mixer from a hose. When it was thoroughly blended and the consistency of the mix was like firm porridge I would position the barrow and pour almost up to the top as the mixer continued to spin. It was then a case of getting the wet mix to where it was needed by Jim or Leon, who were creating foundations and building walls. Getting the mix to them usually involved going up a gangplank, making sure it didn't slop over the sides, or worse, upsetting the barrow. Upsetting the barrow was basically unforgiveable and so I tried not to do it. Then I would rush back with an empty barrow, wash it clean with the hose to prevent a layer of cement forming on the metal surface, and put the next mix on. In this way we worked like clockwork, with any holdup on the part of me or the others affecting the whole system of production.

At one o'clock we would down tools and get into Jim's van for the five-minute drive down to La Herradura and lunch. Usually we went into one of the working men's restaurants – or *comedores* – where you could get a three-course meal with a drink for the princely sum of eight euros. These places were all paper tablecloths and fast-moving waiters, and they filled up with truck drivers, builders and tradesmen of all descriptions. Nobody cared how dirty you were in these places, although that didn't mean they treated you any differently. If you ate fast you could be in and out in twenty minutes, although we usually took a more leisurely hour and a quarter unless we had materials to pick up from the builders' yard on the way back. To escape the worst of the midday heat, many workers took two or even three-hour lunches, as is the custom in southern Spain, but Leon opted for a shorter break so we could leave earlier for the forty-five minute drive back to Órgiva. After a day shovelling sand and gravel in up to forty degrees Celsius I would usually nod off on the way back, as would the others, swaying like a cargo of dead bodies as the rusty old van made its way back up the bendy road into the mountains. We would then pull up outside the Metal Bar and – the best part of the day – sink a few ice cold beers before heading off home, which in my case was an hour's walk up Cerro Negro.

In this way I soon began to feel the benefits of so much physical work. Other than brief stints working on farms, and a month as a bicycle rickshaw driver in Copenhagen, I had never before been paid to use my muscles. The fact that I was doing so in the company of people who had quickly become good friends and in such an idyllic setting made it all the more rewarding. How could it be, I wondered, that at the age of thirty-six working on a building site was the best job I'd ever had?

After a couple of months Leon let me do other things, giving me a break from mixing and pouring concrete. One of the bigger jobs that needed doing was building a stone wall at one end of the annexe. Construction on the new coastal motorway was continuing less than a mile away and sections of the hillsides had been dynamited, resulting in thousands of tonnes of smashed rock at the bottom of a nearby valley. "Look at all those lovely materials going to waste," said Leon casting his eye over it.

And so, for a week, César and I drove my Mitsubishi down a narrow track into the valley and hauled rocks back up again. By then, in contrast to my first disastrous attempt, I had become far more proficient driving off-road and up and down gulleys. Some of the rocks that we found were too large to lift and had to be broken into smaller pieces, so we brought along a couple of sledgehammers for that purpose. It was exhausting work and, dripping in sweat one day as we contemplated breaking up the mother of all rocks, César shared one of his characteristic contemplative thoughts. "Did you see Ethiopia programme on television last night?" he asked. I said that I hadn't. "Pity, you like it. These men, they have giant eagles and they use them to hunt the wolves. The eagles keel the wolves." He paused for effect, a misty look in his eye. "Is … beautiful."

The job with Leon went on for several more months, with the clients asking for more alterations and extensions to existing structures, although I was only called in to work on it when labourers were needed. Afterwards we moved onto another job at a property overlooking the sea in an affluent neighbourhood in the same town. This one was a luxury villa that had recently been purchased by a wealthy young Irishman who'd made a fortune in business. Although there was nothing physically wrong with the handsome-looking building, the buyer's girlfriend had insisted the entire structure needed to be stripped back to a shell and reconstituted with new materials. The plaster on the walls had to be smashed back to the brickwork, the marble tiled floors ripped up and replaced with identical ones, and the whole house had to be rewired with 'fresh' wires before she would move in.

It was a huge job, and also totally unnecessary, but the owner wanted Leon to do it, and Leon needed the money. He brought in several more Romanians, who liked to work for Leon because he paid fair wages and wasn't too tough on them compared to the local Spanish builders. In the previous year there had been a huge influx of Romanians to Órgiva – four hundred by some estimates. Nobody could explain why they had all turned up, least of all themselves. I asked César and he shrugged, saying one had turned up, liked it, and then invited his friends, who also invited their friends, and so on. They were all young, and most of them were skilled in one way or another, sometime highly. Their lot sounded like a tough one though, and none had a good word to say about the country they'd left behind.

One of those on the job at the villa was a newly qualified lawyer, trying desperately to save up the hundred thousand euros he said he needed to pay off the Bucharest Mafia. This was the sum needed for 'permission' to set up a law practice, he said. I asked him how much he had managed to put by, labouring six days a week. "Practically nothing," he said, his head hung low. "When I return to my room each evening I pour myself some whisky, sit in the dark, and I cry."

Another one of my fellow labourers was a Croat named Neven who was biding his time in Spain. Friendly and hard-working, Neven seemed to live off nothing but fresh air, and while the rest of us were eating our three-course lunches he would often sit there with a piece of fruit plucked from some roadside tree or other. "I live in the jungle," he told me one day, explaining how at night he would creep into the ornamental hothouse at the botanical gardens in Nerja and stretch out on a yoga mat beneath a banana tree. Each morning he would stash the mat and his other possessions in some bushes and head off for the day, either to work on a building site or to busk. When I asked him if living in a tropical greenhouse was pleasant, Neven admitted that the situation "wasn't ideal" and that he might have to consider somewhere a bit more orthodox to live in the future, like a van or a shed.

- 47 -

Visitors to Órgiva could hardly fail to notice the aroma of cannabis that hung in the air. What's more, the surrounding hills were filled with secret and not-so-secret plantations, and local lore had it that the *Guardia* could not prosecute you if the plants were no taller than yourself. Órgiva's tobacconist could probably have kept his business afloat with the sale of cigarette papers alone. Every year the *Cannabis Cup* tournament was held in the area, in which competitors presented home grown strands of marijuana in the way English country gardeners entered their marrows and pumpkins into village fêtes. The lovingly created spliffs were sampled by a panel of judges and awarded points on a number of different criteria.

But despite the ubiquity of marijuana, it was still an illegal substance so I was surprised when I saw it growing in a flowerbed outside the *Guardia Civil* headquarters in Órgiva. I made the mistake of mentioning this to Jon, with the predictable consequence that he wanted me to confront the officers about it and write a 'scoop'. I didn't like the idea one bit. "You don't just go around accusing the *Guardia* of growing drugs," I protested.

"Listen," he responded, "if you're going to be a proper journalist you're going to make enemies – it just comes with the territory. Are you a journalist or not?"

I hadn't actually ever claimed that I wanted to be a 'proper journalist' but Jon wasn't listening. "I'll need the story filed with pictures by six this afternoon. Try and get one of the plants with an officer standing next to it. If you can get him to hold up a *fat one* and blow smoke rings you'll get extra points." He hung up.

I sighed. The truth was that, no, I probably wasn't the kind of journalist Jon had in mind. Still, I didn't want to seem weak and foolish so I hardened my resolve and marched into the *Guardia's* fort on the *plaza*. Inside, a duty officer sat at a desk smoking a cigarette and reading a sports newspaper. I made a nervous cough to alert him to my presence. "*Por favor,*" I said, but didn't look up. I began again, "Excuse me, *señor,* I think there are some, er, cannabis plants. Growing outside." The man lazily looked up from the football scores and considered me for a moment with heavily lidded eyes.

"There are *many* cannabis plants growing outside, *hombre,*" he said, perhaps thinking I was a halfwit.

"Yes, but these are growing in your flower borders, right outside the station," I said.

The officer thought about what I'd just said and weighed up whether it was worth getting out of his seat to investigate. He eyed me again: was I winding him up? Eventually he considered that it might be worth investigating, stood up with a sigh and came around the desk.

"Show me," he said.

I led him outside into the bright glare of the afternoon sun and showed him the plants. There were two of them, about a foot high and they were mixed in with the ornamental species. He bent down and had a look at them, rubbing the leaves and smelling his fingers. Then he stood up and frowned at them, stroking his chin contemplatively. "Well, what do you think?" I asked.

"Probably just some *eepees,*" he said. "Flick their butts around and the seeds fall out." He might have been right, I'd noticed them growing in the car park as well, although

I figured it was probably a prank and that the seeds had been planted deliberately.

"So," I asked, "what will the *Guardia Civil* be doing with them?" The man turned around and, seeing I was holding a notepad in my hand and had a camera around my neck, glared at me.

"Why you want to know?" he said.

I gulped. "I'm a journalist. At *The Olive Press*." He looked confused, perhaps wondering what a journalist was doing working at an olive press. He had likely never heard of the newspaper, even though the office was only a thirty second walk away.

"Then you must make a formal complaint against the force," he said. "Please put your camera away, and come back inside, I will need to see your *targeta extranjero*." By this he meant my residency card. I didn't want to show him my residency card. Not that I had done anything illegal, but I didn't really want my name and number being noted down by the *Guardia*.

"Or perhaps you would like to come back later and make your complaint to my boss?" he said, noticing my hesitance.

"Yes, I'll do that," I said, backing away from the station.

"False alarm," I told Jon later. "Turns out they were just some kind of ornamental plant."

"Oh well, it was worth investigating," he replied. "Anyway, remember you told me there was a bunch of skanks selling crack out of a caravan down in the woods by the river in Órgiva? Maybe you can go down there instead and find out what's going on. If they're dealing openly, it probably means they have police protection. Bring a couple of your builder mates with you and expect trouble. And don't forget to take pictures, especially if it kicks off."

"Right you are," I said, and went home to my tea.

- 48 -

One Thursday morning during a dry patch with the building work, I found myself sitting cross-legged on the street at the market in Órgiva. Next to me was a bucket of squirming furry bodies and a cardboard sign saying *'Gatitos gratuitos'* (free kittens). I didn't want to be in this situation but there I was. It wasn't unusual for people moving to Spain to quickly accumulate felines. In our case Michelle had picked up a kitten from someone in Tíjola, and we named her Quark after the design software we had used at the newspaper. A little while later and I'd found an oil-smeared kitten dodging cars in a DIY store car park on the coast. I'd scooped her up, popped in my jacket and brought her back to live with us. Aki, as we named her, grew up fast even for a street cat. She was jumped on by a vicious tomcat when she was only a few months old, producing a litter of six soon after. The same tomcat had got to Quark, and she too had also had a litter of eight before we'd managed to get her spayed. This meant we had gone from having one cat – James, who'd come over with us from Denmark – to seventeen in just under a year. At that rate Los Pechos would soon start to resemble one of those temples in Japan where they worship felines.

So now it fell to me to find new homes for this sudden wave of kittens. This wasn't easy because most people already had several cats. Nevertheless, we figured it wouldn't be too hard to re-home Quark's litter as she had Siamese blood and the kittens looked cuter than those of regular street cats. But Aki's kittens had a problem in that their eyes kept becoming glued shut. This meant they had to be regularly peeled open again and ointment dripped in them. People walked by and looked into the bucket of gummy-eyed kittens, sometimes cooing, but never actually wanting one. My phone rang. It was Jon. I hadn't spoken to him for a couple of weeks, but I'd heard on the grapevine that he was having problems with Marcus and Rick, which could be why he was ringing me. "What are you up to right now?" he asked, as was his custom. I inwardly groaned; the last thing I wanted right then was to be sent off on some 'urgent' assignment.

I explained my predicament with the kittens, saying how nobody wanted them with their eyes glued shut. "Why don't you just do what the Spanish do?" he asked.

"What's that?" I said, sensing that I probably didn't want to know.

"Throw them against a wall. Bam! Far less cruel than drowning them in a sink, or so our gardener says."

I was shocked. "You have a gardener?" Perhaps I'd been living in La Alpujarra too long and had forgotten that people elsewhere generally employed other people to do the mundane things they didn't want to do themselves.

"Too right," he continued. "If you saw my place you'd realise why we need one. Why don't you come over, you can help me put together the next issue. It'd be good to catch up." I thought about his offer. It was tempting. Lately, whenever I hadn't been mixing concrete down on the coast, I had been focusing all my energy on the house and land, digging irrigation channels and dealing with a collapsed terrace that had got waterlogged and caused an olive tree to fall over. In fact, I hadn't been anywhere new for months, and it would be good to reconnect with Jon's newspaper.

"Okay," I agreed. "I'll come over on Sunday evening. There's something we need to talk about in any case."

256

By now it was late morning the market was winding down. I'd only managed to give away one kitten, in this case to a young girl who had begged her mother for it. A Gypsy trader who had a stall selling Afghan coats had been watching me fail to offload them. Eventually, seeing how fed up I must have looked, he came over and lifted one of them up to get a closer look at it. Peering at its gummy eyelids he gave out a dismissive snort. "I will take them," he said, after a cursory glance at the others.

"What are you going to do with them?" I asked.

"I heal," he said. "Many cats."

That was good enough for me. "Here," I said, handing over the rubber builder's bucket. He took the kittens and put them in the back of his van. I didn't know what he was going to do with them, but hoped at least that it wouldn't involve a wall or a sink. On the way home I called in at the vet and booked Aki an appointment to be neutered.

When Sunday came round I drove over to Jon's house near Ronda. Ernest Hemingway had made Ronda famous to foreigners and the place was regarded as a kind of Jerusalem for bull fighting. I had never ventured that far to the west in Andalucía and the contrast with where I lived was stark. The topography was flatter, although still hilly, and vast fields of wheat and red poppies quilted the landscape. The roads were in better condition and the cars using them looked much newer and less battered than those I had become used to seeing. Jon lived in a quiet hamlet outside the historical town. His house, a spacious affair with landscaped gardens, had been newly restored and he lived there with his wife, who was a portrait artist and interior designer. They had a young daughter together.

After I arrived, Jon led me to the upstairs room that doubled as the office where he ran his version of *The*

Olive Press. The walls were decked out with the newspaper cutting of articles he had written in the days when he worked as the showbiz reporter for the *Daily Mail*, as well as other tabloids. It was like a *Who's Who* of celebrity gossip with Jamie Oliver here ("I knew him before anyone had heard of him") and Brad Pitt there ("Bumped into him on set in Morocco, nice bloke") as well as numerous other familiar faces. "I once followed the Spice Girls around for a year," he said. "And Oasis."

I carried on staring at the wall, trying to identify famous faces.

"Prince Charles called me up the other week for a chat," Jon said, matter-of-factly.

"He did? What did he want?" I asked.

"I think he just wanted to check us out. He'd heard about our work preserving local architecture, just wanted to offer us some moral support."

Jon was talking about a real estate business in Ronda that he ran with a friend. They bought old character properties, had them renovated and sold them again for a tidy profit, but I hadn't been aware there was a philanthropic angle to the business.

"Yeah," said Jon. "We preserve all the classical features and stuff, so I suppose it's right up his street."

I had the feeling that he must inhabit a very different universe from the generally uneventful life I lived in Órgiva.

Jon saw me gazing at his tabloid past, arrayed in frames around the room. "None of that stuff matters any more," he said, "this is far more important." He beckoned me over to his desk and pointed at some photos that were displayed on the computer monitor there. He had the golf development at Los Merinos in his sights and was eager to show me the latest information relating to his campaign to save the ancient olive groves and oak trees there.

"Will you look at that!" he exclaimed, pointing a finger at the screen. "That's pure eco vandalism." The pictures showed the stubby bodies of dozens of mature oak and olive trees in giant plastic pots and surrounded by diggers and bulldozers. Sitting in this mangled landscape, the heavily pruned trees looked like a surrealistic nightmare vision of amputees in a battlefield. They were also clearly dead. Perhaps because of the skills he'd learned following the Spice Girls around, Jon had managed to sneak over the fence and take these damning pictures, which he was about to publish in *The Olive Press* as evidence that the developers of the golf course didn't give a damn about following even the slightest rule.

"You know what they do?" continued Jon, "They get these big machines to rip the trees out of the ground and then they put them in pots. It's called remodelling and the developers have to promise to transplant them. All perfectly legal, but the only trouble is the idiots didn't know what they were doing and the trees have been left out in the sun without any water. Now look at them."

It was a story I had heard repeated across the region. Developers often began land clearance before permission had been granted, safe in the knowledge that any objections would take months or years to make it through the court system. By the time the case came up the land would be degraded and ruined and the only victory conservationists could hope for would be a pyrrhic one. The demand was there for even more golf courses, even if the ecological limits of the region's water resources had been breached. At the heart of it was a planning loophole that permitted developers to build blocks of apartments and hotels as long as they were part of a golf course. Jon showed me more pictures, these ones taken from a small plane piloted by an activist from the group *Ecologistas en Accion*. The pictures revealed that the carve-up of the land was more or less complete, with dull yellow tracks running through a landscape of bulldozed earth. Everywhere were the stumps of the trees that hadn't been deemed ancient enough even to stick in a pot.

Shocking as this was, there was still more to come. Jon had teamed up with a consortium of people and groups to oppose the project, from the leader of the Spanish branch of Greenpeace, to local groups and individuals, including the British writer Alistair Boyd, whom Jon had mentioned when I'd first met him.

Boyd had lived a modest life in Andalucía for decades and had written *The Road from Ronda*, recalling a journey from Ronda to La Alpujarra on horseback in the 1960s. Boyd was a high-order misfit, and was perhaps better known in his adopted Spain than his native Britain. In the 1950s, he had escaped a dull career in finance and fled to Andalucía where he opened a language school, which soon failed, before moving to a farmhouse to become what one of his friends called 'an unskilled peasant'. I could relate to him.

But now, following public criticism of the Los Merinos in the left-leaning *El Observador* newspaper, Boyd, along with two other expats were being sued for six million euros by the developers. The logic they were employing was founded on the assertion that some investors had pulled out of the project on the basis of the bad publicity. Jon had also kicked the hornets' nest and was printing damning information about the project, but the developers had focused on the three individuals, presumably because Jon had a well-connected lawyer. Many local people, who knew bullying when they saw it, had rallied around the *'Los Merinos Tres'* (the Los Merinos

Three, as they had become known). Nevertheless it was audacious for a private consortium to sue individuals for expressing an opinion in the open democracy that Spain was supposed to be.

Despite the woeful scenario that was occurring at Los Merinos I had to admire Jon's tenacity in his opposition to it. Since I had left the office six months before I had watched in mute horror as *The Olive Press* I had helped create had turned its back on the local community and many of the serious issues affecting La Alpujarra. I knew that Marcus and Rick were nervous about Jon's deliberate confrontation of powerful interests, and how they felt sooner or later the newspaper would be sued by someone with more clout than just Margaret Moran.

Given that I was still co-owner of the newspaper, even if it didn't feel like it, Jon's bold approach should also have been a worry for me. After all, as publisher I'd probably end up in court along with the rest of them, where I was pretty sure my pleas of innocence would be ignored. Nevertheless, Jon's version of the newspaper, with it campaigns and its lofty rhetoric seemed far preferable to me than the insipid lettuce leaf the Órgiva version had become. Most people I spoke to in town no longer even read it, and it was common to see piles of it lying around unopened.

But Jon's way of running his version of the paper was quite different from how it was done in Órgiva, and although he often catered to the lowest common denominator with articles on celebrity sightings and the like, he said he only did so to widen the readership and prevent being pigeon holed. The logic revolved around the hope that casting a wide net would bring in more readers who would then read about the more important issues, such as ripping up trees at Los Merinos. His maxim, which he repeated often enough, was that "people will always pick up a free newspaper even if there is just a single column they enjoy." And the approach seemed to be working, with new advertisers and writers coming on board with each issue. This was in stark contrast to the Órgiva version that, in all honesty, had turned into a zombie publication, staggering forwards like the risen dead with readers and advertisers fleeing from its advance.

Over dinner that evening I asked Jon if he wanted to buy my fifty percent share in *The Olive Press*. He didn't seem surprised that I wanted to wash my hands of it, and perhaps even expected my offer. "They barely even speak to me any more," I said. "I don't see any point with being connected with it."

He sounded interested but said there would be a long battle ahead as he and Marcus had fallen out over their differing editorial approaches. Furthermore, like the hard-nosed salesman that he could be, he immediately pointed out all the things that were wrong with my offer. He didn't actually say "*You* should be paying *me* to take it off your hands," but he may as well have. But, just like the kittens with the gummy eyes, I was keen to pass the responsibility onto someone else, and Jon seemed like the right person.

I left his place a couple of days later after we had put together his latest issue, and drove back to La Alpujarra, but not before paying a visit to someone I'd been promising to for a while.

- 49 -

After I'd visited Jon in Ronda I went over to see a man in Mijas. To get there I drove along the coast through the Costa del Sol, and stopped for a while at the resort of

Marbella. With its mega-yachts, sports cars and designer clothes shops, the place could scarcely have been any different to La Alpujarra. So it was a relief to get back in the car – which was rather dented and at that time lacking a rear window due to an earlier reversing miscalculation – and drive off into the mountains where the hero of my next eco feature article was fighting an epic battle against developers.

Spain, they say, was once covered in a thick mantle of forest. By the time the Romans arrived most of these trees had already been cut down by the native Iberians and they likened the parched yellow country they found to an old lion skin, pegged out to dry in the sun. One man, however, was on a mission to reverse some of the damage and turn his little patch of Spain green again.

After I'd driven up into the hills from Marbella, Kaj came out to meet me outside the caravan he lived in on a *finca* set in the rolling countryside of Mijas Campo. The place was just inland from the Costa del Sol, but at the same time a million miles away from it.

Kaj Aage Helming was a retired Danish seaman who'd found his land legs in Andalucía in 2003. Since then he'd been on a new mission, and despite his mild manner Kaj was, in fact, fighting a guerrilla war for nature. After introductions and a cup of tea he led me up a hill from where we could survey the scene around us. In one direction lay the urban sprawl of Marbella, punctuated by unnaturally green blobs of over-watered golf courses. In the other direction large billboards announcing the imminent construction of an industrial park crowned the untamed hills. "It's a crying shame isn't it," said Kaj, shaking his head sadly.

How, I asked, could developers possibly build an industrial park in these rugged hills? "Oh, they'll come in with heavy machinery and flatten the terrain in no time.

They blast the tops off the hills and dump the debris in the *barrancos* to level the land. The river will disappear and the land will become parched." As if to illustrate this depressing prospect the sound of a large controlled explosion suddenly reverberated across the valley and a dust cloud rose into the clear blue sky. "Road widening," muttered Kaj, "so they can get the machines in."

Far from being fatalistic about the situation the plucky Dane was taking a King Cnut-like stance against the tide of concrete flowing his way. Thinking ahead, and knowing the insidious nature of urban sprawl, he wanted to protect the land from any future development. By joining with others to take out a legal injunction against the industrial park he had temporarily helped to halt its construction. The second part of his strategy was to plant some one and a half thousand cork oaks on his land, which will in time grow into woodland. Cork oaks – even young ones – were legally protected under Spanish law, so he hoped to save this corner of Andalucía from the ever-advancing bulldozers.

As we strode around his land, with the smell of wild aromatics suffusing the air, Kaj pointed out all the trees he had planted. "This one," he said, indicating a six-inch high bushy twig "will eventually turn into something like that over there." He pointed at a gnarled old oak that stood out on the hillside – a granddaddy of a tree reminiscent of Treebeard in *Lord of the Rings*. "This is one of the oldest corks in the province, and it's even mentioned in a Spanish guidebook on trees," he said.

"In fact, it was sitting under this tree that gave me the idea to protect this land by planting seedlings in the first place, so he's an ally of mine."

Cork oaks, along with their cousins the holm oaks (holly oaks, or *encinas* in Spanish) were perfectly adapted to live in Andalucía. They had evolved there over millennia and were extremely hardy during periods of drought. What's more, they actually hibernated in the summer when it was too hot for them. Their bark has been harvested as a renewable resource for centuries, and is used for everything from bath mats to wine bottle corks. What's more, the trees are ideal habitat for birds and insects and the acorns are a favourite for wild boars. "The first autumn here I collected acorns and planted them in pots. They grew well but died when I planted them outside. So the next year I planted them outside from the start and now they are thriving."

As we wandered around the land together I wondered whether I was meeting a modern-day Elzéard Bouffier, the semi-mythical French sheep farmer whose story is told in the book *The Man Who Planted Trees*. Bouffier, walking alone around the denuded foothills of the Provencal Alps, planted acorns wherever he went, creating over the years a forest full of birds and wildlife. The French authorities, baffled the appearance of a forest described it as 'miraculous' and refused to believe a lone committed man could be responsible for its creation. I asked Kaj to explain how best to plant acorns in order that other people could copy his example and contribute to the greening of Spain.

He explained how you harvest the acorns in October or November, collecting only the good ones that have fallen to the ground, as these are the mature ones. Find a good spot to plant them, preferably sheltered from harsh winds and perhaps in the shade of a small bush. Then, when the first substantial rains have fallen, dig a hole eight inches deep and put a bit of compost in, mixed with soil. Put several acorns in each hole just to be sure, as sometimes only one will grow and other times all of them will. Fill the hole in and wait. The acorns will put down taproots up to a metre long before sprouting upwards the following spring. Don't plant them any closer than thirty feet apart, he said, because eventually they will have huge root systems. If you can, try to protect them for the first summer, and make sure goats or sheep can't get at them.

As if to illustrate the point I noticed a nearby sheep gazing wistfully at the tiny saplings from behind a wire fence. Overgrazing, explained Kaj, was why the trees were unable to reproduce without a little human help. He had asked the local goat herders to keep their animals off his land for a couple of years to give his trees a chance, and they were more than happy to. Instead, Kaj cleared the land by hand with a pair of shears and a handsaw. It must have been quite a task, especially for someone who, like Kaj, was recovering from an operation for cancer. "It keeps me pretty fit and healthy," he said.

By the time I left I had several pages of notes, half a camera full of pictures and a head full of ideas about a campaign that would see expats planting trees all over the region – similar to the one we did to reduce plastic bags.

When I got back to Órgiva I called in on another foreigner who was already doing his bit to increase the tree cover. David Tonge, a translator from Yorkshire, lived with his wife Judy and their young daughter Olivia. They resided in a crooked house on a bend in the road beside a dusty riverbed on the outskirts of town. The Rio Seco (aptly-named 'dry river') had been a grubby channel filled with garbage bags, dumped fridges and masses of building rubble, smashed tiles and lumps of plaster. David couldn't abide all this despoilation so he had managed to persuade the mayor to providing refuse trucks and skips in which to put all the garbage.

But the task proved too big for just one man so David enlisted the help of local volunteers to scour a stretch of river and remove as much waste as possible. I joined him one Sunday morning while they were heaving out rusting microwave ovens, smashed TV sets and bags of garbage. Cleaning the river was one thing, but nothing was growing along its banks save for the pink-flowered and poisonous oleanders.

What the river needed was trees. Trees would provide habitat for birds and insects, they would prevent soil erosion and hold moisture in the land, and they would create shade. In fact, if enough of them were planted they would create their own microclimate and lessen the summer heat in that area.

Again, David swung into action, convincing the municipality to donate several dozen trees that he and the helpers planted one spring day. David volunteered to water them in their first couple of years until the roots had become established, and soon enough the banks of the river were planted up with saplings and the area had taken a small step in the fight back against desiccation. In time the trees would help maintain the water cycle, shading the river to prevent evaporation and releasing cooling moisture during the hot summer months.

When I thought about people like Kaj and David, it made me realise that the impact of their action would persist long after they themselves had left, and that all it took was a little planning and a few seeds.

- 50 -

Sometimes, when I had been working on a building project with Jim and Leon, we'd have a drink or two at Pepe's bar in Órgiva after work. On occasion, we'd then head back to Jim's where there was always a plentiful supply of chilled *Alhambra* beer. Jim, along with his girlfriend Nat, had bought a small run-down house to do up in the quarter where the gypsies lived. Wedged in between two others it was one of the narrowest houses imaginable and the ground floor was not unlike a train carriage with seats at the back. You entered it straight off the street via a thick wooden door that Jim had made himself, and inside it was cosy and snug and ideal for sitting there playing cards and drinking large amounts of beer.

There were not many foreigners living in Jim's *barrio*. Most people considered it too dirty and dangerous, although there was little evidence of the latter. On any given summer evening the streets would be alive with the sound of families, usually shouting to or at one another through open windows, with the ubiquitous flamenco being blasted out of car windows. Life spilled out of the houses onto the streets. One time when I went to visit Jim the pavement was blocked by a fat shirtless man crouching down over a spread of cardboard on which rested a smiling pig's head. He was going at it with a meat cleaver and little spats of blood flew about with each chop, coating his bare stomach and the white cardboard like a shotgun suicide.

"You can see why this place is never mentioned in the Sunday Times property section," observed Jim. "That bloke's always out on the street chopping up animals, I think it's his hobby or something."

And perhaps it was, because a few weeks later I met Jim and he was pale faced and in shock, saying he needed a drink. When he was comfortably seated at the bar with a beer in front of him and a cigarette between his knuckles he told us what had just happened. There had been a great commotion in the street outside his house. People were shouting and something was emitting an unearthly shrieking noise. Jim had stepped outside, at first thinking that two dogs had got themselves stuck together again as often happened in his street when one of the larger randy dogs tried it on with a smaller one, and that people were pulling them apart – always a noisy affair. But this time the screeching was of a different magnitude and chaos seemed to have broken out among his neighbours. Jim took a gulp of beer, looked around, and continued in a low voice. "When I first saw it I thought it was some kind of foetus, perhaps from a donkey or something. It was running around in the street making that screaming noise and the fat bloke was running around after it with his meat cleaver and laughing like a maniac. Some kids were also screaming and throwing stones at him but he didn't seem to care he just kept running after the … *thing* with his meat chopper. And all the dogs were biting each other and the people were shouting out the windows – like I said, it was complete chaos."

Jim took another swig of his beer, clearly not enjoying relating what he had just witnessed. "But then I saw what he had in his other hand. It was a lambskin. The bastard had skinned the lamb alive and it was running around in the street with blood dripping off it and all its muscles and eyes popping out. You should have heard it bleating! Eventually someone managed to catch it and slit its throat. Apparently the bastard said the meat taste better when he does it that way, something to do with the adrenaline."

We sat there in silence taking in what Jim had just told us. When we ordered the next drink Leon asked if they had any vegetarian *tapas* to accompany it.

Changing the subject, we got onto what Jim called the tinfoilers. He had used the term offhandedly once or twice and I asked him what he meant. "You know," he said "people who wear tinfoil inside their hats." I asked him why people would do such a thing and he explained that they generally believed that there was a worldwide government run by lizards that controlled the minds of the masses using mobile phone signals and so-called chemtrails. "I've heard there is a whole group of them living up near the snowline," he said.

After that I always took close notice of people's heads whenever the Thursday market was on. But after a few weeks looking out for exposed scraps of shiny paper jutting from headwear I still hadn't spotted anything. I jokingly brought the subject up at a party and, to my surprise, found one of the other guests staring intently at me. Later he took me aside and explained in a tone of utmost seriousness that I shouldn't make light of such matters. He continued, explaining how climate scientists were in league with George Bush to push up the cost of fuel. The top movers, including various members of the Israeli Likkud Party, were in on the game and had drilled a network of sideways tunnels to suck out the oil from the Middle East without anyone knowing. What's more he claimed to have secret information that practically everything we took for granted was indeed a huge *Truman Show* type simulation.

"Why would they suck up the oil like that?" I asked, slightly baffled.

He gave me an incredulous stare. "Look man, they control the oil in order to keep us all in servitude. They don't want us to know that energy is free – they have all these devices invented by Tesla but they keep them secret, hidden away from mankind."

"Oh," I said. "So what can we do about it?"

"Nothing," he said morosely. "At least not until The Shift comes. The best we can do is just hide out and wait."

"That's too bad," I said.

He himself was building a concrete bunker somewhere up the mountain where he would shelter with his family during the tsunami he said was coming. He eyed me suspiciously. "I don't know why I'm telling you this," he said coldly. "You're something to do with that local rag, aren't you? You're probably getting your directions from *them*."

I never saw or spoke to this man again, although I promised myself that if I did run into him I would keep the conversation firmly focused on the weather.

- 51 -

I had to take a trip to England for a few days to visit my father, and took the opportunity to visit a friend in London. He worked for a tech company that did complex things with databases, and I met him and some of his work colleagues in a swanky bar in fashionable north London. It was Friday night and the place buzzed. I should probably have been enjoying myself but the people I was with seemed to be talking in a strange language that I didn't understand. Having not stepped outside rural Spain for what seemed like half a lifetime, I felt like the country bumpkin that I was perhaps becoming. Over the last couple of years, while I had been learning how to prune olive trees with a chainsaw and master the complexities of my irrigation system, these people had been jetting around the world saying things like "we can help your brand managers design and implement their digital online strategies". Listening to them, my head began to spin, and as I looked at the expensive bottles of lager on the table before me I wished I were sitting in Pepe's Bar in Órgiva, nursing a cold *Alhambra* and listening to Leon outline his latest plan to set up a self sufficient commune in an abandoned Spanish village somewhere.

It felt like I was back home when my plane touched down at Granada airport and I looked out at the city with its background of the mountains rising above it. Soon, I was on the A92 heading east through Santa Fe and looking forward to being back on my own patch again. The setting sun behind the poplar trees cast long shadows that fell like tattoos across the road. I got to thinking about my trip to London and how unnerving I had found it. I mused that perhaps living in La Alpujarra had altered my perception of what was necessary in life and what was just superfluous fluff. In London, for example, it felt like there were a million places to get takeaway food, whereas in Órgiva there was only one such place, and even that was struggling for survival in the face of local indifference.

But when I thought some more about it, it seemed that Órgiva actually lacked for very little, even if there were certain things missing that people elsewhere took for granted. How many towns and cities in the modern world would be okay if there were a sudden shock to food prices or fuel? Could it be that little Órgiva, with its stray dogs, bin-scavenging humans and dysfunctional civic amenities harboured a hidden level of resilience? If half of industrial civilisation suddenly disappeared, I figured, Órgiva could probably still manage on its own better than most places. After all there were still all the traditional artisans in their family-owned businesses – the butcher, the baker, the organic wine maker – and the town was surrounded by productive farmland, with many still employed in small scale agriculture and the preparation of food. What's more, there were people who could fix anything, from leaking pipes to broken laptops, cars, TV sets ... you name it.

Work had begun on building a huge array of solar panels on a nearby hillside, which would provide the town with at least some electrical power, although a lot of people lived remotely and probably had no need for an electricity grid at all. There was a school, a health centre, two dental surgeries, two veterinary surgeries, a language school, churches and a library. There was even a nightclub, although the one time I had ventured inside the place it was half full of old ladies standing at the bar wearing their nighties.

Furthermore, although most Órgiva natives were skilled in their traditional ways, there was also a great fund of 'dropped out' foreigners who could take care of everything from website design to midwifery. This is not to mention a small army of mechanics, welders and blacksmiths, as well as the man would come round and sharpen your knives every week using a rhinestone attached to the back wheel of his scooter. Of course, this is not to say the town would fare particularly well if everything was suddenly cut off, but when I thought of places I knew in England, where almost every shop was part of a much bigger chain (in Órgiva there were none, save the usual banks) and people had been de-skilled to the extent that few knew how to do anything useful and practical, I knew where I would rather be if disaster struck. As I drove into the town that evening over the little bridge, past the metalworking shops and the grocer who never seemed to close, I had a newfound respect for my adopted town.

But this self-reliance would count for nothing if the water were taken away. Water was life, and without it Órgiva would wither and die. A few weeks later a demonstration was held in town against a project to transfer water in a pipeline from one of the rivers to the plastic greenhouse zone, but it was a depressing spectacle and almost everyone attending was either elderly or getting that way. I went along and asked an old man what he thought about the situation. He himself was a farmer who had lived on the outskirts of Tablones his whole life. The old man was despondent about the proposed project, asking "How can they take away our water when we already have so little?" It was clear he and others were at their wits' end, and he knew full well that people like him – subsistence farmers and sharecroppers – had no chance against the politicians and the businessmen.

I watched as the demonstrators, limping old men and long-haired foreigners, marched around Órgiva holding up banners saying things like 'Hands off our water!' but when I asked the old man why there were no young people involved he stated "They do not care about these matters, they think it's just for old folks like us. Their heads are full of fast cars and music."

A case in point was the damage being done by the concreting of the *acequias*. These ancient water channels, which were an astonishing feat of effective but low-tech engineering, were now being 'improved' with disastrous effects. Where before they had been lined with the partially absorbent quartz *launa*, they were now being turned into concrete channels in the name of efficiency. Water flowing through a concrete channel flows faster than it does through a semi-natural one, and it can be more easily measured and regulated. However, the old *launa* streambeds allowed some of the water to seep through to the roots of surrounding trees, which then grew strong and created shaded to prevent evaporation. Now, whenever an *acequia* fell into disrepair the cheapest solution was to replace the *launa* with cement and breeze blocks, thus scoring the hillsides with ugly grey lines and cutting off the water for the cooling trees. Of course, the trees inevitably died, taking their wildlife with them and worsening the problem of evaporation in the process. It was an excellent example of trying to solve a problem and making it worse because of the unexamined assumption that the modern way was better than the old one.

But not everyone was willing to let this happen. I spent part of a day in the hills high above the village of Pórtugos in the company of a man who had taken it upon himself to learn the old ways of restoring the *acequias*. When I met him Alex, from Manchester, was up to his waist in black water and surrounded by hundreds of wasps. "Don't worry, they won't sting you if you ignore them ... much," he called out as I approached. He was semi-immersed in a filthy old irrigation pool, scraping out the rotted leaves and black slime that had accumulated there over the years since the old landowner had died. Nearby, his colleague was digging away at a bank with a spade, clearing out debris.

Alex climbed out of the pond, pulling off his gloves and taking a swig of water from a bottle. "I'll tell you something," he said. "Those Moors knew a thing or two about irrigation, but there were thousands of them and there's only a couple of us." We looked around at the hillsides, which flowed away from us in every direction.

It was an impossibly large task Alex had taken on. He had given up his corporate life working for a multinational oil company ("I'm not going to say which one.") to crawl around in mud and filth and endure wasp stings. His motivation had come when he had seen a film called *El Canto del Agua* ('The Song of Water') that showed how the flora and fauna of the landscape was being threatened by the destruction of the old channels, and he wanted to do his bit to help out. Now, he did contract work restoring irrigation ponds and *acequias*, using traditional methods.

"You see that diagonal green line over there?" he asked, pointing at a distant hill. I could just make it out, a row of small trees or bushes forming part of a zigzag pattern against the yellow background. "Now look at that one over there," he said, directing my gaze to another hill. I tried to see what he was pointing at but couldn't. "Exactly," he said, "it's one that's been concreted in. All the trees have died, there's nothing left." I strained my eyes harder and eventually made out a faint trace line, yellow and brown and practically indistinguishable from the rest of the arid landscape.

It was a salutary lesson in how much this landscape had been changed by mankind, and how losing our understanding of it had had terrible consequences for the other life that lived there. I hoped others like Alex found the courage to step up and try to reverse some of the damage before it was too late.

- 52 -

Around lunchtime one autumnal day I was plastering a wall in a back room when Michelle put her head around the door and said I'd better take a look outside. I put the tools down and rubbed my hands on my overalls, acknowledging consciously something I'd been slowly growing aware of for some time, namely that it had become almost completely dark inside the house. The room I had been working in was windowless; nevertheless light would normally seep through from the kitchen, especially on a bright end-of-summer day like this. What was going on? I had a bad feeling about this.

I walked outside and went up onto a small outcrop above the house that afforded a clear view down the valley to the coast as far as the distant mountains on the border of Malaga Province. The sky had darkened and an eerie pall of silence had fallen across the land. Birds had ceased to sing and in the air there was an anticipatory sense that some sort of unusual act of nature was about to occur. It was a feeling I'd sensed only once before, in the seconds leading up to a solar eclipse. When I climbed up onto the outcrop and looked to the southwest the vision that greeted me was almost apocalyptic. A cloud, dense and threatening, had filled the horizon and obscured the mountains. It looked like something designed in a CGI suite for a disaster movie, and as it moved towards us it was spreading small forks of lightning like fingers feeling the ground.

But apart from the lightning and the density the most striking thing about the cloud was its colour: it was *dark green*. This had been the main thing most people remembered when they talked about it in the weeks that followed: it was the colour of slime dredged up from a stagnant pond, a dark sweating mouldy mass moving with incredible speed in our direction. Although I didn't know it at the time, what I was looking at was a freak tropical storm that had been blow off-course from the Caribbean and was now storming across the landmass of southern Spain. "Holy shit," I muttered.

"Shut the windows," I yelled, running back down to the house as raindrops the size of olives began to fall around me. The drops fell all around me, puckering the summer dust and sizzling on the hot car. As if I didn't know it already, the first crash of mountain-shaking thunder told me that we were in for one hell of a storm. The ground seemed to vibrate as the peal of thunder rumbled on; it sounded like boulders the size of hills crashing together in the ether above. I rushed around the house closing windows and doors, while Michelle dashed outside to rescue the washing and some of the kids' toys. The panicking cats came running in through the front door, tails as rigid as poles.

When the storm hit it was sudden and brutal. The lightning fingers had reached Cerro Negro, feeling out the power lines and the taller trees. Just before they disappeared in sheets of water, I could make out strikes on the Sierra de Lujar, and watched as a tree shone bright and then seemed to evaporate into smoke. And then the rain came. More powerful than anything I had ever before experienced, it hammered the house and caused such a racket I worried how the roof would cope with the onslaught. We stood there looking out of the door in awe, kids clinging onto our legs in fear. It wasn't long before a few drips began to land on us in the kitchen and then a sudden gush of water broke through the plaster in the ceiling. I rushed upstairs, and followed a swiftly flowing stream that was running through a bedroom, finding that it was coming in through one of the back walls directly below a terrace. There was nothing for it but to get outside with a mattock and try to divert the flow.

Once outside I was soaked through in a matter of seconds. I clambered up the muddy bank above the house, which itself had torrents of water gushing off it, and round the back of the building where a concreted gulley ran. I could see immediately that it was blocked by hundreds of desiccated oranges that had fallen from an overhanging tree and accumulated over the last couple of years. There was also a mass of twigs, olives and pomegranate husks, and all this debris had formed a dam which had caused the water to build thigh-deep against the back wall of the house. I leaped in, hacking at it with my mattock until I formed a breach for the water to gush out down the side of the house in a wave of bobbing oranges. As I leapt clear, with the crashing thunder, the rain and the strobes of lightning strikes flickering all around, I had the sudden chilling thought that the house itself could be in danger of being washed away. It had happened to old Gitte, a bit higher up the hill, and it could happen to us too. Just like hers, our house had no foundations and was sitting on top of the rapidly softening terraces that had been hacked out of the clay soil of the hillside.

Looking around it was impossible to imagine the sheer volume of water that was falling out of the sky and soaking into the terraces around me. The storm showed no signs of subsiding and I went back in again where Michelle, the girls and the cats were sitting in the kitchen and looking nervous. I expressed my fears about the house, yet it seemed doubtful that we would feel any safer if we rushed out into the tempest. But as we stood there dithering, the light level outside began to grow stronger and the racket made by the rain on the roof abruptly ceased. Tentatively, I went outside again, finding that only a light rain was falling. All around me were little silver rivulets of water streaming their way down the hillside. A beam of sunlight appeared from around the rapidly retreating clouds, and it seemed like the storm had ended just as suddenly as it had started. The cats yawned, stretched and padded outside to resume their sunbathing as if nothing had happened.

As the clouds cleared and the sun broke through, Technicolor vision was restored to the land, which now looked reborn with all the summer dust gone. Every leaf was polished and every rock glistened, while flowers sparkled fresh in the sunlight and the sky returned to its usual blue. But it wasn't just the dust that was gone, a quick inspection revealed that one of the larger olive trees, which had been growing out of the side of a bank a couple of terraces above the house, had come crashing down. And that wasn't the only tree; a huge eucalyptus next to the irrigation pond had also toppled in the tempest, pulping the unfortunate orange tree it fell on. Looking out across the valley and the sierras, the sides of the mountains were now veined with silver streams and waterfalls – something I had never seen before on these usually dry slopes. Of course, all the communications had been knocked out in the area, so there was no point phoning Jon in Ronda to find out if he wanted me to investigate the damage; I already knew what his answer would be. After a quick change into dry clothes I got in the car and went off to see just how bad the storm had been.

For a start, the track had been badly damaged, with deep fissures and rivulets having been opened up to expose large subsurface stones. Once I'd made it down the track onto the tarmac of the Tíjola road, things weren't much better. Large cactus plants and branches were strewn around and the small gulleys that were normally dry were now flowing full and fast and you needed a four-wheel drive to get through them. Órgiva, when I got to it, looked muddy and drenched but there didn't seem to be too much damage and the electricity had been restored after a brief outage. I stopped for a coffee and watched the rolling TV news in the bar. Reports were coming in of 'extensive damage' down at the coast, especially in Almuñécar, which had been particularly badly hit. I drained my cup and got back in the car. The damage was apparent everywhere as I drove down to the coast, but when I got near Almuñécar it became so bad I had to park up and walk the last mile or so.

Down there on the coast it was the same story with the riverbeds: dry ninety-nine point nine percent of the time, and raging torrents the rest of it. The noise was incredible as the water roared through them, bringing along tonnes of reeds and bamboo, as well as the occasional entire tree. The emergency services were everywhere and shocked-looking people milled around like extras in a disaster movie. As I got closer to the centre of Almuñécar I realised the streets through which I was walking had been underwater only a short time before. Parked cars were still draining out and entire streets were covered in mud, slime and debris. But it wasn't until I got down to the beach that I saw the most extensive damage. Two bridges had been washed away and, incongruously, the sea just off the beach was bobbing with cars. Some were floating upside down with their wheels spinning in the air, while others merely jutted out. Still more lay in various stages of destruction on the beach, some of them on top of one another like humping tortoises. Everywhere was covered in the shattered sticks of sugar cane, which farmers had been dumping in the river beds since the last time they had properly flowed some years before, as well as general garbage and thousands of plastic bags which stuck to lamp posts and plastered fences. People stared at all this destruction with their hands in their pockets. It was like a scene from the end of the world, and it had hit with no warning.

When I read the news about it after, I was relieved to find out that only one person had died during the terrifying deluge. A German expat had died when a wall in his garage had caved in on him, but it was incredible that the death toll wasn't higher. The head of the local government came down to inspect the area, and announced a rescue package to rebuild the damaged infrastructure. The rush of water coming down the Rio

Verde had caused most of the damage, as the river quickly became choked with debris and overflowed into recently developed areas. At the height of the storm some three hundred litres of rain had fallen on every square metre of land in the area – by far the highest level ever recorded – leaving underground car parks accessible only to those with SCUBA diving gear. It was left to the town's fifty or so itinerant Senegalese vendors to clean up the streets over the coming weeks, which they did without complaint.

Meteorologists later explained how the storm had formed in the tropics and how it had become supercharged as it moved into the Mediterranean and hit the Spanish landmass, suitably enough at the Costa Tropical. The hot atmospheric conditions had allowed the clouds to retain far more moisture than they normally would, leading to the unprecedented downpour. Over the following weeks the only ones to do well out of the disaster were the wreckers, who descended on the town offering people a pittance for flood-damaged cars, which were then stripped down and their parts sold on eBay. It seemed as if nature was giving us a wakeup call.

- 53 -

After much horse-trading over selling my shares in *The Olive Press* to Jon, a deal had been reached between all the parties. Jon drove a hard bargain, and so I didn't expect to come away with much compared to what I'd put in. Eventually the day came for us to formalise the sale. A meeting had been arranged at a notary office in the town of Antequera; an inland town situated almost exactly between Órgiva and Ronda. Antequera served as a kind of no-mans-land between the two *Olive Press* tribes as it was easily reachable for all.

It was a rainy winter day as Jon, Marcus and I sat in uneasy silence in the waiting room, watching the drops of water run down the windowpanes to the street outside. A woman sat typing behind a desk and generally ignored us as we waited. Given that he had no transport of his own, I'd had to give Marcus a lift there. Once we had exhausted all small talk in the first few minutes, the rest of the journey had passed in silence.

Carlos, Jon's lawyer, sat hunched over the coffee table between us, examining the contract. Every now and again he would mark something down with a biro and have a brief, explosive, discussion with the notary who was in another office behind a glass wall. Eventually, after what seemed like a long time, we were all summoned to a small cubicle office and the contract was read out to us. The process of washing my hands of *The Olive Press* took barely five minutes, and I watched as my name was erased from the company *escritura* and replaced with Jon's. When everything was signed and the business of the day concluded we went out onto the street. There was a café bar right there but nobody felt much in the mood for marking the occasion. "Gotta shoot, chaps," said Jon, as his lawyer's BMW pulled up against the curb. "There's a great restaurant here that I'm taking Carlos to for lunch. It'll feature in my dining secrets guide when it comes out. Catch you later."

Jon jumped in the car and closed the door. The BMW pulled out and joined the traffic streaming out of town, leaving Marcus and I standing on the pavement. Marcus was no doubt glad to have excised me from the company deeds, but now had to contend with being in partnership with someone else he didn't get along with. Jon had already established another firm using his middle names –

Luke Stewart Media – and he had an agreement that allowed him to print *The Olive Press* under its original title. It was a clever move, meaning the balance of power had now shifted to him.

"I'd better hurry if I'm to make the train," said Marcus. Now that he had done his job signing the contract there was no need for me to offer him a lift back – a lift he likely wouldn't have accepted in any case. "See ya," he said, and I watched as he strode off, a hunched figure wearing a denim jacket merging with the people scurrying along with their umbrellas in the rain.

The money I had got from Jon wasn't a huge amount, but it would give us some breathing space for a while. I was frustrated because I now felt like I had enough experience to start a new newspaper, but it would need to be somewhere fresh. I didn't want to go elsewhere as I loved living in La Alpujarra, nevertheless the thought refused to die and I started to entertain ideas of starting up another newspaper. I would do it *properly* this time, I promised myself.

I looked at a map of Spain and wondered if there was somewhere else that a newspaper like *The Olive Press* might flourish. Catalonia seemed a likely place, but since my visit to Barcelona I'd not felt like going back there for some reason. Galicia and Asturias in the north were also appealing, but there weren't many foreigners living there so demand would be limited. Another option was the Balearic Islands, with Mallorca being the biggest and most populous and therefore a likely base. I had been to Ibiza before and loved its sense of austere antiquity and its hippyish vibe, but I'd never been to Mallorca. Clearly a scouting mission would be in order.

"Do it," said Jon, when I put the idea to him. "It'd be excellent to have another edition of *The Olive Press* up there."

At the time I was reading *The White Goddess* by the English writer Robert Graves. He had moved to Mallorca after the Second World War, living there until his death in 1985. Apart from checking out the island I wanted to spend some time in the northern village of Deia, where Graves had lived. This would form the basis of another episode in the *Writers of Spain* series, which I hoped Jon would publish.

A few days later I was picking up the keys for a hire car in Palma de Mallorca. I put it into gear and headed off on a weeklong island excursion. Mallorca was, unquestionably, one of the most beautiful places I had ever been to. Most of the island was a natural paradise dotted with charming towns and villages surrounded by mountains and verdant green forests. I drove all over, basing myself in Soller, on the north coast, but heading out every morning to explore a different part of the island.

I spent time in Deia, where Robert Graves had lived, visiting the local beaches and olive groves and generally trying to get a feel for how life would have been for him when he lived there. His house had been turned over to a museum, and his writing desk was still in place, while Graves himself was buried beneath a cypress tree next to the church.

I loved Mallorca, but I couldn't see how I could make a newspaper there unless I was already based there. Furthermore, from what I could make out, the foreign population were either wealthy enough to live on yachts or in huge houses behind security gates, or else they resided in places like Magaluf and already had their needs serviced by established newspapers. Most expats there were German-speaking, and the price of property was eye-wateringly high. I simply couldn't afford to live in Mallorca, and so that put an end to any idea of moving there.

I came back to Órgiva feeling deflated and met up with my friend Dan in a bar. Dan, *The Olive Press* web page guru, was an aficionado of Mallorca and had even got married to his wife Jo there. Indeed, he was only living in Órgiva because Mallorca was too expensive a place to buy a house and he felt he had to live *somewhere* in Spain. Over the course of several beers we figured that with his IT skills and my newspaper experience we could launch a new online site in Mallorca that could be run from afar. The more beer I drank, the more my previously strong reservations about the paradise island seemed to evaporate. We were still sitting at the bar in the early hours of the morning, drunkenly discussing the patently silly idea of running a remote-controlled newspaper in Mallorca when one of the local youths, who had been playing pool with his friends nearby, sidled up to us as he ordered another drink. "Did I hear you say Mallorca?" he asked in English. This surprised me because I had thought him to be Spanish. "Hey, I know who you two are," he continued. "You're those newspaper dudes, right?"

"Yes," I said, "and who are you?"

"My name's Liam," he said. "My grandfather used to live in Mallorca. He was a writer, lots of people have heard of him."

"Don't tell me..." I said.

"Yes, Robert Graves."

I almost fell of my barstool. Perhaps I shouldn't have been so surprised, these kind of remarkable coincidences always seemed to happen in Órgiva.

"My dad grew up in Mallorca but moved here later. He's still got a lot of my granddad's books." He took a swig of his beer, bellowed something in Spanish to his mates, and went back to playing pool.

"That's amazing," I said to Dan. "The grandson of Robert Graves here in Órgiva. Who'd have thought it?"

Dan thought about this for a while, his beery eyes seemingly contemplating this remarkable synchronicity. "Robert who?" he replied. "Never heard of him."

Incidentally, Dan and I *did* end up starting a remote controlled newspaper in Mallorca that we named *The Mallorca* (it was supposed to rhyme with *The New Yorker*), but it wasn't until a few years later. And, yes, it did turn out to be a silly idea that we should have left in the bar.

- 54 -

The building work with Leon had begun to dry up and everyone seemed to be concerned about money. I had managed to convince a travel magazine to accept an article an article about the Sacramento gypsy quarter of Granada, accompanied by photographs, and so I boarded a bus to the city one morning in order to do some research. It was still dark when the first bus pulled away and the only other passengers were people who clearly had to make this gruelling pre-dawn journey every day to get to their jobs. They looked as tired as I felt. It wasn't until we were past Órgiva and heading towards Lanjarón that one of the passengers stood up and began to make his way to the front of the bus, which wasn't an easy task given the sharp bends. He was a man, beyond middle age and a bit tubby, wearing a tired-looking baseball cap and moving unsteadily. I recognised him before he had even turned around: it was Paul McGwin, the American writer who had been supplying scattily written articles for the paper since the first issue. I had only ever met him once – that long ago day up in Bubión where he had given me the crushing handshake – but we had communicated often enough by email when he would send me his copy, occasionally on time.

Paul stood at the front of the bus, steadying himself with a hand on the seatbacks either side of the aisle. After clearing his throat he announced in a shaky voice that this was the end of a long foray into the mountains of Spain. He was blessed, he said, to have spent so long where the poet Federico García Lorca – his 'guiding light' – had called home, but that now it was time for him to make his way to other lands.

The passengers were either impervious to the American, or else remained asleep and I saw the driver's eye seeking him out in the rear-view as if pinpointing a troublemaker. This didn't seem to bother the erstwhile *Olive Press* cultural contributor, who ignored the fact that he was being ignored, and continued with his soliloquy. A lengthy farewell to the people of Andalucía ensued, his American drawl peppered at random with whatever Spanish words he had picked up. He spoke of the murmuring streams and lusty fruit trees of La Alpujarra and how the region had drawn him in and spoken to his soul. His time there, he said, had now come to an end, and he felt he must now make his way to Iraq. I wondered if I had heard that last bit right, but figured he must have his reasons. Though he could have been drunk, he seemed genuinely upset and there were tears in his eyes as he concluded his thanks and made his way back down the aisle to his seat. Shamefully, I pulled down the visor of the cap I was wearing and avoided eye contact with him. There was another hour to go on the journey and I didn't want to spend it with an intoxicated American weeping on my shoulder.

We continued the journey in silence until we got to Granada and the last I saw of Paul McGwin was his figure, weighed down with a rucksack and several pieces of hand luggage, as he slipped away into the crowds waiting for the morning buses to Madrid. After he had gone I remembered that he had been writing a book about his life travelling around Europe and San Francisco in the 1960s, and how he had told me in an email that he had 'sweated blood' to write it. Although I barely knew him it somehow felt like a terrible shame that he had departed and yet perhaps he was just one more soul passing through La Alpujarra, stopping a while for soul sustenance like a bee moving from flower to flower.

Perhaps Paul's departure was a harbinger that things were about to change. Another occurred a few weeks later as I was driving back from Órgiva one Friday evening and a black cat ran out from behind an olive tree. There was no time to react and he darted straight under one of the wheels. As far as omens go, that one was unmistakeable.

That weekend the weather was strange and there was a weird feeling in the air. A strong wind blew ceaselessly, causing the doors in our house to slam violently and dust devils to whip across the riverbed in the valley below. The skies were filled with the kind of strange UFO-like lenticular clouds that are caused by pressurised air bouncing off the mountaintops. They hovered there, stationary in the clear blue winter air, and caused people to huddle indoors and remark that no good ever came of them. They were not wrong.

On the Monday morning I met Leon and Jim as usual in a café in town for breakfast. We were working on building an extension to a Swiss woman's house on the outskirts of Órgiva, making the most of the fact that we didn't have to drive down to the coast. In fact, the big job we had been working on, like many projects, was paused as the clients tried to secure more funding. "Terrible thing with that kid at the weekend, wasn't it," said Leon, oiling up a *tostada*. I didn't know what he was talking about. "It happened up near your place," he continued. "Little girl fell in an irrigation pond and drowned."

My mind raced to figure out who it might have been. "I think the parents were called John and Lucy," he continued, taking a sip of coffee. "Apparently it happened in an instant, both of them thought she was with the other."

It was true; the unthinkable had happened and their daughter Molly – a playmate of our daughter Sofia – had wandered off their property and into a neighbour's. There, she had fallen into two feet of dirty rainwater that had collected in an irrigation pond. When the paramedics arrived it was already too late.

Molly's death, and the pain suffered by her parents, sent a shock wave through the community. Parents forbade their children from going near ponds, and fences were erected around properties where before there had been none. Molly's parents were distraught, their lives in ruins. The funeral took place in the church in Órgiva. Outside it, people queued to pass on their condolences to the parents. Órgiva became a ghost town, and all became quiet. It seemed so unfair. Only a couple of months before, we had gathered in the bar opposite the same church with John and Lucy as the clock struck midnight, ringing in 2008. We had clinked glasses and followed the Spanish custom of downing the compulsory twelve grapes in twelve seconds, and hoped for a happy 2008 as our tired and groggy children clung onto us. Molly, not even two years old, had slept peacefully on Lucy's lap.

Now, two months later, the church was full and I doubted the priest had ever had such a mixed congregation. At the end of the service Molly's playmates, including my own daughters, gathered in the transept to sing a final lullaby – *Twinkle Twinkle Little Star* – to the little velvet-clad urn filled with the ashes of their friend. There was not a dry eye in the church. Molly's death had come as a terrible blow, but it did prove one thing; Órgiva was a community, regardless of where you came from.

Elsewhere across Andalucía, a different form of trouble was brewing. Estate agents were reporting fewer people turning up to buy houses, and half of those who did were merely time-wasters harbouring a dream but with no intention of buying. Seeing as the sale of houses was the engine that drove the rest of the expat economy there was a corresponding fall in the amount of work and money available for those who depended on it. At the newspaper, Rick reported that advertisers were harder to come by, and even some long-term clients were trying to back out of their contracts. Others simply didn't pay, and all attempts to reach them proved fruitless.

To that end, Rick had hired a debt collector to help wrangle money out of advertisers. But with valuable time being taken up chasing non-payers, and against a backdrop of faltering sales, *The Olive Press* was starting to struggle again. Internal wrangling was also taking its toll, and Jon said they were locked in an endless round of meetings. At issue was Jon's insistence that he should have editorial equality with Marcus, while he also wanted to be paid a monthly salary. Marcus was digging his heels in over this and relations between the two plummeted further.

Despite the woes of the Órgiva newspaper, Jon's version of *The Olive Press* was going from strength to strength over in Ronda. He was working hard at boosting the distribution network and bringing in paying advertisers and with each new issue the schism between the two versions became more apparent. Jon's strategy of appeasing his readership and coming up with original news content appeared to be paying dividends.

Another twist that didn't help the Órgiva version of the newspaper was that, following a corruption clampdown, there was a new appetite for stamping out illegal building and imprisoning crooked mayors. Unfortunately, many of the illegal buildings that had mushroomed across the province were now occupied by bewildered expat retirees who couldn't see how their property could be judged 'illegal' given that it had all the correct paperwork. The Junta didn't care about their concerns and decided to put on a show of strength, bringing in the bulldozers to raze some of these homes while their owners looked on in horror. Sensing an opportunity, Jon immediately switched the focus of *his* newspaper to report on their plight, demanding an end to the demolitions. Thus, two versions of the same newspaper began not only to campaign *for* the demolition of illegal properties, such as the hideous El Agorrobico hotel built in the Cabo de Gata natural park, but also *against* the demolition of illegal buildings housing British expats. The casual observer could be forgiven for thinking the paper was sounding a bit hypocritical. One critic opined that *The Olive Press* was 'like Frankenstein's monster,' that is, thrown together in a crude manner, possessing a green skin, and out of control.

"It's called compromising your principles," said Vernon, the TV producer, when I met him for a drink. "And having a go at Ryanair, like last week's paper did, was way out of order. It's companies like Ryanair that butter *The Olive Press's* bread," he said, taking a sip of beer.

Vernon was talking about an article criticising the low cost Irish airline for cutting its service to Granada Airport. There had been a number of furious letters from Britons who had bought holiday properties near the airport and now had no way of getting to them at weekends. One woman even said she commuted from Granada to an office job in London and felt that her life had been 'ruined' by the budget airline's strategic decision to pull out of a route that often saw mostly-empty planes shuttling back and forth.

Walking through town one day I noticed that the estate agent where I had worked so briefly had closed its door and the pictures of houses were no longer in the window. Nobody seemed to know where Mel had disappeared to, along with his daughter Emma and wife Nikki, but it was hardly surprising seeing as *The Olive Press* had poached nearly all of their staff. They weren't the only estate agents to suddenly pack up and leave, and other windows were similarly empty.

The bank had changed its manager too. Gone was the friendly man who signed our mortgage and took three-hour long trout lunches at the campsite. In his place was a much less jovial man with a furrowed brow and a look that said 'don't mess'. Letters started to land on people's doormats telling them the cost of borrowing was going up and their mortgages would be adjusted accordingly. Within a few short months, in fact, our mortgage repayments had almost doubled. Michelle and I became increasingly worried about how we would be able to pay the bank while, at the same time, the amount of work being offered to Leon and his crew of builders fell off a cliff.

When things begin to fall apart they usually do so quite quickly, I discovered. It was the Roman philosopher Seneca who noted, *"The path of increase is slow, but the road to ruin is rapid."* Around La Alpujarra, people who had been there for years seemed to suddenly fall into holes they couldn't get out of. Many of them were there one minute and gone the next. Talk in the coffee shops of Órgiva always seemed to be, "Did you know that so-and-so has left?" In the expat bubble people were discovering that when the money stops flowing there were very few options to find a new source of income. Many had buckled when interest rates had been hiked and stories began to circulate of people dropping their house keys through the letterboxes of banks on their way to the airport.

- 55 -

One day I bumped into John '*The Amputee*' Yates in town and he announced in his laconic way that he had quit writing his column as he was about to set sail across the Indian Ocean. Thinking that he might be winding me up, I enquired as to why he was going on such an epic journey. He explained that there was a yacht that belonged to a moneyed contact living down on the coast, and that it needed a new wooden deck. Only the best teak would do for this man's prized vessel and this could only be got in Burma. The plan, John explained, was to set off from Almería, sail through the Suez Canal and Red Sea, and then head out across the Indian Ocean, rounding Sri Lanka before heading up into Bay of Bengal and onto Burma. And then back again. The voyage was expected to take several months, depending on the trade winds.

"Do you think you'll actually make it there?" I asked.

"Oh yes," he replied "but I'm going to need a crew. Do you know anyone? Paid, of course." I thought about it and said I might. Paul, an English builder who'd been doing some plastering work for us, had said he liked boats and was into adventures. What's more, he was looking for work and had recently asked me if I knew of any. I hooked the two of them up.

A few days later I saw the writer Chris Stewart who seemed concerned about John's escapade. Chris himself was no stranger to perilous ocean-crossing voyages and would later write a book detailing several near lethal misses (*Three Ways to Capsize a Boat*), so he probably knew what would be in store for our Antipodean seafaring friend. But he wasn't just concerned for the safety of all on board. "It all sounds a bit ... unethical, don't you think?" he said. "I mean, sailing off to a dictatorship to strip its rainforests of hardwood timber." I agreed that the whole affair sounded a bit dodgy.

Alas, Chris's worries about the seaworthiness of the vessel and John's sailing skills proved well founded. A couple of weeks later I bumped into Paul in the street in Órgiva. Seeing as he was supposed to be crewing a yacht and heading through the Suez Canal right about then I was quite taken aback to see him. He looked ashen and shaky and when he saw me he gave me a look not unlike how a buzzard might look at a vole. For a moment I actually thought he was going to lunge at me and I began to back away nervously. "What's up?" I asked him. His eyes were bulging and he looked angry. "Why aren't you...?"

Paul let out a strangled string of expletives, and I caught John's name repeated amongst them. "Calm down," I said, and offered to get him a coffee so he could tell me the whole story. When we sat down he told me the sorry tale of what had transpired. It wasn't a pleasant story. It started with John, Paul and another crewman departing from Almería a few days before. They had done so against all advice from nautically competent people, setting sail into the teeth of an approaching storm. They were almost immediately in trouble, with the expensive yacht taking on water as the crew lost control just hours out of port. It came as little surprise to hear that the story ended with them all being rescued by the coastguard less than a day later, with their vessel almost sunk, but not before the three wannabe sailors had almost killed one another in a blazing row over whether any of them could actually sail a boat. John, Paul claimed, had ended up barricading himself in the cabin as the vessel lurched around on the broiling sea with a powerful storm raging around them, screaming into the radio and begging to be rescued. "You didn't tell me he didn't know how to sail!" said Paul.

But the good thing was that they'd all come back alive, if a little shaken by the experience, with all three of them vowing never to step off dry land again as long as they lived. What's more, a few trees in the Burmese rainforest probably escaped being cut down.

- 56 -

As the economic mood soured, and with carnage spreading through the Spanish property sector, there were reports of expats who had lost all their money. Numerous investments had been revealed to be no more than scams and Ponzi-schemes, leaving people looking for someone to blame. Many of them had invested in 'off-plan' property developments – that is, they had bought nothing more than images of blueprints on architects' computer screens – in some cases sinking their life savings into projects. Only a few months before it had seemed as if the prices of property in Spain would go on rising forever, but of course, the music had to stop at some point.

During the first half of the Noughties, buying a property off-plan might have represented a sound investment, providing it was sold again before the music stopped. A bar owner in Estepona had told me how she had purchased two off-plan properties on one hundred percent mortgages, and had sold both of them before the first barrow of concrete had been poured, netting a cool hundred thousand in profit. "If you're brave, you can't fail to make money," she had said. Bubble mania had gripped the expat population of Spain and it was the seemingly impossible magicking-up of fortunes out of thin air that had people gravitating towards Spain with euro signs imprinted on their eyeballs. But, inevitably, when the bubble did burst, those who were caught out tended to lose everything.

Jon gave me the whole story about a man who sent Marcus an email one day, telling him he was an investor in a controversial development of holiday flats built next to a tiny hamlet at the eastern end of La Alpujarra. The man claimed to have paid three hundred thousand euros for seven luxury apartments after he saw an investment advert in a UK newspaper. Desperate to secure the apartments, which he intended to sell as soon as they were built, he sold his London home to raise the necessary capital. But when the completion date came and went, the holiday complex was still little more than an abandoned concrete shell on the side of a hill. There was no electricity, water or sewerage connected, and no sign of any builders, or indeed the investment company or the man's money. Clearly distraught about his bad fortune the broken man informed Marcus in measured tones that he was planning 'something spectacular' and invited him come and bear witness. "Bring your camera," he had said, ominously.

A meeting time was established at high noon on a Monday at the abandoned complex and Molly duly drove Marcus to within walking distance. The disgruntled man had warned him to come alone. Marcus walked nervously towards the scene, seemingly the only person around in the huge empty landscape. When he got to the dismal half-built eyesore, surrounded as it was by discarded trash and broken glass, the man revealed himself to Marcus from behind a half-built wall. The first thing Marcus noticed about him was that he was wearing a cardboard box on his head, on which he had painted an angry face with an upside-down mouth. In addition to the cardboard head, a vacuum cleaner tube was affixed to the man's groin region with duct tape, seemingly to allow him to urinate without moving his arms which, Marcus noticed, appeared to be covered in fake blood from two slits in the wrists. It was clear that he had put a lot of thought into the encounter.

"On Wednesday I will kill myself," declared the defrauded Englishman, holding aloft two placards scrawled with a suicide note in both English and Spanish.

"Umm," said Marcus "how are you going to do that?"

The property investor explained that he would remain at the site of his broken dreams and starve himself to death. The only way this could be prevented was if the developers turned up and gave him his cash back, adding that if he hadn't heard anything by Wednesday he would take an overdose of pills to end his life. A blanket hung from a fence behind him on which the man had written instructions about how to deal with his corpse, including a warning to parents to keep their children away from it.

Another blanket implored that anyone who found him in a semi-alive state to "Beat me. Finish me". The 'slit wrists' it seemed, were just for show, and the 'blood' was merely red paint.

I only got to hear about all of this second-hand through Jon, who had been very keen to meet up with the man but was too far away at the time. Instead, Marcus had had to go, and the two of them talked for some time, with the penniless investor airing his grievances. When the man had nothing more to add, Marcus wished him a good day and went back to find Molly.

By the time they got back to Órgiva, having perhaps considered that the man's life lay in his hands, Marcus had entered something like a state of shock. But he didn't have too long to think about it because the man called him almost immediately, saying that due to a lack of local interest in his plight he had decided to bring forward his appointment with death and was intending to end his life the next morning in the manner discussed. Marcus called the police and told them the whole story. When he had given the officer a description of the man he had gone silent for a moment and asked him to repeat it before asking him if this wasn't some kind of joke. Marcus explained how the man looked like a blood-spattered pound-store Cyberman with a vacuum cleaner taped onto his penis, and that he'd given a lot of money to shady investors in some kind of semi-illegal scheme.

The policeman on the other end didn't sound overly keen on getting involved with this sort of thing, but they were duty bound to check it out and gave a promise to do so, leaving Marcus to a sleepless night thinking about the man with a box on his head standing on the side of a hill with a bottle full of pills. The next morning the police called to say that they'd been to have a look but could find no trace of the man. Marcus feared the worst, but shortly before ten o'clock – the time the man had said he would 'do it' – he received a text message stating "I saw the police."

Later on still, the man phoned Marcus again, rambling and confused, saying he was at a public phone in a town whose name he couldn't pronounce. Marcus figured it must be Ugíjar, as that was the nearest unpronounceable town, and persuaded the police to go and pick him up, keeping the man on the line to try and talk him out of killing himself. The situation was eventually defused and the man was picked up. The police took him in for questioning and, after he had calmed down he agreed to return to his family in Essex.

There must have been many more expats left out of pocket and in a similar position, but not many of them could have expressed their dissatisfaction with the Spanish property investment sector in such a dramatic manner. "Nice work," said Jon on the phone to Marcus later. "*The Sun* can have this one."

- 57 -

By the late summer of 2008 Spain was gearing up to full crisis mode. My erstwhile companions at *The Olive Press* were still paying me to shift newspapers down along the coastal routes and sometimes in Granada City, but I got radio silence whenever I offered to write anything for them. I was offered a few days' work here and there mixing cement on a renovation site down in Tablones for a local builder, but this dribble of income meant the financial thumbscrews were tightening. The funds I had got from Jon for selling my share of *The Olive Press* had tided us over for a while but now they were beginning to run out.

I figured that I must be able to make some money online and my investigations led me to editing and proofreading. I'd already tried to sell a few travel articles about Spain to various newspapers and magazines, and had some very limited success, but somehow the eventual payment one received was dwarfed by the effort required to research and write the piece. Proofreading was similarly poorly paid but editing work was something of a niche skill and it was being said that publishing houses were looking to outsource much of the work to qualified individuals, albeit at much lower rates that would be paid to their in house staff. This suited me fine, however, as those lower rates would still allow us to live in southern Spain where costs of living were low. And so, with some of our last money, I decided to do a course in editing.

The course lasted a week and was held at Imperial College in London. There were about thirty people studying for the qualification, which was being taught by a couple of old-school editors in an old fashioned style. They would have nothing to do with computers and insisted we learned the arcane symbols used in a profession that was rapidly going out of style.

Back at home I soon got a job editing and writing a foreword for a dictionary of Spanish building terms, which would hopefully be of great use to Brits wanting to renovate their foreign holiday homes. I started it, but soon got bogged down in the text. Spain being such a diverse place with several sub-dialects meant that building terms could differ substantially from one region to the next. My experience only stretched so far as Andalucía so, for example, I had no idea what a *machihembredo* was called in Galicia or Catalonia. They published it anyway.

After this, what looked to be an extraordinary opportunity presented itself. It would be a dream job by anyone's standards and I could scarcely believe my luck. I was sitting in the driving seat of my now rather battered Mitsubishi Pajero in a builders' yard next to the electricity substation on the outskirts of Órgiva at the time. Covered in dust and sweating profusely in the heat I was doing a job for Leon at a local villa and had agreed to pick up a load of gravel in my trailer. A man in a small dumper was loading the gravel into the trailer, causing the car to rattle alarmingly and sink further on its suspension springs with each load he piled in. My phone rang and I flipped the case open with a grimy, cement-covered hand. It was the call I had been waiting for.

There was a guidebook of unique places to stay in Europe and beyond. Specialising not in luxury hotels – which anyone with a sum of money could build – the types of places covered in the guides had to stand out from the crowd. They had to have been inspired by the vision of their creator and were often one part grandiose refinement and two parts idiosyncratic quirkiness. For some reason the editor of the Spanish version of the guide had left and they were seeking a new one. The interview lasted about twenty minutes and I had to deal with paying the gravel merchant for the materials as I was attempting to describe down the phone why I was the right person for the job. As part of the posting, it was explained, I would need to embark on a grand tour of Spain and stay in every one of their two hundred or so hotels and make sure all the details were up to date. Alongside this, I'd likely have to venture into the nooks and crannies of Spain that other guidebooks didn't reach. Although the pay wasn't great the job sounded amazing and it would throw us a lifeline. The interview went well and fancied I was in with a good chance. The interviewer said as much there and then, given that there was nobody else lined up.

I dropped the gravel off with Leon and raced back to Los Pechos to tell Michelle about the job. I was brimming with excitement – finally, at the last minute and with our funds hovering close to zero, it seemed like we were about to be saved.

But when I got there Michelle was in a state of upset. Our financial situation had become too precarious for her to bear any longer, and her mother had sent her some money to fly back to Denmark and bring the kids with her. I was devastated.

Within a week they were gone and I was alone in a large half-finished farmhouse with only three cats for company.

- 58 -

In September it was being reported on the news that two large banks in America had collapsed, sparking off a full-blown global economic crisis. I wasn't the only one in dire straits. The financial crisis in Spain was getting worse and there was almost no work to be had anywhere. Leon, with his wife Rebecca and their two children (baby Inca had just been born) had been particularly badly hit and were now struggling to find enough money to live. As Leon had helped me out with a job in my hour of need, I wanted to return the favour and asked them if they wanted to move into Los Pechos with me. At least they would be able to grow food, and there was plenty of space. By way of rent, Leon could do some building work whenever he had the time, assuming we had materials.

I moved into one of the small bedrooms at the back and continued in my efforts to pick up bits of work wherever I could find them. I knew that if I got the travel guide job, which I felt had practically been promised to me, I would need some sort of vehicle to live in while I was on the road. To finance this I sold the Mitsubishi and looked at campers for sale in the UK, where vehicles are far cheaper. I soon found one located in Devon, and made an offer on it.

Once again I found myself travelling to England out of necessity. I flew to Gatwick and took the train to Exeter having arranged to meet the seller of an old but apparently functional left-hand-drive VW camper van in a pub in the city centre. I waited for an hour but there was no sign of him. I rang him, and when he found out I was waiting he said, "Oh, sorry mate, I didn't think you'd actually turn up." When he eventually arrived I could immediately see he was a wide boy wheeler-dealer. I didn't trust him one bit.

He drove me to an industrial unit beside the M5 motorway and showed me the camper. On the way we stopped off at his house so he could pick something up and I made a note of his address in case I needed to trace him. The van was in a worse condition than he'd implied previously, but at least it went and I had to make the ferry from Portsmouth to Santander the next evening so was keen to get away. I took it for a test drive, money changed hands and I drove off towards the motorway, happy at least to get away from the foul character. And that's when my troubles really started.

Driving it round a roundabout onto the motorway ramp, there was a sudden clunk and I felt the transmission go. I managed to steer it over to the side but it was still blocking the flow of traffic, which was getting heavy as rush hour approached. It began to rain heavily and all I could do was put on the hazard lights and peer underneath the van for signs of obvious mechanical dysfunction. I rang the vendor several times and he eventually answered. "What do you want?" he said. I told him I'd only been driving it for two minutes before it broke down, and now I was stuck. "It's a done deal, mate, not my problem," he said, and hung up.

The police arrived and asked me to move the van, which was causing a tailback. In fact, if I didn't move it in twenty minutes it would be towed away and I'd be billed. I rang the vendor again and told him I had the police with me and that I'd be giving them his details if he didn't come and help me, saying that I had his name and address. Within minutes he had reappeared, now with a surly mechanic who dived underneath the vehicle with a set of spanners while the police watched us from their patrol car. The hellish situation of annoyed drivers, heavy rain and the police breathing down my neck took a turn for the worse when the mechanic rounded on the dealer, shouting "I told you it was fucked and dangerous to drive but you never listen to me do you?" He then turned to me and said, "Don't drive this, mate. It's a death trap."

The police came over again to see what all the fuss was and an angry encounter ensued, with me demanding a refund and the vendor trying to placate both the mechanic and me while the police decided whether to book anyone. After a short while the vendor handed me back half of my money and made out a cheque for the balance (which, of course, bounced). The police told us all to get lost and so I decided to cut my losses and leave the ugly situation behind. I started walking back along the main road to Exeter in the rain.

It took me at least an hour to get to the city centre and by the time I got there I was soaked through and felt thoroughly depressed. I sat in a café and ordered a pot of tea and scones while I looked at other vehicles for sale on the Internet. I was damned if I was going to go back to Spain without something that would enable me to do the job that might save us. There was a dealership on the outskirts of north London and, when I called them, they said they had a couple of left-hand-drive campers for sale. I told them I'd be there the next morning to take one of them. The next train to London wasn't until about nine o'clock in the evening but I got on it anyway and settled back into my seat. However, my problems weren't over yet and the train ground to a halt at Salisbury. After quite a long period of immobility there was an announcement to the effect that the heavy rains had caused problems with the track and the train would be terminating there.

I got off and wondered what to do. Salisbury seemed completely dead at that time of night. I wandered towards the centre, drawn towards the immense cathedral that was lit up like a beacon in the night. Where was I going to stay? I had no idea. The hotels I walked past looked far too fancy for my limited budget, and so booking somewhere to stay online seemed like the only option open to me if I didn't want to sleep rough. I managed to find a site on my phone, which had basic Internet functionality. The address was Salisbury, but I didn't know the city at all so I sought out a taxi and asked the driver to take me there. "Are you sure?" he asked when I gave him the name of the cheap hotel. Yes, I was sure, I said.

It was about a twenty-minute ride and we headed not into the city but away from it, pulling up somewhere in the countryside at a building that would be called a motel in America. I paid the driver and arranged for someone to bring me back to the train station the following morning. I then checked in and was relieved to collapse blissfully onto a bed covered in starched white sheets. I fell asleep almost instantly, but not before noticing two things: the room was kitted out with orthopaedic equipment, and there was a huge faded picture of Stonehenge at the end of the bed.

The next morning I pushed some bacon and eggs around on a greasy plate in the dining room as my fellow guests and diners sat in silence. One or two were measuring out pills from dispensers and a husky voiced old American lady was berating her downcast husband in a half-whispered growl. I polished off the food, drank some bitter-tasting instant coffee and looked at my phone. According to the map I was only about two miles from one of Britain's most sacred ancient sites. I had never seen Stonehenge except in pictures and I had an hour or so before the taxi was due to pick me up again.

Jogging along the main road in the grey morning light towards a stone circle, bacon and eggs sloshing around in my tummy as commuters whizzed past me wasn't an average kind of morning for me, but then again I felt as if my life had taken a turn for the bizarre of late. A heavy drizzle was falling, making my clothes wet and misting my glasses, but at least it was invigorating. At a certain point I rounded a bend and the stones came into view in the middle distance. I stopped and looked at my watch. There probably wouldn't be enough time for me to jog all the way to them so I ducked into a field off the main road and gave myself five minutes to simply look at them from afar.

They weren't as big as I'd expected, but then again I was probably half a mile away standing in a windswept field in the rain, so perhaps the perspective was distorted. Despite the cars and vans flying past along the A303, the landscape nevertheless seemed to hold onto a sense of timelessness. The fields and hills were rounded and bare with almost no trees, giving the sense that the stones were poking out of the hard earth like the teeth of a skull.

The scene was strangely alluring in a way I couldn't put my finger on, as though this landscape was both unfamiliar and familiar at the same time. As I stood and stared, I regained my breath and felt a sense of being grounded. Half walking, half jogging I made my way back along the busy road so as to be in time for my taxi pickup. I wasn't sure why, but it felt as if events had somehow conspired to bring me to this unlikely spot on my unplanned journey.

Back on the train again and heading east I arrived in London at around lunchtime and made my way out to the northern suburbs to locate the next car dealer. When I found what I was looking for it turned out to be a trio of Pakistani brothers with a used car lot in a shabby industrial estate. I asked to see the camper van I'd spoken to them about the day before but they said, unfortunately, it had 'gone missing' and must have been a computer error. This was getting very frustrating – surely there must be at least one left-hand-drive camper van somewhere in Britain? "Loads mate," said the dealer, "but they get snapped up by the Aussies touring Europe. You'll have to go down to Kings Cross on a Sunday to find one, but it won't be cheap."

I asked him if he had any left hand drive vehicles, and he said he had one. It was a little Renault Twingo that had sat out the back for the past year. I went and had a look. The tiny French car was pretty much the opposite of a camper van, but at least the steering wheel was on the correct side so I would be able to import it onto Spanish plates without too much of a problem. I could buy a tent and, that way, I'd still be able to carry out my mission travelling around Spain and writing the guidebook. The only slight problem was that the car reeked of cigarettes. Not just that but the ashtray was overflowing with butts and there were even some of them in a glass balanced on the dashboard. My bearded friend looked bashful "Sorry pal, this car's been the office smoking room for the past year. I'd have got it cleaned up if I knew you were coming."

Two hours later I was whizzing along the M25 in the direction of Portsmouth in my nippy little French car. It had been given an MOT in record-breaking time, and the dealer had hung a lemon-scented air freshener on the rear-view mirror. I had only a couple of hours to make the Santander ferry, and I didn't mean to miss it. When I got there, with only minutes to spare, the man at the docks scrutinised my ticket, noticing that it was for a camper van and not a car. "So what," I smiled "a car's smaller." He sighed and muttered something about protocol but there was a line of drivers behind me so he just waved me on board.

The sailing down to Spain's north coast took a night and a day. I spent most of it sitting on the deck looking out for whales in the Bay of Biscay and reflecting on how my life seemed to be spinning out of control. I wondered what, if anything, I could do anything to salvage our Spanish dream. I hadn't managed to get a camper van, but at least I now had a set of economical wheels to get me around Spain, and this would allow me to earn some money. Nevertheless, I couldn't shake the feeling that I was hanging on by my fingertips, and that my increasingly fragile situation could be cut short at any minute.

When I eventually arrived back in Órgiva, having driven right down through Spain, Leon and Rebecca said they had run out of money and needed to find ways of getting food quickly. To that end they had decided to get chickens. This sounded like a great idea to me and I'd always wanted to have chickens roaming around the garden. This way we could have fresh eggs on a daily basis for no cost.

First, though, we had to build a chicken coop and we only had a budget of around twenty euros to do so. To that end, Leon, Jim and myself set out early the next morning in Leon's van to look for materials in Motril. As a sprawling port Motril wasn't particularly beatific but at least it had industrial estates, meaning there would plenty of waste materials up for grabs. We found what we were looking for out the back of a factory where some men were unloading pieces of machinery from a truck and tossing the wooden crates into a skip. They seemed happy for us to take them so we strapped them to the roof and went off to search for more scrap materials. Both Leon and Jim were connoisseurs of scavenging, and Leon possessed a mental map of Granada province on which he had noted abandoned items thrown into ditches or left at the side of roads. Meanwhile, Jim's favourite hunting ground was Nerja where, he said, you found a 'better class of skip'.

Although Nerja's dumpsters might be good for antique doors and furniture, these items would be of little use for our chickens and so we headed off along the coast in the direction of Almería. Here, construction workers had been building a number of bridges in order to straighten the roads and make it easier for the big trucks rolling out of the province laden with salad. Wherever a bridge had gone up, the *barranco* below was cluttered with discarded waste materials. Although this was an environmental disgrace, for us it was something of a treasure trove. The area we were looking in was quite remote and nobody saw us as we loaded up the car roof with long pieces of building steel and discarded planks of wood. On a previous visit, Leon had taken away a wooden drum used to coil high voltage cable, which he had sanded, oiled and polished to the point where it resembled a bespoke Scandinavian designed kitchen table. He was good at things like that.

When the three of us returned to Los Pechos we set about constructing the chicken coop the same day. Using instructional videos on YouTube, we built it up against the large concrete water tank on the top terrace. The tank, which had cost us so much, had developed a crack that kept the ground around it moist and therefore covered in green plants. In addition to this, olive trees shaded the area so it was the perfect spot for some chickens to live. Jim, with his carpentry skills, set to work building a hen house from scraps of wood and quickly knocked together a boxy yet fine-looking dwelling vaguely reminiscent of an Italianate villa. Next we draped chicken mesh from the top of the tank down to ground level, burying the edges a foot under the soil and in-filling with rocks to keep out foxes. This wire was the only thing we had to buy, but we figured we couldn't do without it. An old broom handle provided a spacious perch for the hens, and a sawn-in-half wooden door salvaged from an abandoned farmhouse provided entry to the new walk-in chicken coop.

We stood back and looked at our work. It was a job that we could be proud of, but there was a certain something missing: some chickens. These were harder to come by that one might expect as, since the outbreak of avian flu the unlicensed sale of fowl had been tightened up. Before, it had been easy enough to find men selling chicks from the back of vans, but those days were now gone. Nevertheless, this being Órgiva, Leon asked around in the bars and soon obtained a number of hens and a cock, which he brought back in a cardboard box.

And so the chickens settled into daily life at Los Pechos, roaming around the terraces during the day and returning to their secure cage at night when the foxes were out. It was great to see them getting used to their new home, strutting about and pecking away at the leaves on the terraces. By allowing them to wander free, and only putting them back in the coop at night, they were performing the valuable service of removing insects such as the blighted palm weevils and *scolopendras* from the land, and along with kitchen scraps we fed them the chickens were soon providing us with eggs.

- 60 -

What had been a bad situation in Spain had become a whole lot worse, with many people in La Alpujarra finding themselves without any money at all. Practically all work had dried up in the area and nearly everyone was struggling to some extent. The only people who seemed to be okay were those who received money from abroad every month in the form of a pension or some other payment. By contrast everyone who had to work for a living was having a job putting food on the table. Spanish unemployment was skyrocketing, estate agents were closing by the day and foreign expats were abandoning their properties and leaving in droves. It was an economic collapse.

Times might have been hard but living as low-key as possible had its compensations. Growing and eating fresh food at Los Pechos was still a sublime pleasure, and less work meant more time for working on the land and indulging in pastimes such as reading and gardening. Leon and Rebecca had started to rear goats, which could provide us with milk. The solar panels gave us enough electricity to power computers and music systems (but not much more), and the mountain springs still spilled out cold, pure water, just as they always had. I found out you could eat fairly well on the three basic ingredients of potatoes, eggs and olive oil. Spanish peasants had known this for centuries, of course, which was why so many of the local dishes were variations on this theme. Antonio, our olive-farming, goat-raising, wild boar-eating neighbour, was so used to what outsiders might call 'hardship' that he claimed not to have noticed the economy had collapsed.

But it was hard work, harder than most people were probably willing to realise. And with no money for luxuries, or – often – petrol, living with solar powered electricity was okay as long as the day wasn't a cloudy one. Several cloudy days in a row meant no electricity at all. The enamel on my teeth was starting to wear off from drinking too much orange juice (because one thing we were never short of was oranges and lemons) and in the evenings we slumped in the kitchen while Rebecca cooked up a hot pot of whatever was to hand. There was ample time for reflection.

The promise of the job working for the guidebook hung tantalisingly close, but the start date was forever being put back for one reason or another. I began to entertain the idea that it wasn't going to happen. Nevertheless, I tried my best to hang on, selling our grapefruits to the health food shop in Órgiva for fifty cents apiece. There were no end of almonds and olives to pick and sell, although they didn't fetch much so it was better to just use them for personal consumption. We were never really short of food as the trees on our land and the roadside bushes provided generously, with figs, pomegranates, prickly pears, *nisperos*, oranges and lemons in abundance. I found a few bits of online work, and carried on delivering newspapers down on the coast, but that was it. One day, with no petrol in the car, I walked into Órgiva to drop off my latest load of grapefruits and pick up some money I was owed from the office. When I got there the mood was frosty. It was usually strained whenever I appeared, but this time I could sense something had changed. Jayne told me there was no money left in the kitty, and that others would be paid ahead of me.

I left empty-handed. If they couldn't pay me they would have to find another newspaper boy. It was the last time I ever went into the office or saw any of them again. So it goes.

The occasional day of building work turned up for Leon, and I'd help with mixing the concrete or shifting materials or rubble. Working cash-in-hand and seeing those eighty euros peeled off and handed to you at the end of a long, sweaty day made you feel temporarily rich. On pay days such as this, myself, Jim, Leon, along with whoever else was working with us at the time, would load up with food at the big coastal supermarket on the way back – making sure to pack in plenty of the absurdly cheap bottles of *Alhambra* lager – and then spend the rest of the evening eating Rebecca's *chorizo* stew, listening to trippy ambient music and getting very pleasantly drunk and stoned. The next day I would inevitably find myself moneyless once again, and with a hangover to boot, but at least I'd have another week's food in the cupboard and it was impossible to stay glum for long in the beautiful Alpujarra.

Three months after my family left, I was feeling tired, beaten and lonely. Michelle was back in Denmark, working as a cleaner for the local council and living in the spare room at her mother's house. She started work at four o'clock every morning and her wages covered our mortgage payments. By then, mortgage payments were rising steadily month-by-month as the banks tried to avoid collapse.

There were no two ways about it – life in Spain was getting tough for those without a safety net. There were reports of families splitting up, people having mental breakdowns and even some suicides. Those foreigners who could afford to take the financial hit and get out when they could did so, but many more were left in limbo; unable to afford to move back to somewhere they could earn a living, and yet stuck somewhere they could not. The huge machines blasting roads through the mountains had ground to a halt as the EU cash spigot had been turned off, while rows of cement trucks accumulated unused in vast dusty parking lots, and *Se vende* signs appeared on houses everywhere. Spain's economic boom was dead.

I had to face the painful truth: making a go of living in Spain had failed, and I would have to leave before things got any worse.

- 61 -

Wₕen it was time for me to go, Leon and Rebecca organised a leaving party for me and transformed one of the terraces into an improvised party scene, complete with fairy lights, huge rounds of olive wood for chairs and a fire pit for cooking food over. People from the hillside turned up and we talked, drank wine and played music under the stars until the early hours.

The next day, I packed the Twingo with everything I could fit into it. I hoped the couple of hundred euros in my pocket, would buy enough petrol to see me back to distant Denmark. Dave and Judy, our tree-planting friends who lived down by the dusty river, slipped me a fifty euro note and told me to get at least one decent night's rest on the way back rather than sleeping in the car. I thought about the motel in Barcelona I had stayed at on my first night in Spain …

There was a light rain falling as I left. When I looked back, a rainbow had appeared over Cerro Negro – the only time I had ever seen one there. I figured this must be goodbye. I set out with a heavy heart, wondering if I would ever return. I didn't know what the next few years of my life would hold, although I sensed there would be a lot of rebuilding to do.

Instead of taking the most direct route north, I decided to take a slight detour to the east. I had promised myself one last night in Cabo de Gata, a place where I felt a strong connection to Spain. It took about three hours to get there, and I drove the car all the way to the edge of the sea where the century plants stood like skeletal sentinels in the evening light.

The beach was wide and empty. I walked along it, remembering the time we had gone there on my birthday. I recalled the sense of optimism and excitement we'd felt about our new life in Spain and the little newspaper we had created. Coming to the volcanic-looking hill where we had seen so many goats, I climbed up to the top in order to see one last Spanish sunset. Sitting on a pile of stones as the shadows lengthened and the fiery orb of the sun slipped into the hazy sea, I could feel what Laurie

Lee had called 'the long arm' securing a comfortable grip on the scruff of my neck. For sure, my adventures in this magical land were coming to an end. I looked out over the sea as the sun sank below the horizon and then, as the sky bruised purple and red, I turned and left.

***

Epilogue

It could sound like a cliché but Spain had seized me by the heart. I had known this from the first day when I'd awoken in Pampaneira and watched the sun touch the mountains with something far beyond what we know merely as light. There was something heightened and expanding about the experience of being present in such a natural arena, an ineffable feeling of lightness.

I went there with an open heart and an open mind, and I had treasured every moment of being there and calling Spain my home. I loved the cacophonous chaos of Órgiva on market day, with its gypsy traders, New Agers and Sufi mystics, mixing with the staid and conservative grandmothers and the noble kind-eyed souls who'd lived through times so hard most people would struggle to comprehend. I loved the peace of the mountains and the fragrant herb-strewn hillsides and the oleander-choked gorges where the silence could be intense and otherworldly.

There were plenty of things not to like about Spain though, not least the too-common cruelty towards animals and the despoliation of its once beautiful coasts. But even here, the horror of dripping blood and spewing concrete somehow served to heighten and enhance the aspects that were the flipside of the coin. It was as if Spain were a catalyst in some grand alchemical experiment where good and evil had been mixed together and brought to a simmer, the essence distilled into drops. Nobody spoke of the civil war any longer, but the bones were beginning to poke out of the *barrancos* and a reckoning was long overdue.

And I loved the sense of freedom, the idea that a man and his family could live the life they had been ordained to live, mostly free from interference. In the sleepy villages and towns of Andalucía the measure of a person was in how they treated their friends and neighbours – a yardstick that has been lost elsewhere. The concepts of loyalty, honour and cultural convention cling on tenaciously, for right or wrong.

But I also recognised that one must earn one's place there, and that it took time and patience and fortitude. It was funny in a way that our economic premise had been so flimsy, and to learn how easy it was to be knocked off your perch and find yourself in a mess on the floor.

Compared to the neighbours we had had when we lived there, Julio and Antonio in particular, I was not a person of that place. I was, in this case, a misfit, no matter how much I tried to fool myself otherwise. Julio, in his good-natured way, had not let me forget that fact while we lived in Pampaneira. I knew nothing of the ways of making young wine from the wild vines that grew in the gorge, just as I would have lacked the strength or the knowhow if it came to holding down and slaughtering a fully-grown pig during a *matanza*. It was absurd for me to assume that I could just roll up and expect to be a part of village life when it was clear that I'd always be an outsider, and yet none of this seemed to matter to Julio or the other people of the mountains.

Back in Denmark we had nowhere to live, so we all crowded into my mother-in-law's spare room for a few months until the local municipality deemed us homeless and allocated us a flat in a dull suburb near the airport. This was all quite a change from our lives in Spain but it could have been a lot worse and at least we were still together as a family. Ironically, the day after I got back I was finally offered the job working for the guidebook. I had to turn it down. Instead, I got a job doing layout for a newspaper, rising to the position of editor over the following couple of years and launching another 'green' newspaper – but that's a whole other story. It took us over five years to sell Los Pechos, as well as our house in Pampaneira – oddly enough we received offers on the same day. We sold Los Pechos to a couple who had taken early retirement, and they completed all the projects I'd had to leave half-finished, soon turning the place into an enviable smallholding. I was happy that it had fallen into good hands.

I returned to Órgiva several times over the next decade, noting all the changes. The main difference was a visual one, with the newly elected female mayor embarking on a spending spree that not only gave the dirty old town a major scrub and facelift, but also upgraded the local infrastructure and breathed new life into the place. Sitting outside our old office at Café Galindo on Calle Doctor Fleming in April 2019, it was easy to recognise the same town where, fourteen years previously, the barefoot beggar woman would play mellifluous notes on her tin whistle and helmetless youths would roar up the road on their 125cc bikes, even if the place had been transformed in the meantime. Now, there were public art installations, landscaped flowerbeds, a swimming pool, a museum, functional traffic lights, a supermarket and many other things. Órgiva was far less rough round the edges and it had become more connected to the wider world, although it was certainly not gentrified and had lost none of its vibe. In fact, it seemed to have settled into its transition from a hard-up ex-mining town to a burgeoning centre for alternative lifestyles and the arts. People were arriving every day to start a new life there, many of them yoga teachers.

Over the years people had come and gone from La Alpujarra. Various ill-conceived businesses had gone bust, while new ones were just starting up. Some people had passed on while others had been born. Sadly, John, aka *The Amputee*, had been killed when his car tumbled off a mountain with himself and his wife inside after he had lost control while trying to jump-start it. Thankfully, his wife survived. Julio, my erstwhile neighbour in Pampaneira, had also departed this life, having been found dead from a heart attack with his mule standing beside him – far too young, in his early fifties. Michael Jacobs, the best and yet most under-appreciated travel writer on the Spanish speaking world in recent decades, had died from liver cancer at a hospital in London not long after his friend Manolo 'El Sereno' similarly bought his ticket to the Great Beyond. Michael's last book *The Robber of Memories* is a poignant farewell about travelling through Colombia by river while facing up to mortality. Others, who didn't make it into the pages of this story, had similarly passed on.

The New Labour MP for Luton South, Margaret Moran, who had unsuccessfully tried to sue *The Olive Press* after we published photographs of a threatening note she had written on House of Commons notepaper, was later found guilty of falsifying parliamentary expenses. That simple note she had placed on Jake's motorcycle had been the first marker of what would become an all-engulfing parliamentary expenses scandal that brought down Tony Blair's government. Moran was found guilty of fraudulently claiming £53,000 on expenses, mostly for her various houses, although she never stood trial in court. She claimed that the stress of the situation had caused her to suffer a mental breakdown, and was deemed unfit to stand trial. In absentia, she was found guilty of false accounting and forgery and was given a two-year supervision order, with the judge commenting that some people would feel that she had "got away with it". Ironically, by attacking *The Olive Press*, she had helped it get noticed.

I was saddened to find out that Aspen had died from a tumour, leaving David to ponder whether to continue with their Semilla Besada project or hand it over to someone with fresh energy. In the end he opted for the latter, and Semilla Besada still thrives, showing others how to turn a dry region green again.

Jim was now a proud father and, since the building work had dried up, he and his now-wife Nat had moved up to the north of Spain and bought a tumbledown farmhouse for a song. Meanwhile, Leon and Rebecca had continued to live in Los Pechos and had amassed several goats, an expanding flock of chickens and a donkey, while Leon had acquired a white horse that he sometimes rode into town instead of using a car. Nevertheless, even with their degree of tenacity and inventiveness the constant grinding lack of money got to them in the end and they reluctantly moved back to the UK where Leon retrained as a past life regression hypnotist and now runs his own practice in Herefordshire.

Although, I never saw them again, I gleaned from others that Marcus and Molly's version of *The Olive Press* had stumbled on for a few months with a much-depleted readership, with their food and wine magazine having never made it off the starting blocks, as far as I know. The office in Órgiva was closed and operations were moved up to the village of Bubión, where they lived along with Zac the husky. There it resided for a while before collapsing in a heap of red ink and unpaid bills. Marcus's name, as well as my own, appeared of a 'wall of shame' outside the tax office in Granada, as a warning for others not to do business with either of us.

Meanwhile Rick had retreated to an off-grid stone cottage that he and Jayne had built in one of the more remote parts of La Alpujarra, starting a family. There he worked selling insurance products online to people in the UK and no doubt earning a lot more money than the newspaper could ever have hoped to pay him.

Jon had switched much of the focus of *The Olive Press* to tabloid news in order to boost readership numbers, especially on the Costa del Sol, which enabled the newspaper to grow and expand its territory. Nevertheless, he continued to run a number of campaigns that focused on protecting the local environment. Within ten years *The Olive Press* had become the largest English language newspaper in Iberia, and now had several more regional offices, including one in Mallorca, one on the Costa Blanca and another in Gibraltar.

As the first foreign journalist on the scene in the Madeleine McCann missing child case, Jon had continued to be associated with the investigation and was featured prominently in a Netflix documentary about it. The fight with the developers of Los Merinos golf mega-project had claimed the life of Alastair Boyd, with friends saying the stress of being sued by the developers had got to him.

It was on one of my visits back to the region and was sitting outside a café in Órgiva when I noticed a copy of *The Olive Press* lying on the next table, its pages fluttering in a light breeze. I reached over and opened it up. It was still recognisably the same newspaper, but now it looked far slicker and a bit fatter. As I turned the pages a large headline jumped out at me. It read:

Olive Press Given *Beacon of Hope* Award and Cited as an Inspiration in Fight to Save Our Environment

THE Olive Press has been handed an award for its environmental campaigning.

The paper was singled out by Green group Ecologistas en Accion in Priego de Cordoba for its consistent reporting on issues affecting the environment.

In particular, it singled out the paper's plastic bag and walking campaigns, as well as its "fearless" reporting on the controversial Los Merinos golf course case in Ronda.

Presenting the award inside Priego's castle during the town's annual festival, Ecologistas en Accion spokesman Pepe Reyes, said: "The Olive Press has fast become one of the very few truly responsible papers when it comes to the environment.

"Independent and fearless, it has consistently reported on corruption and illegal construction over the last few years.

"As well as a series of hard-hitting campaigns, it has also brought international attention to the controversial Los Merinos golf course scheme near Ronda, as well as other illegal golf course schemes around Andalucía."

Accepting the award, alongside Subbetica National Park director Baldomero Moreno, Olive Press editor Jon Clarke told 200 locals that he felt that the paper was having a positive effect on not just the expatriate community but also the local Spaniards.

In Spanish, he explained: "Andalucia is one of the most beautiful places in the world and it is vital that it is not ruined by developers and corrupt mayors."

Clarke was then given the honour of lighting the beacon to lead the town's annual nocturnal walk in defence of the area's green spaces.

As for me, I figured the whole thing could make the basis of an amusing tale. And so, sitting in my council flat in Copenhagen over the course of numerous evenings one harsh winter I jotted down the bulk of this book. I tried to sell it to publishers, and at one point even had an agreement with one, however, they became nervous and wanted me to cut out much of the story, including any mention of miscreant politicians, missing children and plastic greenhouses, and so I reluctantly withdrew it.

Nobody else seemed interested, and I was busy with other projects, so I saved my story on a memory stick that had a logo of Hanover Airport embossed on it, stuck it in a drawer and forgot about it for the best part of a decade. I found it again when clearing out my study, which by then was in Cornwall. I inserted the memory stick into my computer to see if there was anything worth keeping, but discovered that most of the files had been corrupted. Nevertheless, I salvaged what I could and found other ways to rescue other parts. Re-reading what I had written I found myself laughing out loud at this tale of hapless misfits, inflated egos and quixotic capers and that, dear reader, is why I decided to share it with you – I hope you have enjoyed it.

***

Acknowledgements

Although this book features myself as narrator and storyteller, it would not have been possible without a whole host of others. Stories have their own curious internal logic and they need a range of characters. The main character in this book isn't me, it's the oddball publication known as *The Olive Press*, which was birthed by the mountains and the rivers and valleys of La Alpujarra, and somehow chose me as one of the midwives. Other people present at the birth were Marcus and Molly, who provided the initial spark and without whom the newspaper would never have been conceived; Rick, who rescued the fledgling publication from destitution; and Jon, who nurtured it through it's troubled youth. There are, of course, a supporting cast of hundreds, including all those who have written for, worked with, featured in or financially supported *The Olive Press*. From my own perspective, I would like to thank my wife Michelle, who has seen me wrestle with the manuscript for so long, and my sister, Joanne, who helped with the proofreading. Last but not least I'd like to thank the modest and welcoming people of Órgiva and La Alpujarra for continuing to host all us misfits in such a tolerant manner and providing us with a place of refuge in this crazy world.

Note: Throughout the story I have referred to the region as La Alpujarra. Although this is technically correct, most people refer to it as Las Alpujarras – while English speakers invariably call it The Alpujarras – pronounced *al-poo-haar-uz*.

Please consider giving your support to the efforts of the Ecosystems Restoration Camp in the Altiplano to the north of Granada, which is an inspiring non-profit project run by dedicated individuals:
www.ecosystemrestorationcamps.org/camp-altiplano/

And lend your name to the campaign to prevent hundreds of massive electricity pylons being built across La Alpujarra and the Lecrin Valley:
www.dinoalastorres.org/es/

Disclaimer and note
The Olive Press: News From the Land of the Misfits is an original work by Jason Heppenstall and is not in any way affiliated with the newspaper *The Olive Press*. All events related in the story are factually accurate to the best of the author's recollection, and yet this remains a work of fiction in that the requirements of storytelling dictate that events may not have occurred in the order they have been portrayed, and some aspects of the story have been highlighted while others have been omitted. All dialogue is, of course, paraphrased, and some names have been changed to protect identities.

The Path to Odin's Lake
By the same author

Several years after he left Spain, Jason Heppenstall set out on a journey of discovery from his old home in Copenhagen. Unsure of where he was going or even why he was doing it a series of bizarre happenings leads him to believe he is being drawn towards a lake in a Swedish forest where the Norse god Odin was once worshipped.

More than just a travel story *The Path to Odin's Lake* is a mixture of philosophical meditation, psychedelic adventure and spiritual quest that will have you pondering the deeper meaning of being alive in a chaotic universe.

"... a sane man's response to an ever maddening world ... It is a journey of gradual reawakening to the power and beauty of nature and its place of healing in the human psyche." – Maddie Harland, Editor of Permaculture Magazine

Available from online stores

Seat of Mars
- Dystopian Sci-fi -

Hell-bent on preserving the privileges of the wealthy in the face of a looming resource crisis, the British government executes a false flag terrorist attack and shuts down the electricity grid. In the ensuing turmoil, a shadowy cabal watches on from a bunker buried deep beneath the frozen Arctic, and readies to roll out "the experiment" across the world.

Seat of Mars follows the fortunes of a handful of ordinary people flung into extraordinary times. Could something beautiful emerge from the glowing embers of chaos?

"Great book! So possible, that it was scary. Yet, solutions abound, if one has courage and a bit of knowledge. Mr. Heppenstall is obviously a writer with talent." – Amazon reviewer

Available from online stores

About the author

Jason Heppenstall grew up in the English Midlands and went on to study economics in London. After years spent travelling and living in different countries he now resides with his family in Penzance, Cornwall, where he nurtures a coppice woodland and continues to write.

Printed in Great Britain
by Amazon